The History of Street Gangs
in the United States

The History of Street Gangs in the United States

Their Origins and Transformations

James C. Howell

LEXINGTON BOOKS
Lanham • Boulder • New York • London

Published by Lexington Books
An imprint of The Rowman & Littlefield Publishing Group, Inc.
4501 Forbes Boulevard, Suite 200, Lanham, Maryland 20706
www.rowman.com

Unit A, Whitacre Mews, 26-34 Stannary Street, London SE11 4AB

British Library Cataloguing in Publication Information Available

Library of Congress Cataloging-in-Publication Data

Howell, James C.
The history of street gangs in the United States : their origins and ransformations / James C. Howell.
p. cm.
Includes bibliographical references and index.
ISBN 978-1-4985-1132-2 (cloth : alk. paper) -- ISBN 978-1-4985-1133-9 (electronic)
1. Gangs--United States--History. I. Title.
HV6439.U5H6794 2015
364.106'60973--dc23
2015010286

∞ ™ The paper used in this publication meets the minimum requirements of American National Standard for Information Sciences Permanence of Paper for Printed Library Materials, ANSI/NISO Z39.48-1992.

Printed in the United States of America

Contents

v

Acknowledgments

I am deeply indebted to Walter B. Miller for mentoring me on gangs across a span of thirty years, from the early 1970s to his death in 2004. Miller became the nation's foremost expert on the prevalence of gangs by virtue of a cumulative series of multi-city studies that he conducted in the 1970s and 1980s. Both the 1967 President's Commission on Law Enforcement and Administration of Justice and the 1969 National Commission on the Causes and Prevention of Violence opined that gangs in the United States had died out in the 1950s and 1960s. Miller's pioneering studies debunked that widely accepted conclusion. He actively lobbied the U.S. Congress to support long-term gang research and a national level gang survey. As a result of his persistence, the 1992 Amendments to the Juvenile Justice and Delinquency Prevention Act granted new gang authority to the federal Office Juvenile Justice and Delinquency Prevention (OJJDP), including the collection and dissemination of information on gangs. Barbara Tatem Kelley prepared the task force report that moved the national gang center concept and a national gang survey forward. Thus, Miller's research led to the establishment of both a federal gang center and a National Youth Gang Survey that would gather information on cities' and counties' gang activity, thereby producing reliable data that would connect the past with the present.

The National Gang Center is located in the Institute for Intergovernmental Research (IIR), the nation's premier law enforcement support organization, in Tallahassee, Florida. The foresight of IIR's leaders, Emory Williams, CEO, and Bruce Buckley, General Counsel, made this possible. The first National Youth Gang Survey was launched in 1996, and it was conducted annually up to 2012 by the National Gang Center. John Moore and subsequent leaders of the National Gang Center, Meena Harris and Trelles D'Alemberte, recognized the importance of gang history in crafting solutions. Several colleagues at the U.S. Department of Justice also have been steadfast advocates of an historical perspective on gangs, particularly Barbara Tatem Kelley, Phelan Wyrick, James Burch, and James Chavis.

Research projects such as this book inevitably build upon one's prior work. My first offering, only a brief synopsis, titled the *History of Street Gangs in the United States*, published in 2010 by the National Gang Center, elicited a sufficient positive response to encourage me to continue in this endeavor. Next, my gang textbook, *Gangs in America's Communities* (Sage, 2012) introduced segments of the story to university classrooms. After favorable feedback, the second edition of that book was expanded, giving me the opportunity to begin sketching an historical framework that encapsulates key phases of gang emergence and transformation. I gratefully acknowledge Jerry Westby, Publisher, SAGE Publications, Inc., for encouraging me to continue developing my historical account begun in *Gangs in America's Communities*.

Several research colleagues have encouraged my continuing interest in an historical perspective of gangs including Beth Bjerregaard, Becky and Richard Block, David Curry, Finn Esbensen, Adrienne Freng, Amanda Gilman, Rachel Gordon, Elizabeth Griffiths, Mark Fleisher, Karl Hill, Lorine Hughes, Ron Huff, Barbara Tatem Kelley, Andrew Papachristos, Dana Peterson, Irving Spergel, Terrance Taylor, George Tita, and Diego Vigil. Importantly, Ron Huff, Irv Spergel, and Diego Vigil, more than any other gang scholars in the modern era, have utilized a variety of forums to drawn national attention to public policy implications of gangs along with well thought out solutions.

Ron Huff reviewed my first draft and encouraged me to move forward with this project. Bruce Buckley's critique of a later draft greatly improved the precision and completeness of my manuscript, and for this I am most grateful. My long-time friend and historian extraordinaire, Larry Riggs, reviewed and provided helpful insights on sections with which I struggled, particularly immigration patterns and settlement of the Southwestern region of the United States. I thank Jana Hodges-Kluck, Associate Editor, Lexington Books, for anticipating that this volume could make a worthwhile contribution to the field of criminology. Sarah Craig, Assistant Editor, Lexington Books, expertly managed preparation of the manuscript to the production-ready stage and Ashli Mackenzie, Assistant Editor, Production, skillfully carried it to print-ready.

I owe special thanks to Dan Oates, Library Director, and Suzanne Sinclair, Librarian, Health Sciences Library, First Health of the Carolinas, for greatly assisting me in securing resource publications. Ms. Sinclair displayed unusual research skills in locating reports in the gray literature, and with extraordinary dispatch.

The most valued support of my gang history research and writing has come from my wife, Karen, and our daughter, Megan Q. Howell, both of whom steadfastly encouraged me to persist in this challenging historical research. I thank Karen for her gracious indulgence and helpful discussions, and Megan for her insightful critiques and encouragement.

James C. (Buddy) Howell
Pinehurst, North Carolina

Introduction

The term *gang* had no negative connotations its earliest usage. In Old English, gang simply meant "a going together" and a gang was "in other words, a group" (Haskins, 1974, p. 8). Hence, the term *gang* simply referenced groups that gather on city streets. The first known use of the term in the English language in a disparaging sense was with reference to pirates in 1623.[1] A widely respected chronicler of British crime, Luke Pike (1873), reported the first active gangs in Western civilization, highway robbers in England during the early part of the seventeenth century. However, it does not appear that these gangs had the features of modern-day, serious street gangs. Later in the 1600s, London was "terrorized by a series of organized gangs calling themselves the Mims, Hectors, Bugles, Dead Boys [and they] fought pitched battles among themselves dressed with colored ribbons to distinguish the different factions" (Pearson, 1983, p. 188).[2] These likely were the first traditional sort of gangs.

At the time of the American Revolution, there were no reports of street gangs[3] in the United States. The question that arises, then, is this: How did the observed steady growth in street gangs come about? To provide a satisfactory answer to this question, we take a regional approach, for three reasons. First, the early accounts of gang emergence display a regional sequence of development, beginning with the Northeast, followed by the Midwest, next, in the West, and lastly, in the Southern region of the United States. This time-ordered sequence is unmistakable. However, this pattern does not suggest a sequential progression with one region influencing the next and so on. Rather, it is apparent that—though similar in many respects—conditions that gave rise to gangs were endemic to each region. Our second justification for taking a regional approach is that a few very large cities stand out in three of the four regions for rapid development of gang problems within their urban centers, particularly in New York City, Chicago, and Los Angeles. Each of these epicenters of gang activity had such enormous populations that with continuing growth, they spawned gang activity outward from their urban center. The Southern region had no single epicenter. Third, taking a regional approach should help to isolate key conditions and events underlying the emergence of gangs and fueling their expansion. In this sense, a regional perspective has some comparative benefits. Therefore, this volume examines social and historical events associated with the emergence of gang activity in four major regions of the United States: the Northeast, Midwest, West, and South.[4]

NOTES

1. *A New English Dictionary* (Oxford, 1928).

2. Aside from England, gang activity was reported in Western and Eastern societies for centuries including: Albania, England, Scotland, Germany, Italy, Kenya, Tanzania, South Africa, Australia, Brazil, El Salvedor, Hong Kong, Kenya, Mexico, Papau New Guinea, Peru, New Zealand, South Korea, the Soviet Union, Taiwan, Tanzania, and the People's Republic of China (Spergel, 1995).

3. A distinction is maintained in this volume between youth gangs and street gangs (see chapter 3). The *youth gang* term is useful for drawing attention to younger gangs. The street gang term makes a point of emphasis, denoting older gangs that have a presence on city streets the use violence to claim territory, maintain power, and further their goals particularly assault, robbery, gun crimes, and murder.

4. The U.S. Bureau of the Census nomenclature is used here to reference these main regions, as well as the classification of states within each of the respective regions.

Chapter One

Emergence and Development of Gang Activity in the United States

GANG EMERGENCE AND EXPANSION IN THE NORTHEAST REGION

The Dutch immigrants arrived first on New York City's Ellis Island, in the early 1600s, and they promptly stole Manhattan from the indigenous inhabitants of the island (Bourgois, 2003). Immediately following the American Revolution, English Protestants were the first large immigrant group, and they represented more than eight out of ten residents by 1790 (Pincus & Ehrlich, 1999, p. 224). Other peoples in the first U.S. census, in descending order of numbers, were Scottish, German, Dutch, Irish, French, and Jewish. The first great wave of Irish came to the United States following the American Revolution, and another million Irish Catholic immigrants began arriving in 1854, fleeing the potato famine in Ireland, settling mainly in New York City and Boston.

Altogether, some five million immigrants arrived in the United States, mainly into New York City, Boston, Philadelphia, and San Francisco, by the 1850s (Pincus & Ehrlich, 1999). In the second large migration to the United States, from 1865 to 1890, approximately eleven million immigrants came from mainly northern and western Europe, especially Great Britain, Germany, and Scandinavia (Denmark, Norway, and Sweden). Next, a third group (1890–1930) doubled the U.S. immigrant total, coming from countries of Southern and Eastern Europe—the Poles, Italians, Austrians, and many others. The arrival of each of these unusually large immigrant groups overwhelmed the young U.S. seaboard cities in the Northeast, and the unanticipated impacts created conditions that gave rise to street gangs.

First Period of Gang Emergence in New York City: 1783–1860s

New York City's Ellis Island was the major port of entry to the United States from the 1820s to the 1920s (Pincus & Ehrlich, 1999). The lower side of New York City—particularly the Five Points area—fell victim to rapid immigration and ensuing political, economic, and family disorganization (Anbinder, 2001; Sante, 1991). Largely consisting of low-skilled, low-wage laborers seeking factory work in the United States, the large Irish immigrant surge overwhelmed the housing and welfare capacity of the young city, contributing directly to slum or ghetto[1] conditions and the accompanying crime problems, gangs included. The only New York City neighborhood that would accept them was the Five Points district—surrounding the intersection of five streets. The back rooms of several local grocery stores in Five Points, called *speakeasies*, illegally sold cheap liquor and thus became hangouts for small criminal groups that were attracted to busy port cities along the eastern seaboard—pirates, sailors who had jumped ship, derelicts, drunks, pickpockets, and cargo thieves. In the nearby "deviance service centers," the majority of dives typically featured a bar, a dance floor, private boxes, prostitution, and robbery (Sante, 1991). These centers catered to the demand for illicit sex, alcohol, guns, protection, and even murder for hire (Hagan, 1995). To be sure, fights that spread into the streets were a common thing. The isolation and marginalization of very poor immigrants in the rapidly growing New York City prompted them to establish a small secure area where group control of resources and spaces could provide a buffer against the uncertainty, chaos, and dangerousness of many city streets.

In the early 1820s, the Five Points district was a hellish place where it was every man for himself and his family. There, the impoverished Irish first formed true New York City street gangs, and these gangs were early products of New York City's "battle with the slum" (Riis, 1902/1969). The initial gang, made up largely of local thieves, pickpockets, and thugs, formed around 1825 in the back room of Rosanna Peers's greengrocery (Haskins, 1974). Named the Forty Thieves, it was the first armed gang, and it was "the first to have a definite acknowledged leadership, to adopt a common name, and to work together for many years" (p. 26). The second gang to have formed in the area, the Kerryonians, named themselves after the county in Ireland from which they originated (Asbury, 1927). For the most part, the earliest gangs were Irish men and adolescents, joining together in the face of poverty, squalid conditions, and great prejudice (Haskins, 1974). "As a social unit, the gang closely resembled such organizations as the fire company, the fraternal order, and the political club, and all of these formations variously overlapped" (Sante, 1991, pp. 197–198).

Inter-ethnic conflict was prevalent already, and street gangs grew as turf wars became commonplace in neighborhoods, and the Irish gangs—who incidentally brought with them hatred of the English who controlled New York City—soon took center stage. The New York City Police Department was not effective in maintaining order. Gangs and other criminal groups were virtually unfettered from forging their own wedges in the social and physical disorder. Colorful gangs quickly formed in the Five Points area, including the Chichsters, Roach Guards, Plug Uglies, Shirt Tails, and Dead Rabbits (Sante, 1991). The latter gang's battle symbol was a dead rabbit impaled on a pike. In local jargon, a dead rabbit was a super tough fellow. The Plug Uglies, named after their large plug hats with flaps that, when stuffed with leather and wool, protected their heads in battle as blows to the head were common in gang fights, from the use of brick bats and clubs. Most notorious were the Roach Guards and Dead Rabbits who constantly fought one another, but they set aside their differences and united with other Five Points gangs when fighting outside gangs.

Another cluster of gangs formed in speakeasies and on the streets within the nearby Bowery area, the largest and most vicious of which was the Bowery Boys. In time, the Bowery Boys produced dozens of gang sets or off-shoots including the True Blue Americans, American Guards, the O'Connell Guards, and the Atlantic Guards—all principally Irish. Battles between the Bowery Boys and Five Points gangs (claiming more than one thousand members each) were legendary, each of which was supported by smaller gangs they had spawned. "The weapons the gangs used were deadly and imaginative. Some were fortunate to own pistols and muskets, but the usual weapons were knives and brickbats and bludgeons. For close work there were brass knuckles, ice picks, pikes, and other interesting paraphernalia" (Haskins, 1974, p. 31). From the 1830s to the 1860s, these gangs fought one another almost weekly, sometimes in battles that lasted two or three days, in endless melees of assaults and murder.

Altogether, the Bowery Boys waged as many as two hundred battles with Five Points gangs over a span of ten years, beginning in 1834 (Asbury, 1927, p. 37). A 2002 movie based on Asbury's book, *Gangs of New York*, vividly depicted their reign, with some exaggerations and distorted history in "a blood-soaked vision of American history" (Gilfoyle, 2003, p. 621). In time, the Bowery Boys replaced the Five Points gangs. By the 1870s, few gangs remained in Five Points.

A third cluster of gangs operated along the docks and shipyards on the East Side River of Manhattan, including the Short Tails, the Border Gang, Day Break Boys, and the Swamp Angels (Asbury, 1927; Haskins, 1974). These gangs were far more violent than either the Five Points or Bowery Boys gangs. This observation comes as a surprise because these gangs were made up of much younger members (average age around twenty years) than the other groups, as many participants joined by age fifteen or sixteen, and even younger in some cases. Nevertheless, virtually every one of the adolescents had killed someone, and murder or robberies were committed regularly as they pirated cargo on the ships and docks. Occasionally, they battled nearby gangs, almost always victoriously. These gangs were destroyed by police by the time of the Civil War because they did not have the political protection that downtown gangs enjoyed.

Shrewd businessmen and politicians immediately recognized the valuable asset that the street gangs could be in the chaotic conditions of the city, in protecting their interests (Haskins, 1974). Adamson (2000) coined the term *defensive localism* to describe the role gangs played, particularly in ensuring that white neighborhoods remained that way. In the early 1830s, several politicians (ward and district leaders) bought grocery stores in Five Points as well as saloons and dance halls in the Bowery. In return for their assured protection of the gangs' operations from police, and financial rewards offered to the gang for their loyalty, gang leaders were paid for taking care of jobs like Blackjacking[2] political opponents of sponsors.

For twenty years before the Civil War, corruption and vice were rampant in New York City, and a governmental and political organization, Tammany Hall, was at the center of much of the corruption—even aiding and abetting gang activity (Haskins, 1974). Gang membership grew enormously during this period. By 1855 it was estimated that there were at least thirty thousand people who owed allegiance to the gang leaders and, through them, to politicians of various affiliations. At every election the gangs burned ballot boxes, beat up ordinary citizens trying to exercise their right to vote, and themselves voted many times over (pp. 34–35) .

Police were powerless to arrest the growing number of gang members; they were also beaten when they attempted to guard polling places. However, police too were corrupt. In 1857, police corruption was so widespread that the state legislature abolished the city police department and set up a new Metropolitan Police Force under the control of a special board appointed by the governor.

Philadelphia and Boston could also lay claim to having substantial street gangs before the Civil War (Adamson, 2000; Miller, 1966/2011). Boston's earliest gangs—comprising white Catholic and predominantly Irish youth, with a few Italians—were first reported in the 1820s (Woods, 1898), likely having evolved from the fighting street corner groups (Miller, 1966/2011; Whyte, 1941, 1943a, 1943b). Numerous White turf-defending Philadelphia gangs were identified in1848 by *New York Tribune* reporter George Foster (Adamson, 2000). Gangs quickly became a fixture on both the western and northern streets of the City of Brotherly Love; virtually all of which were Blacks in ghetto-like neighborhoods.[3] However, these early Philadelphia gangs do not appear to have been well organized and certainly not as ferocious as the New York gangs, although that assessment soon would change (Miller, 1975).

Second Period of Gang Growth in New York City: 1860s–1930s

In 1860, the population of New York City numbered more than eight hundred thousand, one-fourth of which were Irish—the largest group of foreign born inhabitants—and most of them were very poor (Haskins, 1974). By 1900, residents of the Manhattan and the Bronx boroughs (the old city) numbered two million, more than two-thirds of which lived in tenements (Riis, 1902/1969, p. 81). Tenement houses created as a temporary solution had become permanent. "The tenement is the basic façade in New York, the face of the slums, a slab of tombstone proportions, four to six stories, pocked by windows" (Sante, 1991, p. 23). Conditions were so deplorable that members of the 1857 Select Committee of the Assembly came to the city to observe conditions first hand and witnessed that people were housed in crowded, filthy tenements with "dark, damp basements, leaking garrets, shops, outhouses, and stables converted into dwellings" (cited in Riis, 1902/ 1969, p. 12). No consideration or public support was given to the tenants; they were on their own, at the mercy of slum landlords.

> Reckless slovenliness, discontent, privation, and ignorance were left to work out their inevitable results, until the entire premises reached the level of tenant-house dilapidation, containing, but not sheltering the miserable hordes that crowded beneath smoldering, water-rotted roofs, or burrowed among the rats of clammy cellars. (Select Committee, cited in Riis, 1902/1969, p. 13)

These conditions predated the formation of the city Health Department, viable social services, and the Children's Aid Society. Future gangsters were set adrift from weakened families and inadequate schooling as well.

The next event that changed the orientation of gangs in New York City was the Civil War draft riots—the first significant racial/ethnic riots in the United States.[4] These were precipitated in large part by young Irish street gang members (Haskins, 1974). An 1863 Federal law (the Conscription Act) gave President Lincoln the power to draft American citizens (men between ages twenty and forty-five) into the Civil War, with a clause that exempted persons who paid the U.S. government $300, an option that was not available to very poor residents of Five Points and the Bowery. The initial draft was scheduled to begin in New York City on July 11, 1863. Two large Irish gangs led the protest, as fifty thousand to seventy thousand mobsters (mostly age twenty or younger) participated in the rioting throughout the city, and continued for several days, after quickly turning into a racist event (Haskins, 1974; Sante, 1991). "The controlling inspiration of the mob was to destroy the city, and secondly to destroy the City's Negro population" (Haskins, 1974, p. 39). Altogether, eighteen Black men were lynched, and as many as seventy of them "vanished without a trace," and "perhaps hundreds were forced from their homes, which were burned or otherwise rendered inhabitable" (Sante,

1991, p. 351). Altogether, more than one thousand rioters were killed, and more than one hundred buildings were burned. The so-called Draft Riots continued for several years, and 1877, called "the year of the riots," saw the biggest outbreaks in Pittsburgh, Cleveland, and Baltimore.

Following these riots, along with the growth of anti-Black sentiments and the Civil War, the city's gangs "branched out, diversified, and merged, absorbing smaller and less well-organized units and encompassing ever-larger swaths of territory" (Sante, 1991, p. 217). The Whyos (named because of a bird-like call the members used to alert one another) is said to have been "the most powerful downtown gang between the Civil War and the 1890s" (Sante, 1991, p. 214). This far more criminal gang actually had a take-out menu of its services, including punching ($2), nose and jaw bone broken ($10), leg or arm broken ($19), shot in the leg ($25), and "doing the big job" ($100 and up) (Sante, 1991). After the Whyos dissolved in the early 1890s (from jailings and deaths), a small number of very large gangs, organized as umbrella formations made up of smaller ones, came to dominate the scene—yet still under the control of the adult gangs. One of these gangs, the Forty Thieves, birthed a juvenile gang called the Little Forty Thieves that was led by a girl, Wild Maggie Carson, until "she was persuaded to go straight by a concerned minister" (Haskins, 1974, p. 56).

A few gang alliances were longest-lived on the Lower East Side of Manhattan in the post–Civil War era: the Five Pointers, the Eastmans, the Gophers, Gas Housers, and the Hudson Dusters (Haskins, 1974; Sante, 1991). Many other independent gangs controlled small areas within the broad turfs of the larger gangs, and territorial disputes and reorganizations were commonplace. Overall, the gangs of the 1870s, 1880s, and 1890s were not very different from those of the 1920s, 1930s, and 1940s, and while the earlier gangs met in back rooms of greengroceries, or saloons, these new gangs had their "clubrooms," usually in tenements, where they drank, played cards, slept, and organized their raids (Haskins, 1974, p. 47). Haskins also notes that, unlike their predecessors, the newer gangs were quite frequently drug users, often cocaine. Also, the beginning of the twentieth century brought with it the beginning of widespread gang firearm use.

Chinese gangs were the first Asian gangs on the East Coast (Chin, 2000). These Chinese immigrants were recruited beginning in the late 1800s to work in factories and on railroads. They brought gang culture with them, in the form of secret associations (*tongs*) that soon put the street gangs to shame in running a criminal operation that controlled opium distribution, gambling, and political patronage. "The Tongs merged the functions, resources, and techniques of politicians, police, financiers, and gangsters, and enforced their levy with no opposition" (Sante, 1991, p. 226). But most of the youth gang conflict mirrored long-standing ethnic, political, and commercial crime rivalries that were rekindled by in influx of immigrants from different regions of China (Greene & Pranis, 2007). Crime increased significantly among Chinese people, and gangs formed among them in Boston, New York City, and San Francisco. Soon, highly organized New York City Chinatown gangs had established a notable street presence as a result of their active involvement in extortion, robbery, debt collection, and protection of Asian-owned vice businesses, and they steadily grew into the 1990s (Chin, 2000). Most of the Chinese gang-related street-level violence, however, has historically been fueled by traditional sorts of conflicts over turf, status, or revenge within Chinatown.

In the first decade of the 1900s, another 8.8 million Europeans migrated to the United States (Pincus & Erlich, 1999), largely into Northeast and Midwest cities, where there were insufficient homes for the enormous influx. The tenement houses created as a temporary solution had become permanent. The arrival of the Poles, Italians, Austrians, and other peoples in New York City in the period 1890–1930 created even worse slum conditions. Ethnic invasion, dominance, and succession processes (Park, 1936) churned the melting pot of immigrant groups (Riis, 1902/1969; Sante, 1991). As new immigrant groups moved in, they took their place at the bottom of the economic ladder, in the worst housing available, succeeding peoples that had garnered sufficient resources to move outward to better neighborhoods.

Gangs and other criminal street groups were virtually unfettered from ruling the streets, and they thrived amidst the squalor. Around 1913, "there were more gangs in New York than at any other period in the history of the metropolis" (Asbury, 1927, p. 360). Irish gangs controlled the west side of Manhattan, and Italian and Jewish gangs controlled the east side, while the Lower East Side was dominated by adult criminal racketeers (Yablonsky, 1997). Gang leaders were no longer Irish; in one case, an Italian fellow took over the reins of an existing Irish gang. An epic gun battle between the Eastman Gang and the Five Pointers that yielded three deaths and seven serious wounds led to the first known gang truce, negotiated in 1903 by politicians whose predecessors fueled them (Haskins, 1974, pp. 57–58). But police "smashed" most of the large gangs in the first U.S. "war on gangs" by beating and arresting them, and the criminal courts imprisoned more than two hundred of the most important gang leaders by 1916 (p. 67).

Two important developments led to the demise of Caucasian gangs in New York City. First, White ethnic immigration had begun to decline sharply around 1910 with World War I, followed by a series of restrictive immigration laws enacted between 1921 and 1924 (Haskins, 1974; Pincus & Erlich, 1999), thus they no longer had large groups of European immigrants from which to recruit. Second, cultural and social assimilation of the European immigrants steadily progressed (Telles & Ortiz, 2008). Soon, "the gang situation downtown had entered its decadent phase. Gangs were splintering into tiny groups, while bands of juveniles and amateurs were coming up everywhere" (Sante, 1991, p. 231).

Third Period of Gang Growth in New York City and the Northeast Region: 1930s–1980s

Two immigration patterns exacerbated Northeast gang activity in this period: the arrival of more Black migrants from the South along with Latinos from Puerto Rico.[5] Blacks had come North in "the great migration" that extended from the beginning of World War I to the early 1970s for expanded employment opportunities in factories (Hamilton, 1964). During the 1930s and 1940s, the most intensive gang activity in New York City shifted to the north (the Bronx and Harlem) and southeast to Brooklyn from downtown. Gangs already were present in East Harlem, quite likely having grown out of ethnic Irish and Italian clashes (Bourgois, 2003), and that area soon would be a gang hot spot. More fighting gangs took root after the arrival of Latinos from Central America, South America, and the Caribbean in the 1930s and 1940s. These peoples settled in areas of the city originally populated by European Americans—particularly in East Harlem (Bourgois, 2003), the Bronx (Curtis, 2003), and Brooklyn (M/Sullivan, 1993). Three-way race riots were common in the 1940s in Harlem, then dubbed *El Barrio*, or Spanish Harlem. The riots were prompted by ethnic invasion, dominance, and succession (Bourgois, 2003). Gang fights between the White (of European extraction) Jets, and the Sharks (comprised of Puerto Ricans) were featured in Leonard Bernstein's classic musical, *West Side Story*. Violence continued on the West Side of New York City in the 1950s.

Meanwhile in South Brooklyn, Italians were provided housing in Carroll Gardens, a neighborhood of brownstones, adjacent to multiple-level Red Hook Houses where Blacks were concentrated. Interracial violence occurred there for more than thirty years, having commenced in the 1940s (Adamson, 2000). The ill-advised public policy of housing them in racially segregated high-rises soon would exacerbate gang problems, as this way of consolidating the population served to structure ongoing territorial gang conflicts by providing a convenient base of operations. Post–World War II urban renewal, slum clearances, and ethnic migration pitted gangs of Blacks, Puerto Rican, and Euro-American youth against each other in battles to dominate changing New York City neighborhoods, and to establish and maintain their turf and honor (Schneider, 1999). In the 1960s, many of the City's neighborhoods experienced a "radical transformation" with migrants from Latin America and the Caribbean replacing traditional European Americans (Curtis, 2003). Overall, by this time, more than two-thirds of the New York gangs were Puerto Rican or Black, and just 11 percent were White (Gannon, 1967).

By 1960, it was estimated that New York City had more than five hundred "fighting gangs" by accounts taken from detached workers (Geis, 1965).

Owing to economic growth in the Northeast, a steady stream of millions of Blacks in the great migration northward (Hamilton, 1964) enlarged slums of Philadelphia, Boston, and New York City between 1940 and 1950. These and other Northeast cities saw widespread Black–White conflict from then onward for several decades. The second northward Black migration spawned violent gangs in Philadelphia, surely from clashes with White ethnics. Miller (1974b) reports that the Black West Philadelphia gangs which emerged in the 1930s were still continuing in the 1970s, no doubt buttressed by the arrival of new recruits. Blumin, a *New York Tribune* reporter, described the northern suburbs of Philadelphia in 1948 and 1949 as "swarming with gangs" (in Davis & Haller, 1973). The city's status as a thriving manufacturing city spiraled downward with "deindustrialization," the large-scale shift from an industrial-based economy to one linked to automation and computerized production that replaced the assembly line, leaving only lower-paying service type positions for working class persons (Ness, 2010). Over three decades, the city lost more than 250,000 manufacturing jobs (McKee, 2004). Severe economic distress followed (Wilson, 1987).

By the late 1960s and early 1970s, Philadelphia had "youth gangs of every description—large and small, violent and peaceful, male and female, Black and White" (Miller, 1974b, p. 226). Philadelphia was experiencing a wave of gang violence which "probably resulted in more murders in a shorter period of time than during any equivalent phase of the highly-publicized 'fighting gang' era in New York" (Miller, 1966/2011, p. 237). Following the growth of Black gangs in Philadelphia to about one hundred violent gangs by the late 1960s, police reported about forty gang-related killings each year in the mid-1970s (Miller, 1975). For a time, broadcast media dubbed the city the "youth gang capital" of the nation (Ness, 2010, p. 32). The great bulk of gang clashes there involved Blacks versus Blacks, accounting for the vast majority of injuries and homicides (Miller, 1974b).

In the meantime, gang violence subsided in New York City in the late 1960s. Two well-conceived programs had been put in place by city officials, the Mobilization for Youth (MFY) project (launched in 1962) and the Lower Eastside Neighborhood Association (LENA). The MFY had some success in addressing urban disorganization and improving service delivery to distressed communities (Greene & Pranis, 2007). Staff in the latter program successfully negotiated several gang truces and coordinated other local services. As a result, the cycles of violent attacks and retaliation were disrupted to a considerable extent (Schneider, 1999). Together, these two programs played a central role in diminishing gang activity somewhat by the mid-1960s (Schneider, 1999). By then, authorities decided that gangs were no longer a serious social problem. Gang activity appeared to have been displaced by the rapid spread of heroin among New York's adolescents (Greene & Pranis, 2007). However, that assumption proved to be fool's gold. The 1970s saw a revival of gang activity in the South Bronx. Therein, youth gangs carried on the traditional battles over turf, but interestingly, "they also organized against the drug trade, mounting aggressive campaigns to drive heroin dealers and junkies out of their neighborhoods" (p. 18).

Expansion of Northeast Gang Activity to the Present

Before 1970, it appears that female gangs had remained auxiliaries to male gangs. An exhaustive effort of the New York City Youth Board's street workers to classify gangs city-wide in the mid-1960's documented more than two hundred New York City street gangs, but girls had not yet established independent cliques (Gannon, 1967). However, by the mid-1970s violent female gangs were reported there (Campbell, 1984, 1991), along with Black female gangs in Philadelphia (Brown, 1977), and White ones in Boston (Miller, 1973, 1980).

Along with the emergence of gangs in boroughs outside the Bronx, New York City saw rapid gang growth in the early 1970s, to an estimated twenty thousand gang members by the mid-1970s (Miller, 1975). Throughout the 1970s, a mixture of youth gangs remained in both the northern and southern areas of New York City (Curtis, 2003), though their energy was sapped by the Civil Rights movement, creating a lull in gang violence between 1965 and 1971 (Schneider, 1999). Greene and Pranis (2007) insist that "cycles of gang activity have continued to the present time, with periodic episodes of gang violence flashing above the tipping point in one distinct area of the city after another" (p. 18), with deadly gun violence among New York City youths reaching a crescendo in the 1980s—though most of it was not gang related. The notorious Brooklyn gangs (largely poor Puerto Rican Latino) were classic fighting youth gangs that drew widespread media attention for the large number of murders in Brooklyn in the early1980s (Sullivan, 1993).

During the 1980s, another immigrant surge occurred in the Northeast and West regions, "with greater cultural diversity than in earlier periods" (Pincus & Erlich, 1999, p. 225). Immigration of Mexican-Americans into New York City, including Harlem, increased sharply in the 1980s (Bourgois, 2003). Many of the new migrants into Brooklyn were Asian and non–Puerto Rican Latinos—especially Dominicans, followed by Central and South Americans (Lobo, Flores, & Salvo, 2002; Sullivan, 1993). The newer Mexican-American and Latino groups began to succeed Puerto Ricans. "In fact, by the late 1990s, Hispanics[6] had replaced Blacks as the largest minority group in the city" (Lobo et al., 2002, p. 704). By the turn of the century, 51 percent of Harlem residents were Latino/Puerto Rican, 39 percent were African-

Americans, and the remainders (only 10 percent) were Whites and other groups (Bourgois, 2003).

In 1980, 24 percent of known gang-problem cities across the United States were in the broader Northeast region (Miller, 1982/1992, p. 33). Hence, New York City was no longer the epicenter of serious street gang activity as was the case in the early 1900s. Boston already had developed a serious and widespread, largely Irish, gang problem that grew enormously after 1965 (Miller, 1974b), involving numerous gangs in lower-status White districts such as East Boston, Charlestown, and South Boston, and two of them compromised primarily Black youngsters. Gangs in Boston remained White at least through the early 1970s (Miller, 1974b), and they were sufficiently serious in the view of agency representatives (Miller, 1975) that it is quite possible that they had diffused around Boston by this time. Miller (1974b) discovered that gangs were present in all thirty-seven cities adjacent to municipal Boston. The district within Boston that had the most persistent gang problem was the predominantly Irish district of South Boston, in the past a neighborhood of eminent political families. The few Black gangs, in Roxbury, were considerably less active than in comparable lower-class areas in White districts such as East Boston, Charlestown, and South Boston. But Boston's Black gangs would continue to grow.

As might be expected given its underpinnings, Philadelphia continued to thrive as a gang center in the Northeast (Ness, 2010). By 1980, authorities in Long Island, in nearby New Jersey (Newark and Jersey City); eastward on Long Island; northward in Albany, Cambridge, Hartford, New Haven, and Springfield; westward in Pittsburgh; and southward in Baltimore also reported gang activity—expanding the scope of gang activity in all directions within the region (Miller, 1982/1992, pp. 157–159). Pittsburgh's gang history was intertwined with drug trafficking gangs that first formed there in the early 1990s in communities where violence associated with the drug trade was most widespread (Cohen & Tita, 1999). Violent urban street gangs calling themselves Crips and Bloods began to take hold there during the latter half of 1991 (Tita & Cohen, 2004). In fact, all of the hard-core sets had Black gang members (Tita, Cohen, & Engberg, 2005). Gang emergence continued through 1993 and stabilized in 1994–1995 with no new gangs forming and no gangs desisting.

The first decade of the current millennium saw enormous gang growth in the Northeast region. By 2008, an estimated 640 street gangs with more than 17,250 members were criminally active in the northernmost area of the New England region that extends northward from the New York border (Federal Bureau of Investigation [FBI], 2009). However, most of the recent gang activity in the broader Northeast region was in the 222 Corridor—so named because Pennsylvania Route 222 bisects five cities in the state.[7] In the decade following the late 1990s, "each of these cities experienced a dramatic increase in gangs and their associated criminal activities" (Easton Gang Prevention Task Force, 2007). This Task Force has insisted that "violent gang members from major metropolitan areas such as New York City, Newark, Philadelphia, and Baltimore travel to and through the 222 Corridor using the smaller urban communities as part of their drug distribution networks" (p. 1). Another important trend in the broader Northeast region is increasing gang-related violence as a result of competition among gangs for control of territories (FBI, 2009). According to the FBI (2009, 2011) and the National Alliance of Gang Investigators' Associations (2009), the most significant gangs operating in the broad East region in recent years are Crips, Latin Kings, *Mara Salvatrucha* (MS-13), *Ñeta*, and United Blood Nation (UBN). According to these same sources, the most significant gangs operating in the smaller New England region are Hells Angels, Latin Kings, Outlaws, Tiny Rascal Gangster Crips, and UBN.

A total of twelve Northeast cities with populations greater than one hundred thousand reported persistent violent gang activity from 1996 to 2009 in the National Youth Gang Survey, each with approximately 40 percent of their total annual homicides as gang related (Howell, Egley, Tita, & Griffiths, 2011). These cities are Hartford, New Haven, and Waterbury, Connecticut; Boston, Springfield, and Worchester, Massachusetts; Elizabeth and Patterson, New Jersey; Buffalo, Syracuse, and Yonkers, New York; and Pittsburgh, Pennsylvania.[8] In recent years, Newark, New Jersey has emerged as an extremely high-rate gang homicide city (Centers for Disease Control, 2012). Philadelphia police did not consistently report gang homicides in this period, but Miller (1982/1992) reported that up to 1980, only Los Angeles and Chicago saw more gang homicides than Philadelphia. Still, the Northeast had the smallest proportion of "chronic" gang cities of all regions from 1996 to 2009, as less than half (45 percent) of the large cities (with populations greater than fifty thousand) in the Northeast were so classified (Howell & Griffiths, 2016).

GANG EMERGENCE AND EXPANSION IN THE MIDWEST REGION

In many respects, gang emergence in Chicago replicated the process of immigrant invasion, dominance, and succession seen in the Eastern region, though one-half century later because of the delayed influx of large migrant groups into the U.S. heartland. As in the Northeast region, gang emergence in Chicago was prompted by extreme social isolation of ethnic groups with fixed lines of demarcation. But racial/ethnic segregation was more restrictive in Chicago (Hagedorn, 2006). This policy fomented racial tensions, both when additional immigrants sought housing in tightly restricted areas, and when long-time residents attempted to move out of poor areas to more desirable ones.

First Period of Gang Emergence in Chicago: 1860s–1920s

As in New York City, Chicago's gangs developed among White immigrants along ethnic lines. Chicago gangs began to form after the city emerged as an industrial hub between the Civil War and the end of the nineteenth century. City officials had recruited a massive labor force from the peasantry of Southern and Eastern Europe, becoming "a latter-day tower of Babel" (Finestone, 1976, p. 6). The city increased enormously and quickly, from fewer than 30,000 residents in 1850 to 1.7 million by 1900 (Berkin, Miller, & Cherny, 2011). First Irish, next German, and then Polish immigrants came (Thrasher, 1927/2000, p. 4). The social tensions and family stresses associated with such a traumatic move from Europe to the United States weakened families and other social institutions. The gang, Thrasher observed, "is one manifestation of the disorganization incident to the cultural conflict among diverse nations and races gathered in one place and themselves in contact with a civilization foreign and largely inimical to them (p. 76)." Merely mischievous groups at first, by the 1860s more menacing gangs of Irish and German juveniles emerged. In the 1860s, these embryonic European ethnic gangs did nothing more than mischievous deeds such as breaking fences and stealing cabbages from the many small family gardens. Thrasher reports that the first bona fide gang of about a dozen Irish fellows, ages seventeen to twenty-two, formed in 1867, and spent much of their time together gambling and sometimes robbing workers on their way home, for which some of them went to prison. More serious Irish and German gangs had more street presence in the late 1880s around the stockyards, fighting among themselves, and terrorizing new immigrants who had begun settling in the area. Aside from fighting constantly among themselves, these White gangs sometimes united to battle other nearby gangs.

Black immigrants began arriving following the U.S. Civil War, to escape the misery of Jim Crow laws and the sharecropper's life in the Southern states. As long as their numbers were small, Black families were scattered around Chicago. But with the great migration northward beginning around World War I (Hamilton, 1964), because of the economic growth in the Midwest, Chicago received large numbers of Black immigrant families. As their presence increased, Blacks were kept out of White Chicago neighborhoods until 1948 by racially restrictive real estate covenants, allowing them to take residency only within the Black Belt of Chicago (a thirty-block stretch of substandard housing along State Street on the south side), and for decades to follow by the informal practices of realtors (Hagedorn, 2006). The first Black gangs formed there in the early 1900s, as turf-defending gangs against the violence of White intruders (Adamson, 1998; Cureton, 2009). "While other ethnic groups followed a path of invasion, succession, and assimilation, Black Chicagoans were forcibly segregated" (Hagedorn, 2006, p. 195).

A major impetus for Black gang growth in Chicago was the race riot of 1919. This particular riot surely was the most serious of at least two dozen such riots throughout the United States in the "Red Summer" (meaning "bloody") following World War I (McWhirter, 2011; Voogd, 2008). These were precipitated by the flood of Black migrants northward, fleeing the degrading sharecropping system, Ku Klux Klan lynchings, and ongoing racial strife in the Deep South that stemmed from Jim Crow laws. However, race riots occurred in both the North and South (Boskin, 1969, 1976).[9] Stretched out over a half century (1900–1949), there were thirty-three major interracial clashes. McWhirter (2011) documented numerous race riots and lynchings in the Red Summer[10] of 1919, the year in which the riots peaked.[11] With few exceptions, it was White people that sparked the incident by attacking Black people—usually when Blacks attempted to change residential patterns, or were perceived as attempting to do so.

The bloody Chicago riot (culminating in thirty-eight deaths and hundreds of injuries) was precipitated by three related events. First, Black men who had migrated from the South to Chicago took jobs vacated by White ethnics when they joined World War I. Once the White soldiers returned and found their old jobs were occupied by Southern migrants, violence commenced. Second, in the spring of 1919, White gangs called Social Athletic Clubs (SACs) had begun fire-bombing Black homes in the so-called "neutral zone" between White and Black residential areas (Chicago Commission on Race Relations, 1922). The capture and murder in the Black Belt of two Black men by a White gang further stirred Black unrest. Third, the death of a Black youth who had been swimming in Lake Michigan ignited the riot (Tuttle, 1996; Voogd, 2008). After drifting into an area demarcated for Whites only, the Black youth was either stoned to death or drowned. Police refused to arrest the White man who led the attack. This angered Black observers. Sporadic fighting broke out between gangs and mobs of both groups. Gangs frequently served as nuclei for the rioting mobs that included sailors in uniform, augmented by civilians (Chicago Commission on Race Relations, 1922).

Following the riot, gangs of White youths brutally attacked Black residents for several days on foot and in automobiles, and shots were fired in forays into their neighborhoods. Violence escalated with each incident, and for thirteen days Chicago was without law and order, as even the state militia could not quell the riot. To be sure, the 1919 riot contributed directly to Black gang formation in Chicago as Black males united to confront hostile White gangs who were terrorizing the Black community (Cureton, 2009; Perkins, 1987). Chicago's police chief admitted to the Chicago Commission on Race Relations, "There is no doubt that a great many police officers were grossly unfair in making arrests. They shut their eyes to offenses committed by White men while they were very vigorous in getting all the colored men they could get" (p. 34). Twice as many Blacks as Whites were arrested.

SACs were very active in the riots and aftermath. These gangs emulated the New York City "voting gangs" (Hagedorn, 2008). As in New York City, the Chicago SACs were composed of Irish lads and men, with political patronage. However, the Chicago SACs were far more plentiful, numbering at least five hundred according to Thrasher (1927/2000, p. 26), almost one-third of all enumerated gangs. Thrasher observed that most of the SACs were transformed from small street gangs, stimulated by city politicians. According-ing to the Chicago Commission on Race Relations (1922), the worst of the White gangs was "Ragen's Colts," sponsored by Cook County Commission-er Frank Ragen. This gang's members boasted that they were "protected" and "tipped off" by police. The politicians also protected the SACs, in return for electoral support in the future. In time, the SACs came to play an active role in running rackets, and controlled them until Al Capone's consolidation of power in the Prohibition years (Hagedorn, 2008).

Second Period of Gang Growth in Chicago: 1920s–1940s

The second period of gang growth in Chicago is amply documented in Thrasher's (1927/2000) monumental study. In a departure from Darwinian explanations of gang members as primitive forms of life, Thrasher stressed the ecological features of gang emergence, pointing out that gangs tend to thrive in "interstitial areas" of Chicago, lying between adjacent commercial and residential neighborhoods. More specifically, the term *interstitial* per-tains to spaces that intervene between things. Urbanizing processes them-selves produced interstitial areas, as explained in Thrasher's insightful de-scription: "In nature, foreign matter tends to collect and cake in every crack, crevice, and cranny—interstices. There are also fissures and breaks in the structure of social organization" (p. 6). Hence, Thrasher regarded the gang "as an interstitial element in the framework of society, and gangland as an interstitial region in the layout of the city" (p. 6).

In his 1927 book, Thrasher plotted on a map of the city the location of the 1,313 early gangs (with a total of some 25,000 members) that he studied in Chicago over a seven-year period.[12] Thrasher's unparalleled study—to this day—revealed Chicago's "gangland" (see the In Focus). During the "Roar-ing Twenties," violence among warring Caucasian gangs was a frequent occurrence in Chicago. Some of the early White Chicago gangs were headed by notorious criminals and rum-runners (Thrasher, 1927/2000), and orga-nized crime groups were very prevalent (Landesco, 1968; Lombardo, 1994), the most notable of which was the Al Capone gang (Peterson, 1963). Street gangs were said to "prosper in the very shadow of these institutions" (McKay, 1949, p. 36), and some youths graduated to participate in them. Interestingly, the Capone gang, better known as the Capone Syndicate, originally comprised largely non-Italian men; the Italian requirement came much later when organized crime began to recruit from Italian communities in the United States (Lombardo, 1994). Instead, these racketeering groups emerged from the urban "social conditions and factors within American society itself" (p. 291).

IN FOCUS

Chicago's Gangland

Gangland first stretched in a broad semicircular zone about the central business district, called the Loop of Chicago, and in general forms a sort of interstitial[13] barrier between the Loop and the better residential areas (Thrasher, 1927/2000). Thrasher mapped the gang regions as the "Southside badlands," the "Northside jungles," and the "West Side wilderness."

The Southside badlands produced the earliest serious street gang in the city, the origins of which Thrasher traced back to 1867 in available urban documents. The unnamed gang was said to have killed and thrown some victims into a creek. This slum area also gave rise to a number of small criminal organizations and unofficially was dubbed "the aristocracy of gangland" (p. 5). Indeed, Ragen Colts, a notorious Irish gang that flourished on the Southside during the period 1912–1927, eventually claimed as many as three thousand members.

Gangs in the Northside jungles continually waged war across river bridges with their enemies, gangs in the West Side wilderness. But the most notorious gangs in the Northside jungles were found in "Little Sicily," which came to be known as "Little Hell." Notably, "Death Corner" in this area was the scene of frequent murders. A Polish gang, Pojay Town, received considerable respect there.

The West Side wilderness was a slum of fifty thousand people per square mile with "a gang in almost every block" (p. 2). This area was home to the Polish Blackspots, a perennial community terror, and the fighting "West Siders," who constantly battled the Pojay Town from the Northside jungles. "The notorious and daring 'Deadshots' and the adventure-loving Irish and Italian 'Black Handers' [were] among the groups which [carried] on hostilities with the [Black] gangs from Lake Street and the Jews to the west and south" (p. 3).

Source: Thrasher, 1927/2000.

More organized ethnic gangs—particularly in the Irish ones—emerged from SACs that were organized around sports and paved the way to success for Irish, Polish, and other White ethnic men as firemen, policemen, and in other respected occupations. Soon, street gangs became entrenched in the patronage networks operated by ward politicians who sponsored many of these SACs (Adamson, 2000), and the city's gangs thrived on political corruption. The Hamburg Athletic Association (Hagedorn, 2008) a particularly tough gang, had among its members an Irish youth named Richard J. Daley who soon became this SAC's president—and later, the longest serving mayor in the history of Chicago (Arredondo, 2004). This particular gang came to be Chicago's "most prominent institutionalized gang" (Hagedorn, 2008, p. 72).

To be sure, politically powerful adults transformed gangs into the most significant community policing agents (Adamson, 2000; Hagedorn, 2006). These adults "approved of the youth gang's role in keeping strangers, especially Blacks, off their streets and beaches, and out of their parks, baseball diamonds, swimming pools, salons, and dance halls" (Adamson, 2000, p. 278). Dubbed "voting gangs" (Hagedorn, 2006), these organized groups ensured the elections of their political patrons by stuffing ballot boxes and intimidating potential voters (Diamond, 2009). Both Mexican-American and Black youth were attacked by Ragen's Colts in marking the racialized boundaries of "their" space. Other Irish gangs applied harassment tactics similar to those of Ragen's Colts and the Hamburgs, frequently assaulting Mexicans and Blacks (Arredondo, 2004, 2008).

More formidable Black gangs emerged in the second period of Chicago gang growth. Between 1910 and 1930, with the "Great Migration" of more than a million Blacks from the rural South to the urban North for employment opportunities, Chicago gained almost two hundred thousand Black residents (Marks, 1985; B. Miller, 2008), giving the city an enormous urban Black population—along with New York City, Cleveland, Detroit, Philadelphia, and other Northeast and Midwest cities. But Chicago received the largest number of Black migrants of all northern cities, as their population doubled in the Windy City.

None of the Chicago gangs that Thrasher (1927/2000) classified in the 1920s was of Mexican descent. This changed after these people's massive migration into Chicago. Beginning around 1916, Mexican laborers began to appear, "having leapfrogged from the interior of Mexico to the Midwest industrial centers" (McWilliams, 1948/1990, p. 169). The first major wave of Mexican migration occurred during the years 1916–1930, instigated by the revolutionary period in Mexico and new employment opportunities in Chicago, particularly in the meat-packing factories, steel mills, and rail yards (Arredondo, 2004, 2008; McWilliams, 1948/1990). Railroads in Mexico linked with the rails in Texas and elsewhere in the Southwest, and these connected with multiple railways leading to Chicago (via Nuevo Laredo, San Antonio, and Kansas City). Taking track work and rail-related jobs with a variety of railroad companies, the first significant numbers of Mexicans worked their way to Chicago, reaching twenty-five thousand by the 1940s (McWilliams, 1948/1990). By then, Mexicans had established more than thirty businesses in the city (Diamond, 2009). In the next twenty years, Mexican migration into Chicago steadily increased, reaching fifty-six thousand by 1960, prompting some observers to dub the city as the "Mexico of the Midwest" (Garcia, 1996). They also settled in Indiana, Kansas, Michigan, Minnesota, Missouri, Nebraska, Ohio, and Wisconsin. But the Mexican migrants' experience in the Midwest was unlike their settlement in the Southwestern United States and California, because the Midwest was never part of Mexico. Hence, in several respects, the Mexican experience in the Midwest resembled that of other immigrant groups.

Nevertheless, Arredondo (2004) makes a strong case that, because of constant deportation threats, Chicago Mexican-Americans were disadvantaged more severely than European ethnics. The majority of Mexican migrants settled on the near west side of Chicago in the Back of the Yards industrial and residential neighborhood and also in south Chicago, where they clashed with European White ethnic groups and Blacks (Arredondo, 2004). Because they settled among similarly stigmatized Polish and Italian immigrants, as might be expected, they experienced multiple social obstacles to adjustment, of "becoming American." "From the outset of their settlement, Mexicans had a harder time finding affordable housing in White neighborhoods, which pushed them closer to African Americans in many parts of the city" (Diamond, 2009, p. 104). In short, "Mexicans found that by the end of the 1930s they were not only a nonwhite racial group but also foreign, that is, outside the ethno-racial borders of Chicago, on the margins, un-absorbable" (Arredondo, 2004, p. 401). Thus, small Mexican-American gangs first formed in Chicago during the 1930s, a second-generation product of conflict, avoidance, and defiance (Diamond, 2009). No doubt, the city's zoot suit riot that occurred there in 1943 instigated more attacks on them by White and Black youths and provided even more impetus for gang formation in defense (McWilliams, 1948–1990).[14] Only a decade would pass before Mexican-American gangs were very prevalent in Chicago. With the growing presence and strength of Black and Mexican gangs, the White ethnic gangs of the 1920s came to an end, largely "a one-generation immigrant ghetto phenomenon" (Moore, 1998, p. 68).

Third Period of Gang Growth in Chicago and in the Midwest Region: 1940s–1980s

From 1940 to 1950, the Chicago Black population nearly doubled, from 278,000 to nearly 500,000 (B. Miller, 2008). As noted earlier, virtually all immigrant Blacks in Chicago were forced to settle in the area known as the "Black Belt." But the expanding Black population could not be contained in this relatively small area. Interracial conflict escalated along with hostility from the largely Irish police, in battles over the use of schools, playgrounds, parks, and beaches (Hagedorn, 2006). The focal points mainly were on the borders between the White "no-go zone" and the Black Belt. With continued immigration and expansion of Black residential zones in "hyperghettoization" (Adamson, 1998), and growing resistance to conflicts with White gangs, the established Black gangs began to form multi-neighborhood branches, and this change "was the first step in Black gang institutionalization" (Hagedorn, 2006, p. 201).

A few White gangs continued to thrive in Chicago. Perhaps most fearsome among these, the 42 gang of west side Chicago's Little Italy, was considered one of the most violent juvenile gangs in history (Taylor, 1990b). Shaw and McKay (1942/1969) tracked the forty-two members—more than thirty of whom eventually were maimed, killed, or sent to prison for such crimes as murder, rape, or armed robbery. Several of the members of this gang graduated into the lower ranks of the Capone mob. As in Northeast cities a century earlier, "defensive localism" fueled White and Black gang growth in Chicago during the 1940s and 1950s, "when the influx of southern Blacks created a tidal wave of urban racial transition" (Adamson, 2000, p. 281). Adults in Chicago and Detroit formed neighborhood improvement and homeowner associations that mobilized gangs to do much of their "dirty work," pulling Blacks off streetcars and attacking University of Chicago students who supported integration. "White youth gangs targeted Black teenagers in [various Chicago neighborhoods] that were undergoing partial or complete racial transition" (Adamson, 2000, p. 281).

The largest and most cohesive Black gangs formed in the 1940s in the "Black Ghetto" of the highly segregated Black Belt (Adamson, 1998; Diamond, 2009). The first formidable Black gang, the Deacons, was "largely a product" of the Ida B. Wells Housing Project, one of the first Chicago public housing projects (Perkins, 1987, p. 27). In addition, Perkins insists that the first Black gangs did not actually pose a threat to the Black community. Rather, in many respects, these gangs acted as guardians of their community as they would retaliate against White gangs that brazenly came into the Black community to terrorize its residents. These "early Black street gangs took great pride in showcasing their gang symbols and colors by wearing colorful jackets and sweaters. This attire was proudly displayed and worn by gang members with little concern or fear of police reprisal" (Perkins, 1987, pp. 26–27). Social events were special for both gang and individual recognition. "Not unlike the White ethnic gang subcultures of the late 1930s, the gang subcultures in the 1940s were structured around 'raising hell' and 'having a good time'—pursuits that also corresponded to the fashioning of masculinity" (Diamond, 2009, pp. 148–149). Being one of the most segregated cities, in the nation, "extreme ghettoization" in Chicago "ultimately cut African American youth off from White areas of the city so that African American youth gangs began to prey on each other" in the massive public housing projects in the middle of slum areas (in the 1940s–1960s)" (Adamson, 2000, p. 282).

The likely first Black female gang in Chicago, the Deaconettes, was reported in the Chicago Black Belt in the 1940s (Perkins, 1987).[15] This teenage gang began as the female contingent of the largest Black gang at that time, the Deacons. The Deaconettes acted independently with its own leadership, however, and battled other female gangs in the 1950s such as the Noblettes, a counterpart of the Italian Nobles gang (Diamond, 2009). But Perkins notes that the prevalence of Black female gangs was short-lived, becoming practically nonexistent by the 1960s, with their roles limited to auxiliary functions to prominent street gangs.

The post–World War II period also saw another surge of Mexican-American and Latino workers move into Midwest cities, including Chicago and Detroit (Pachon & Moore, 1981; Taylor, 1990a). Puerto Rican settlements grew in Chicago, such that "the hostile reception of Puerto Ricans in the mid-1950s, articulated by numerous near-riot situations precipitated by Italian street-corner youth groups, presaged the increasing separation of Italian and Mexican youths in this area" (Diamond, 2009, p. 208). Mexican-American gangs began expanding in the late 1950s after the Mexican members of Italian Dukes and Nobles separated and formed their own gang, Clay People, a racially suggestive name drawn from traditional Mexican pottery. By 1960, nine other Mexican-American gangs had formed on the near west side and lower west side of Chicago: Latin Counts, Spartans, Morgan Deuces, Gents, Play Boys, Harrison-May Boys, Taylor Saints, Saratogas, and Royal Kings (Diamond, 2009, p. ii). Later, toward the mid-1960s, Mexican immigrants spread into two Chicago communities that had long been settled by the Irish, Germans, Czecs, and Poles (Pilsen and Little Village), wherein Mexican-American gangs grew to join the ranks of the most violent gangs in the city (Spergel, 2007).

Following World War II, a seeming "wave" of potentially violent Black youth began to emerge in large numbers in Chicago (Perkins, 1987). "It was probably during this period that the passion of turf took on a greater significance and became crucial to a gang's identity" (p. 27). Several major street gangs formed between the 1940s and early 1960s including the Devil's Disciples (later renamed the Black Gangster Disciple Nation), P-Stones, Vice Lords, and the Latin Kings. The Latin Kings originated in the oldest Mexican-American neighborhoods (Block, 2000). Two of these gangs, Black Gangster Disciple Nation (BGDN) and the Latin Kings grew to become the most widespread and violent of all Chicago gangs (Block, 2000), and the BGDN came to account for more than one-third of all drug-related crimes in Chicago (Block & Block, 1993).

Ironically, well-intentioned public housing policies further expanded gangs' base of operations. To alleviate the housing shortage and better the lives of poor city residents, from 1955 to 1968 the Chicago Housing Authority (CHA) constructed 21,000 low-income family apartments (90 percent of which were in high-rise buildings), the best known of which are Governor Henry Horner Homes, Cabrini Green, and Robert Taylor Homes (RTH). The latter complex, the largest of the three, consisted of 28 sixteen-story buildings in uniform groups of two and three along a two-mile stretch from the industrial area near downtown into the heart of the Black ghetto on the south and west sides of Chicago (Venkatesh, 2000). Believed to be the biggest public housing project in the world, RTH was also dubbed "the largest contiguous slum in the U.S., for it housed approximately thirty thousand Black poor people, and 90 percent of the adults reported welfare as their sole source of support. The miserable ghettos turned into "spaces of revolt" (Castells, 1983). Gang wars erupted, and Chicago's largely Black gang problem "exploded" in the 1960s and 1970s, a period of increased gang "expansion and turbulence" in Chicago (Perkins, 1987, p. 74). Gang membership was then estimated at fifty thousand in the city, leaders became local icons, and several of the gangs were attracted to Black nationalist groups.

Erecting the CHA high-rise complexes dramatically changed Chicago's gangland. Before these buildings were constructed, the city's Black street gangs were small, localized adolescent peer groups involved in only petty delinquency. This setting provided a strong base for gangs, and also brought them into regular and direct contact. "Gangs increased in size, boasting several thousand Black ghetto males, many of whom had remained members into their young-adult years" (Venkatesh, 2000, p. 133). Inadvertently, the high-rise complexes facilitated the cohesion that gangs had sought on the streets. Chicago's Black street gangs grew quickly, to such proportions that they posed a serious threat to the Black community as well as to one another.

> [These gangs] were being perceived as predators who preyed on whomever they felt infringed on their lust for power [and] they turned to more criminal activities and the control of turf became their number one priority . . . by controlling turf, gangs were able to exercise their muscles to extort monies from businesses and intimidate the Black community. (Perkins, 1987, p. 32)

In the 1960s, the Black and Latino gangs replaced the Outfit as the main drug distributors (Hagedorn, 2008). A key to the success of the gangs' foray into drug trafficking was having a defensible space—the high-rises—in which to sell their products, including cocaine (Venkatesh, 2008). In short order, the public housing high-rises became gang incubators and drug turf battle-grounds—amply documented in the RTH (Venkatesh, 1996, 2000, 2008; see also Kotlowitz, 1992). Soon, RTH came to be widely recognized as the hub of Chicago's gang and drug problem. In short, placing the high-rise units adjacent to each other proved disastrous (Moore & Pinderhughes, 1993). In time, given the isolation of most Black housing projects and the Mexican-American settlements in major cities, in many settings, Blacks could only fight other adjacent Blacks, and so it was with Mexican-Americans, fighting among themselves, largely over territories they shared (Adamson, 1998).

Large-scale acceleration of Mexican migration to Chicago began only in the late 1960s and early 1970s, and it has continued unabated since that time (De Genova, 2008). As was the case with White European ethnics, wide-spread gang joining commenced with second-generation children of immi-grants (Thrasher, 1927/2000). So it was with youth of Mexican heritage (De Genova, 2008), producing continuous gang growth. But the immediate Mexi-can gangs that had formed in the 1950s and 1960s were plenty menacing, as they were drawn into battles with European American and Puerto Rican gangs in the Lawndale, Near West, and Near Northwest Side (Diamond, 2009). In these barrios of one of the most segregated cities in the United States, "the struggle over space that the gangs enacted was an everyday affair" (De Genova, 2008, p. 143). If gangs were to survive, they must maintain current members and recruit replacements. Children often got caught in the crossfire. Chicano children "were likewise the premier targets for the gangs' recruitment efforts as they sought to reproduce themselves in subsequent generations of membership" (p. 153).

De Genova relays that he commonly witnessed teenage male gang mem-bers actively cultivating gang identifications among small boys, as young as six or seven years of age, educating and mentoring them in gang signs, symbols, and rivals. In time, the most dangerous Latino gangs formed in Pilsen (the 18th Street barrio) and Little Village (the 26th Street barrio): the Latin Kings and the Two Six (De Genova, 2008). These two gangs soon would join the ranks of the most violent ones in the city. The Latin Kings had an estimated one thousand two hundred members, and the Two Six had some eight hundred members, and each gang was composed of fifteen subunits, or sections, that operated on the streets in their respective territories (Spergel, Wa, & Sosa, 2006). These two gangs accounted for about 70 percent of the gang violence in Little Village by the turn of the century.

Somewhat later than Chicago, St. Louis first saw the emergence of gangs around 1878 (Huff, 2007). Populated by youth of Irish and German descent, these gangs dissolved in time. As Huff explains, permanent gangs did not appear there before the 1950s, growing out of rapid changes in the demographic and socioeconomic structure of the city. These were a mixture of predominantly White and also Black gangs. Cleveland and Minneapolis reported gang activity by the 1920s (Thrasher, 1927/2000).

Detroit also had gangs by the 1920s (Taylor, 1990a). These White ethnic groups were made up of Polish, Jewish, Sicilian, and other groups. Like the earliest groups in New York City, Detroit's were scavenger gangs. These gangs would persist, transforming themselves into territorial and corporate gangs in due course.

Expansion of Midwest Gang Activity to the Present

Ongoing racial unrest contributed to continuous Black gang growth in Chicago (Cureton, 2009; Diamond, 2009; Perkins, 1987). Gang wars began to occur frequently among Chicago's large gangs in the late 1960s, producing a high volume of gang homicides between the mid-1960s and late 1970s, reaching a peak in 1970, followed by another one in the early 1980s, and a third one in the early 1990s (Block, Christakos, Jacob, & Przybylski, 1996). These peaks are evidence of episodic spurts of violence from gang-on-gang wars (Block & Block, 1993). The Blocks report that, overall, most gang violence in this period was related to emotional defense of one's identity as a gang member, defense of the gang and gang members, defense and glorification of the reputation of the gang, gang member recruitment, and territorial expansion. Small Latino gangs tended to specialize in violent offenses, almost entirely from turf battles for prominence over the constricted boundaries of small neighborhood areas, whereas Black gangs tended to specialize in drug offenses (Block & Block, 1993). In addition, gang lore in Black and Mexican-American gangs never let members forget the failure of law enforcement and the criminal justice system to protect them from the early Irish gangs. An ill-timed Chicago Crime Commission (1995) report, *Gangs: Public Enemy Number One*, rekindled that memory. It was viewed as a "most irresponsible document" (Venkatesh, 2000, p. 314), not only because it reminded residents of Mayor Daley's war on gangs, but particularly for having been released under the helm of Chicago Mayor Richard M. Daley, son of Richard J. Daley, who earlier was head of a SAC, the Hamburg Athletic Association, "Chicago's most prominent institutionalized gang" at that time (Hagedorn, 2008, p. 72).

The hot spots of gang violence in Chicago proved more important than the highly publicized gang affiliations. By 1991, 51 percent of the city's street gang-motivated homicides and 35 percent of nonlethal street gang-motivated offenses occurred in ten community areas on the west and south sides—largely gang turfs, controlled mainly by the Disciples, Latin Kings, and Vice Lord gangs (Block & Block, 1993). In 2011, 27 percent of all homicides in Chicago were gang related (Chicago Police Department, 2012). Still, in 2011, the overwhelming majority of gang homicide victims were Black (75 percent), followed by Hispanics (19 percent). But the estimated number of gang members in Chicago has not diminished,[16] and gang homicide perpetrators and victims remain predominantly Black.[17] A partial explanation is available. Mexican-American barrios in Chicago "were historically scattered throughout metropolitan areas, and this pattern still remains," and only two large cities permitted any immigrants to "leapfrog out to areas of second settlement" on the edge of the city, namely, New York and Chicago (Moore & Pinderhughes, 1993, p. xxxiii). Conditions of hyperghettoization of Blacks persist in Chicago (Alexander, 2011).

The diffusion of gang culture in the Midwest region was not as straightforward as broadcast media reports imagined. First, Huff (1993) noted that the presumed migration of gangs from Los Angeles (Bryant, 1989; McKinney, 1988) was unfounded. Huff's (1989) research in Columbus, Ohio and studies in other cities in the Midwest region—including Evanston, Illinois (Rosenbaum & Grant, 1983) and Milwaukee (Hagedorn, 1988)—refuted broadcast media reports on proliferation of Los Angeles gangs. Rather, as Huff (1993) notes, in each of these cities, "gang graffiti and other gang symbols were decidedly influenced by Chicago gang graffiti and symbols" (p. 8). Moreover, "from 1986 to 1988, every identified Ohio gang leader who had moved to Ohio from Los Angeles, Chicago, or Detroit was in Ohio because his parent(s) had moved there" (p. 8; see also Huff, 1989).

Interestingly, the main outside infusion of gang culture into St. Louis came mainly from far away Los Angeles rather than from nearby Chicago, along with gun access from Los Angeles and Detroit (Decker & Van Winkle, 1996). Monti's (1993) informants revealed that there were twenty-four gangs in St. Louis in the mid- to late 1980s and thirty-six by 1990 (Monti, 1993). Nine of these St. Louis gangs had either disbanded or were absorbed by other gangs. One gang (the North Side Posse) split into three gangs or sets after rapid membership growth and disagreements over drug transactions. Four new gangs had emerged in this period, named after Los Angeles-based Hoover Crips (i.e., Redbud, 49 Crips, Rolling 60s, and 49 Hoovers). Three of the new gangs were all female (the Switch Blade Sisters, El Control, and West Side Possettes), and the latter two gangs had close ties with specific male gangs. By 1990, several St. Louis gangs had added the Crip or Blood names of Los Angeles gangs to their own name. However, "the only nonlocal gang that seemed to have established a successful bridge across several different towns was the Gangster Disciples" (p. 245). Nevertheless, St. Louis gangs grew to be quite violent. In a three-year field study of active youth gang members in St. Louis, Decker and Van Winkle (1996) reported that 81 percent owned guns. The mean number of guns owned was more than four.

Two-thirds of gang members had used their guns at least once. The most common use was in gang fights; infrequent use was reported in drive-bys, defense against attacks by strangers, and other incidents.

A gang intelligence expert, Starbuck, documented hybrid gangs in the Midwest region in the early 1980s (Starbuck, Howell, & Lindquist, 2001). Kansas City soon had approximately five thousand documented gang members and affiliates and numerous Chicago- and California-style gangs in the metropolitan area. Motivated to come to Kansas City for drug trafficking opportunities, they brought with them the gang culture from their cities of origin. Soon other cities and towns in the region had gangs that bear names of old time Los Angeles gangs such as Rollin 60s Crip, Inglewood Family Gangster Bloods, or Chicago origin gangs such as Latin Kings and Gangster Disciples. However, a large percentage of these gangs have little or no real connection to the original gangs and often put their own variations into the way they operate in cities in which individual gang members had relocated.

Detroit, Cleveland, and Minneapolis reported substantial gang activity by the 1920s (Thrasher, 1927/2000). By 2006, nineteen gang turfs were scattered around Chicago, throughout Cook County (Chicago Crime Commission, 2006, p. 119). The Chicago gang culture soon spread to nearby cities, south to Gary, Indiana, southeast to Columbus, Ohio, and north to Milwaukee, Wisconsin (Cureton, 2009; Huff, 1993). Actually, Milwaukee's gangs formed much earlier, among second-generation children of immigrants—German, Polish, and Italian—and growing out of social disorganization attendant to their overcrowding in this "quintessential U.S. factory town" (Hagedorn, 1998, p. 121). Violence increased there in the same pattern seen in Chicago, as Blacks, Puerto Ricans, and Mexican-Americans arrived. In 1980, just 7 percent of known gang-problem cities were in the North Central region of the United States (Miller, 1982/1992, p. 33).

Chicago remains the epicenter of gang activity in the Midwest. "Chicago gangs tend to be larger in size, more organizationally sophisticated, and more heavily involved in large-scale drug dealing than gangs in other cities" (Papachristos, Hureau, & Braga, 2013, p. 422). In 2008, the largest street gangs in Chicago included the Gangster Disciple Nation, Black Gangsters/New Breeds, Latin Kings, Black P. Stone Nation, Vice Lords, Four Corner Hustlers, and Maniac Latin Disciples (Chicago Crime Commission, 2006, p. 11).

In time, other cities in the surrounding Great Lakes Basin[18] reported large numbers of gang homicides, particularly Green Bay, Wisconsin; South Bend, Indiana; Grand Rapids, Michigan; Akron and Toledo, Ohio; and Buffalo and Rochester, New York (Howell et al., 2011). From 1996 to 2009, two-thirds of the ninety-five Midwest gang problem cities with populations greater than fifty thousand were classified as "chronic" gang cities (Howell & Griffiths, 2016). Much of the span of gang activity in the Great Lakes Basin is attributable to the enormous growth of gangs in Chicago and also in Illinois prisons.

To be sure, the exploding gang problem in Chicago was heard far and wide, for it was dually driven by handgun violence and enormous youth gangs based in high-rise forts that law enforcement could not penetrate. Never before had street gangs received such extensive and diverse media coverage. It can be said with certainty that media presentations make gangs seem very appealing. No doubt, many street-oriented young people took notice and in the surrounding region as well. Gang culture has long been widely diffused in the United States (Diamond, 2009; Ro, 1996). Often integrated with youth culture, it is evident that "fads and fashions that begin among the ghetto poor diffuse to middle- and upper-class young people and vice versa. Styles of music, dance, and dress diffuse widely. Artifacts of affluence, such as shoes and gold chains, become symbols of status among the less affluent" (Short, 2002, p. viii).

A total of sixteen Midwest cities with populations greater than one hundred thousand have reported persistent violent gang activity over the past fourteen years in the National Youth Gang Survey—approximately 40 percent of total annual homicides were identified as gang related (Howell et al., 2011). These cities consist of Wichita, Kansas; Independence, Missouri; Aurora, Chicago, Elgin, Joliet, Springfield, and Peoria, Illinois; Fort Wayne, Indianapolis, and South Bend, Indiana; Minneapolis and St. Paul, Minnesota; Akron and Toledo, Ohio; and Madison, Wisconsin. With a less serious gang problem, Detroit reported about 20 percent of total annual homicides as gang related over the past fourteen years in the National Youth Gang Survey (Howell et al., 2011). Taken as a whole, these cities form a large Midwestern concentration of gang violence.

GANG EMERGENCE AND EXPANSION IN THE WEST REGION

Developments leading up to emergence of the first street gangs in Los Angeles and elsewhere the West region began to materialize centuries beforehand.[19] The cultural history surrounding the Spanish-speaking population in the territory that would become the southwestern part of the United States dates back to the sixteenth century, when people of Indian and Spanish heritage inhabited a broad region that was then northern Mexico and is presently the American Southwest. Having colonized the Mesoamerican cultural region that extends from just north of the central plateau of Mexico City to Central America, Spanish forces moved northward.[20] The Spanish expeditions (or *entradas*) for the discovery, conquest, and colonization of new territory were devastating for native Indian tribes and Mexican inhabitants (McWilliams, 1948/1990). "With neither armor nor horses, the Indians were simply no match for the Spanish" (p. 37). Less heroic than folklore suggests, possessing a clear superiority of weapons, there was nothing to stop the

Spaniards. Enveloped in a feudal, caste-like social system that the Spanish brought to the Southwest, and supported by Catholic clergy, eventually, Spanish conquerors succeeded in establishing a few permanent settlements within the area that later would become New Mexico, including Santa Fe.[21] However, the broad Spanish-speaking and acrimonious "borderland" between the United States and Mexico extended from California to Texas. McWilliams graphically envelops that area by imagining "a fan thrust north from Mexico with its tip resting on Santa Fe." Gradually the fan unfolds— eastward to Texas, westward to California—with the ribs of the fan extending northward from the base in Mexico. The bulk of Spanish-speaking people in the United States resided inside this fan of influence for several centuries.

The United States' boundaries had not yet been fully established. In fact, a half century would pass after the United States was formed before its border with Mexico was agreed upon. A war between these countries that commenced in 1846, the MexicanAmerican War, was settled by the 1848 Treaty of Guadalupe Hidalgo. Under this agreement, the Mexican government ceded a large southwestern region to the United States. Those Spanish and Mexican citizens residing within the ceded domain—essentially the entire fan of Spanish-Mexican influence that we now know as California, Nevada, Utah, Arizona, Texas, and residents in parts of New Mexico and Colorado—were to become U.S. citizens if they failed to leave the territory within one year of treaty ratification. Only an estimated seventy-five thousand Spanish-speaking people were living in the Southwestern region at that time; the great majority of which were of mixed Spanish-Indian blood (McWilliams, 1948/1990). However, a total of 180,000 Indians lived there— whom McWilliams called the "forgotten link," for they would not be granted statehood. Instead, Anglos moved westward, in "Manifest Destiny" as the industrial revolution undergirded growth and development. Anglo-Americans took over all administrative, trade, and cultural activities, and neither the Indian natives nor the Mexicans had any influence on government policy (Campa, 1993).

Despite the Treaty of Guadalupe Hidalgo, migration of Mexican citizens from deep in Mexico to the Southwest area annexed by the United States steadily increased. First, this custom had long been commonplace for relatives. Second, the Mexican Revolution that began in 1910 sent large numbers of Mexican peoples northward, populating the area with Mexicans, no longer Spaniards—although some called themselves Spanish Americans in an effort to ease assimilation (Vigil, 1998). "For many Mexican Americans, however, assimilation was a sad experience because dominant Anglo society was so exclusionary" (p. 207). *Pachucos* was the name given large numbers of Mexican males in Southwestern schools (girls were called *Pachucas*). To be sure, these names were symbolic of the plight of Mexican youth—caught between two cultures.

From another perspective, Chicanos emerged from the Mexican Revolution. Their revolutionary spirit soon would be intensified in the Southwest region and later brought to a boiling point in Los Angeles, in the 1960s, with the Chicano Movement. As Rendon (1971, pp. 2–3) explained, "It is closer to the truth that there has always been a Chicano revolt. That is, the Mexican-American, the Chicano, as he calls himself and his *Carnales*, brother and sister Chicanos, has never ceased to be a revolutionary all the while he has suffered repression." With the Anglo-American dominance in the Southwest region, Mexican-Americans who wished to protect and maintain ethnic traditions formed barrios (ethnic enclaves) in towns and *colonias* (colonies) in rural area in the 1920s and 1930s (Vigil, 1998). "Thus, some rejected separatism, assimilation, and acculturation—or were forced out of these patterns by poor treatment—and continued a life of resistance" (p. 170). Gradually, most Chicanos in the United States adjusted to the new industrial order and settled mainly in cities.

By 1930, the total number of Mexicans in the United States had grown to number 1.4 million, nine-tenths of which resided in just five states: Texas (48 percent), California (26 percent), and the remainder in Arizona, Colorado, and New Mexico (McWilliams, 1948/1990). The relatively large contingent in California, in particular, felt resentment that they were no longer Mexican Nationals. Even though they were naturalized citizens, they often were treated as second-class citizens and were told to go back to their home, Mexico. In their mind, they *were* home, but now their homeland was part of the United States because of the annexation. "The trail from deep inside Mexico through El Paso to its northernmost boundary had long been a well-traveled road with a multi-generation tradition of migration to and from Mexico and the United States (McWilliams, 1948/1990; Vigil, 1998). But the "new" Mexican immigrants into Los Angeles[22] were pushed into barrios just east of the center of the emerging city after a flood of Anglos arrived in the late nineteenth century. In time, these *barrios* were scattered throughout the metropolitan area, near migration routes, and later, as outgrowths alongside rail lines that employed Mexican workers in the West region (McWilliams, 1948/1990).

Mexican immigration was greatly accelerated by the Mexican Revolution (1910–1920), Mexico's new rail system, and the labor needs of the Southwest and the Midwest U.S. regions. These three factors combined to draw 700,000 legal Mexican immigrants to the United States from 1911 to 1930 (Telles & Ortiz, 2008). Vigil (2011) maps the expansion of Mexican migration routes in three stages, beginning with El Paso as the major immigration route up to the 1920s (p. 190); next, via Tijuana in the 1940s (p. 203); then, all along the Southwest-Mexico border in the 1960s (p. 263). Yet two forces served to incubate street gangs of Mexican origin in Los Angeles and in other

Western cities: physical and cultural "marginalization" (Vigil, 1988, 2002, 2008).

The barrios in which the earliest and most firmly established gangs developed were well-demarcated settlements of Mexican immigrants. "They were located in geographically isolated areas that other settlers and developers had bypassed as less suitable for habitation, and were further isolated by cultural, racial, and socioeconomic barriers enforced by ingrained prejudices of the Anglo-American community" (Vigil, 1993, p. 95). Conflict with groups of youth in other barrios, school officials, police, and other authorities solidified them as highly visible groups (Moore, 1993; Vigil, 1993).

First Period of Gang Emergence in the West Region: 1890s–1930s

Widely recognized experts on Mexican-American gang origins report that the first gangs in the Western region evolved from the *palomilla* (see the In Focus). These were well-established, non-territorial, age-graded friendship associations, the equivalent of embryo gangs, that had long been a tradition in Mexico and continued to appear along a route from southwest Texas (Rubel, 1965) north through the Rio Grand Valley[23] to El Paso and onward to Los Angeles (Redfield, 1941; Rubel, 1965; Vigil, 1998). Gangs had not yet formed in Mexico, likely not before the late 1950s (Lewis, 1961). Twenty to twenty-five gangs composed of three hundred to four hundred Mexican boys—80 percent of whom were under fifteen years of age—were reported in the Mexican section of El Paso in 1924 (R. E. Dickerson, cited in Thrasher, 1927/2000, p. 130). Having been active for eight or nine years, their delinquency involvement in stealing and property damage had landed many of them in state correctional facilities.

The first reported Mexican-American gang members, in El Paso, were called *Pachucos* (a Mexican-Spanish word for a young Mexican living in El Paso, especially one of low social status who belongs to a more tightly knit group, a street gang, *pachuco*, a term that replaced *pandilla* and *banda*; see In Focus: *Palomilla, pandilla,* and *banda*). The gangs in Los Angeles grew from this base, with continuing migration from Mexico via El Paso in particular (McWilliams, 1948/1990; Moore, 1978, 1998; Paz, 1961/1990; Vigil, 1990, 1998). In time, *pachuco* and "zoot-suiter" became synonymous terms that replaced the word Mexican (McWilliams, 1948/1990). Zoot suits were a fashionable clothing trend, stylized for fast dancing maneuvers in the late 1920s and popularized in the nightclubs of Harlem (McWilliams, 1948/1990). The exaggerated zoot suit included an oversized jacket with wide lapels and shoulders, and baggy pants with cuffs that narrowed at the ankles, typically accompanied by a wide-brimmed hat.

IN FOCUS: *PALOMILLA, PANDILLA,* AND *BANDA.*

An anthropologist, Arthur J. Rubel (1965), observed a custom in Mexican society that contributed to gang formation. Social groups of young men were called *palomilla* after a word that is derived from the Spanish *palomilla* (dove), thus meaning a covey of doves, and by extension, a company of young men. Rubel observed *palomilla* in Mexiquito, a neighborhood in the Southwest Texas town of New Lots, in Hidaldo County. It was customary in Mexican society for *palomilla* to bridge the transition from childhood to adulthood for young males. "It is in the *palomilla,* rather than in his family, that a boy becomes a man and learns to express himself as such" (p. 93).

Of course, for the most part, the *palomilla* simply were congenial and stable associations of friends (*comprades*) who hung out together, drank, partied, shared amorous adventures, and discussed personal problems of mutual concern. But important cultural traditions were maintained in two critical life events, marriage and death. The *palomilla* played a very important role in celebrating marriage, often with ceremonial barbeques and dances. In addition, "so important is the role of the *palomilla* during bereavement that . . . the rites of intensification at funeral services as clearly apply to the relationship between the bereaved and his *palomilla* as between the former and his families of association and procreation" (p. 95). The funerals of fallen gang *comprades* are not only well attended, and commemorated with the salute, R.I.P. (rest in peace), but gang lore honors deceased members.

It is readily apparent from research on Mexican-American youth groups that the *palomilla* customs remain influential. The crystallization of street gangs from these traditional associations was commonplace in Los Angles, and *palomilla* customs serve to maintain the traditions and strengths of Mexican-American gangs. "A 'gang' of Mexican boys in Los Angeles is held together by a set of associations so strong that they often outweigh such influences as the home, the school, and the church" (McWilliams (1948/1990, p. 216).

Based on a visit to Los Angeles, Paz (1961/1990) observed that youths of Mexican origin had adopted unique forms of speech, personal deportment, and clothing, notably the zoot suit. In time, the innocuous term *palomilla* was "dropped from colloquial and academic usage, to be replaced by the terms *pandilla* and *banda.* The 1968 Mexican Penal Code "considered *pandilla* to be akin to a criminal organization, motivated, strategic, and undertaking hard-core gang behaviors, whereas *banda* was shorthand for social relations that might be ascribed as gang-like or gang-lite" (Jones, 2014, p. 260).

Sources: Jones, 2014; Rubel, 1965; McWilliams, 1948/1990; Paz 1961/1990

The first bona fide Chicano[24] gang crystallized in *El Hoyo Marvilla*[25] (in Belvedere, East Los Angeles, Boyle Heights area) in the 1930s (Moore, 1991, p. 27). This gang was named *El Hoya Marvilla*, after the barrio by the same name, as was the tradition with the Chicano gangs. These gangs seemingly coalesced under urban social pressures and discrimination in schools (McWilliams, 1948/1990, pp. 216–217). Belvedere was the area of "first settlement" for most immigrant families. Other Chicano gangs soon formed in the nearby Pico Gardens housing project (Vigil, 2007), and a major one, *Cuatro Flats*, is described in some detail later in this volume. Female Chicano gang cliques also were prominent in that area by the 1930s (Moore, 1991). Although most of them were attached to male cliques, several were independent of the boys but sometimes were attached to a barrio. Eight female cliques of the *El Hoya Marvilla* and White Fence gangs formed by the 1960s (p. 28).

The Chicano tradition of settling in *barrios* and *colonias* gave permanence to gangs, in that the process became perpetual. "Each new wave of immigrants has settled in or near existing barrios and created new ones, [providing] a new generation of poorly schooled and partially acculturated youths from which the gangs draw their membership" (Vigil & Long, 1990, p. 56). In this way, isolationism and stigmatization were major contributing factors to gang regeneration and growth (Moore, 1985). The intense bonding to barrios and gangs is unique to Los Angeles and other Southwestern cities because of their long-standing youth subculture underpinnings. The three long-standing "classic barrios" that formed gangs in East Los Angeles are *Marvilla* cliques (1930s), White Fence (1940s), and *Cuatro Flats* (1940s) (Moore, 1991; Vigil, 2010). Each of these have two or three cohorts defined by age and status in the gang; typically twelve to fourteen year olds in middle school, fourteen to eighteen year olds in high school, and eighteen to twenty year olds, seasoned *veteranos*, who may play this role into their thirties.

Second Period of Gang Growth in the West Region, Los Angeles: 1940s–1950s

Following a hiatus during the Great Depression, Mexican immigration accelerated again beginning in the early 1950s, bringing almost 1.4 million more persons to the United States by 1980 (Telles & Ortiz, 2008). The Mexican-origin population in the United States grew from 2.5 million to 8.7 million during this period. The Los Angeles area received the most Mexican immigrants. Partly as a result, the city grew enormously "between 1930 and 1990, adding more than six million people for a total of nearly nine million residents" (Moore & Vigil, 1993, p. 30), becoming the second-largest city in the nation. Los Angeles became heavily populated with an unusual mixture of native-born urban Americans, Mexican-Americans from other parts of the

Southwest, Salvadorians, Guatemalans, and other Latin Americans (Moore, 1978, Vigil, 2002). By the 1950s, fights (more so rumbles than shootings) were a common occurrence among the Cuatro Flats and other gangs in Pico Gardens and the broader Boyle Heights area. Gang violence escalated there in the 1950s and 1960s. Still, guns were rarely used. "The key figure in these disputes was the gang's toughest leader, who was considered . . . the baddest dude of the gang and the person who best understood the gang's place in the larger context of the barrio" (p. 43).

Two historic social events proved pivotal in the growth of Mexican-American gangs in the West: the Sleepy Lagoon murder and the zoot suit riots. Mexicans had come to replace the Japanese as a "scapegoat" people (McWilliams, 1948/1990). As part of the stereotype, Mexican immigrant youth were called "zoot-suiters." But the stylish outfits also served a purpose for the stereotyped youth. "They were often used as a badge of defiance by the rejected against the outside world and, at the same time, as a symbol of belonging to the inner group" (McWilliams, 1948/1990, p. 219), which also contributed to gang formation in Denver, CO and Ogden, UT (Durán, 2012). Broadcast media continued their derogatory characterization of Mexican youth with these captions: "Pachuco Gangster" or "Zoot-suit Hoodlum," one and the same.

In July 1942, the newspapers prominently featured a fight between the Belvedere "gang" and the Palo Verde "gang," and the stories stigmatized the "Mexican character" of the youths (p. 207). A Mexican youth was mysteriously beaten to death the next month around a place that a reporter dubbed "Sleepy Lagoon," a popular swimming hole in what is now East Los Angeles. Police quickly swept up twenty-four members of the 38th Street Mexican-American gang. The criminal trial was more of a ceremonial lynching than a trial in a court of justice, and seventeen Mexican youths were convicted and jailed or imprisoned (McWilliams, 1948/1990). "From the very outset, a 'gang' was on trial," stereotyped in every negative way possible by prosecutors (p. 209). Two of the boys were sent to San Quentin Prison. Confinement of these innocent youths served to unite the Mexican community in a common cause, a battle against the establishment. They maintained their dignity and demonstrated a type of gang pride and resolve never seen before, and this elevated the incarcerated 38th Street gang members to folk hero status in the Mexican community. A Sleepy Lagoon Defense Committee eventually got all charges dismissed to great joy in the Mexican community (McWilliams, 1948/1990).

Using the derogatory "Pachuco Gangster" and "Zoot-suit Hoodlum" terms to distinguish Mexican immigrant youth (Chicanos) apart from native Mexicans, police and newspapers teamed up to create a moral panic centered on the Mexican-American gangs. Soon, the media developed a full-blown stereotype of the Mexican gangs as comprised of gun-toting, drug-dealing, drug-using youth who presumably coerced other youngsters into committing robberies and other crimes (McWilliams, 1948/1990). The exaggerated image of them as a savage group led to the first moral panic over gangs in the United States. In the context of heightened tensions toward these youth, they were accused of attacking a group of servicemen while on leave. Instead, the boys were first attacked by a non-Mexican group according to McWilliams's (1943) historical investigation of the incident. But police accused a group of the Mexican boys and threatened to round them up in a community-wide raid in the Mexican barrio. Following this event in June, 1943, military personnel on leave and citizen mobs organized themselves and, initially in taxi cabs, chased and beat any Mexican youth wearing colors—during a five-day riotous period (Vigil, 2002, p. 68). This was but the first of several "zoot suit riots." Other similar anti-Mexican riots followed in the summer of 1943, notably in San Diego, Philadelphia, Chicago, Detroit, and Harlem (McWilliams, 1948/1990). But the worst riot was in Los Angeles. "During the riots, the press, the police, the officialdom, and the dominant control groups of Los Angeles were caught with the bombs of prejudice on their hands," and the riots left a residue of resentment and hatred in the minds and hearts of thousands of young Mexican-Americans in Los Angeles (p. 231). To be sure, the riots facilitated gang recruitment and greatly fortified the resolve of Chicano gangs.

Black gangs had a distinctively different history in Los Angeles. These gangs continuously formed in Los Angeles in three phases (Alonso, 2004, 2013): (1) in the 1920s and early 1930s (strictly juvenile gangs), (2) in the 1940s (growing out of school-based conflicts), and (3) in the 1960s onward (growing out of segregated housing conflicts). Relatively well-formed Black gangs emerged beginning in the mid-1940s (Alonso, 2013). Several observers report that these gangs formed as a defensive response to White violence in the schools (Alonso, 2004; Davis, 2006; Vigil, 2002). The first interracial gang conflicts were reported at Manual Arts High in 1946, at Canoga Park High in 1947, and at John Adams Junior High in 1949 (Vigil, 2002). Once the Black gangs had formed, the victimized youths were better able to defend themselves against Whites over the social space of the schools and entertainment areas.

Third Period of Gang Growth in the West Region, Los Angeles: 1950s–1980s

At the beginning of this period of gang growth in the West region, the development of Black gangs in Los Angeles followed a pattern similar to the emergence of their counterparts in Chicago—stemming from large-scale westward Black migration into that region in the 1950s (Hamilton, 1964). Migration of Blacks westward from the South had not commenced before this time, as economic opportunities in the Northeast and Midwest were more plentiful beforehand. "Southern Blacks were simply looking for a better life, and the West was considered the land of prosperity because of employment opportunities in factories" (Cureton, 2009, p. 355). Instead, institutional inequality (particularly in housing, education, and employment) and discriminatory housing covenants legalized in the 1920s rendered much of Los Angeles off-limits to most minorities (Alonso, 2004; Cureton, 2009). Black social clubs began to challenge the restrictive housing covenants, leading to conflicts between White and Black clubs. "Fear of attack from Whites was widespread and this intimidation led to the early formation of Black social street clubs aimed at protecting Black youths against persistent White violence directed at the Black community" (Cureton, 2009, p. 664). As White clubs began to fade from the streets, the Black clubs—first organized as protectors of the community—began to engage in conflicts with other Black clubs. Comprised largely of older youths, Black gang activity soon represented a significant proportion of gang incidents across Los Angeles (Alonso, 2004).

Serious Black gangs were well established by the 1960s in low-income housing projects, including Jordan Downs (700 units housing 2,940 people), William Nickerson Jr. Gardens (1,110 units housing 4,662 people), and the Watts slum, which had 26,000 residents, one-third of whom lived in public housing by the end of the 1950s (Vigil, 2002; see also Vigil, 2007). The effects of residential segregation (particularly in public housing projects), police brutality, and racially motivated violence in the aftermath of the 1960s Civil Rights conflicts created a breeding ground for gang formation in the early 1970s (Alonso, 2004). Beginning as early as 1940 (Vigil, 1988), low-income housing projects helped to curb social problems for impoverished Los Angeles families, but these large-scale settlements also contributed to gang growth among Black and Mexican youths alike. Five such projects in East Los Angeles "have become barrios in their own right" (p. 21). The most notable one that housed Blacks was Jordan Downs, in the Watts section.

Influential gang members successfully galvanized Black youths into "revolutionary soldiers" in the Watts Rebellion of 1965, and this signaled "a turning point away from the development of positive Black identity in the city" (Alonso, 2004, p. 668). The deeply racialized context undergirded the resurgence of new street groups between 1970 and 1972—in large part because of poverty and high unemployment rates prevalent among Black youth and the collective self-defense against police brutality—particularly in the Watts race riot—and social injustices (Alonso, 2004; Davis, 2006). By the 1970s, many Blacks were able to escape the ghetto to surrounding communities, and in doing so, they not only widened the ghetto's boundaries but also the expanse of gang territories (Vigil, 2002). Unlike the Mexican-American gangs, which were located in more geographically restricted barrios, territorial boundaries were less important to the Black gangs, allowing them to encompass a wider area, "creating gangs that were more so confederations than single entities" (Vigil, 2002, pp. 68–69).

The Watts riots commenced in August 1965 after a California Highway Patrolman pulled over in the Black Watts neighborhood a Black man for drunken driving and impounded his vehicle, refusing to allow the fellow's brother to take possession of it (Zilberg, 2011, p. 270). This catalyst ignited the Watts revolt, after which street rivalries were set aside for a period of three to four years (Vigil, 2002). But the intensity of the "great rumble" of 1965 had a lasting effect. Many street youths were attracted to the Black Panthers and their mantra, "Black power!" underscored with clenched fists.

The emergence of a wide variety of street groups also expanded the base of Black gangs into two camps, Crips and Bloods (aka Pirus). There are competing accounts of how Bloods and Crips gangs formed.[26] Prominent among these is Cureton's (2009) research, indicating former Black Panther president Bunchy Carter and Raymond Washington formed the Crips in 1969 out of disappointment with the failure of the Black Panther Party to achieve its goals. According to Cureton, the Crips originally were organized to be a community self-help association; however, following Carter's death, the Crips' leadership shifted its focus to "drug (marijuana, heroin, and other drugs) and gun (Uzi, AK-47, and Colt AR-15 assault rifles) sales that involved much violence and crime" (p. 356). Street gang feuds soon erupted. "Crip identity took over the streets of South L.A. and swept Southside schools in an epidemic of gang shootings and street fights by 1972," first involving eighteen Black gangs, that multiplied to sixty by 1978 and to two hundred seventy throughout Los Angeles County by the 1990s (Alonso, 2004, p. 669).

The Crips gang also spread southward at that time, into Compton and Inglewood, spawning more independent gangs (Alonso, 2004).[27] Bloods formed in defense against the Crips. The Bloods became particularly strong in the Black communities in South Central Los Angeles—especially in places on its periphery such as Compton—and in outlying communities such as Inglewood, Pacoima, Pasadena, and Pomona, and Crippettes soon formed as the female counterpart (Vigil, 2002). Crips wore blue clothing; the Bloods chose red. Both the Bloods and the Crips drew large memberships in the public housing projects built in the 1950s—and Blacks made up nearly 95 percent of the membership of these two gangs (Vigil, 2002, p. 76). These two gangs were the largest of more than five hundred Los Angeles gangs in the 1970s. The public housing projects had become their neighborhood turfs and the hyper ghetto conditions therein sustained them. Inevitably, the introduction of public housing into the ghetto to fill the need for affordable housing, as well as the concentration of poor and low-income peoples in these areas "further contributed to an increase in the number of unsuccessful residents, thus ensuring that available positive role models were kept to a minimum and that the role models that were around belonged to the street" (p. 77).

Expansion of Western Gang Activity to the Present

Other Latino and Asian people began migrating to Los Angeles in the late 1970s, causing major demographic shifts throughout the greater Los Angeles area (Vigil, 1990, pp. 126–127). These first-generation residents replaced earlier Black and third-generation Latino ghettos and barrios, respectively. They soon established new barrios in multistoried low income apartments while changing the appearance of the downtown shopping district. In general, they transformed the spatial and social fabric of greater Los Angeles.

Black gangs in Los Angeles expanded enormously from the early-1970s to the 1990s, having increased in number by fifteen-fold (Alonso, 2004). This proliferation was associated with a gang homicide epidemic that raged from 1979 through 1994 (Hutson, Anglin, Kyriacou, Hart, & Spears, 1995). Alonso (2004) attributes the enormous increase in Black gangs to the "racialization and disenfranchisement" of Black youth in Los Angeles—particularly in the legal system, policing practices, and White-Black youth conflicts. Crips and Bloods gangs have remained strong for more than thirty years. Yet neither of these groups (or affiliations) has been unified to the extent of the Chicago People and Folk "nations."

The President of the California Gang Investigator's Association, Wesley McBride, said in 2005,

> In Los Angeles there are over 200 Crips sets and maybe a 100 Bloods sets, there is no common leader among any and they war on one another. [Most gang violence involves] Crips on Crips, Bloods on Bloods. There is no evidence of a Crips or Bloods nation in California. They do not understand that concept of gang nations. Each gang is totally independent of other gangs. (cited in Howell, 2012, p. 33)

One would be mistaken in assuming that all that these gangs do is fight; for Hoover Crips in South Central Los Angeles, gangbanging is a way of life, but one that also has a human side (Cureton, 2002, 2008). Distinctive clothing and symbols distinguish them to the present time. In the 1990s, these gangs adopted expensive warm-up or jogging suits as preferred clothing, particularly sports apparel. "Expensive clothing, 150 dollar sneakers, beepers, and flashy cars imply that one is 'rollin' (making money by dealing drugs), whether or not that is actually the case" (Huff, 1993, p. 12). An interesting feature of these gangs—unlike Chicano gangs—is that little loyalty is demanded of Bloods and Crips gangs.

The enormous growth of gangs and related violence in Los Angeles in the mid- to late 1980s prompted Police Chief Daryl Gates to declare "war on gangs" and form the nation's first gang unit (Davis, 2006). Based on his overstated fear that gangs represented an enormous threat to public safety—even perhaps national security—the initial Los Angeles Police Department (LAPD) gang units specialized in "crackdowns" (Klein, 1995, pp. 162–163). Chief Gates's Community Resources Against Street Hoodlums (CRASH) unit was first activated in south central Los Angeles in 1988, when a force of a thousand police officers—in "Operation Hammer"—swept through the area on a Friday night and again on Saturday, arresting presumed gang members on a wide variety of offenses, including existing warrants, new traffic citations, curfew violations, illegal gang-related behaviors, and observed criminal activities. But only sixty felony arrests were made, and charges were filed on just thirty-two of these. As Klein describes it, "This remarkably inefficient process was repeated many times, although with smaller forces—more typically one hundred or two hundred officers" (p. 162). Ten years later, the CRASH unit was shut down because of corruption among the police officers, the use of excessive force, and civil rights violations (Katz & Webb, 2006).

Some Mexican-American gangs have continuously grown in the community where they first emerged in the 1930s (cf. Moore, 1991; Brantingham, Tita, Short, & Reid, 2012). "Until the 1980s they were a predominantly adolescent phenomenon" (Moore, 1998, p. 69). But many gangs expanded with age-graded cliques in East Los Angeles. Altogether, twenty-nine street gangs were active in 2002 in the Boyle Heights area of East Los Angeles (previously called Belvedere). In general, the growth of Mexican-American gangs from the 1960s onward was fueled by three historical developments: the Vietnam War, the War on Poverty, and the Chicano movement of the 1960s and 1970s (Vigil, 1998). Vigil notes that the Vietnam War depleted the barrios of a generation of positive role models. The ending of the War on Poverty also eliminated jobs and increased marginalization. Perhaps most important, the Chicano civil rights movement brought attention to the overall plight of the Mexican-American people, particularly long-suffering barrio populations. Its climax occurred with region-wide participation in the Chicano Moratorium march in East Los Angeles on August 29, 1970 (Moore & Vigil, 1993). "The event ended in death and destruction: a crowd dispersed by police and tear gas reacted by looting and destroying stores in the commercial section of East Los Angeles" (p. 37).

Gang activity was first noted in San Francisco as early as the 1960s, and these early gangs were mainly African-American and Asian with a mixture of Mexican gangs later into the early 1990s (Joe, 1994; Miller, 1975; Waldorf & Lauderback, 1993). Asian gangs in San Francisco's Chinatown were visibly dangerous as early as the 1970s (Joe, 1994). Other Latino and Asian groups began migrating to Los Angeles in the late 1970s, causing major demographic shifts throughout the metropolitan area; establishing new barrios in segregated areas and multilevel downtown apartments while generally transforming "the spatial and social fabric of greater Los Angeles" (Vigil, 1990, p. 127). Vietnamese immigrants who fled Communist-controlled Vietnam began arriving in the United States in 1975–1977, following the Vietnam War, and settled in major metropolitan areas in California, including Los Angeles (Hong, 2010). These people brought gang culture with them (Vigil & Yun, 1990). To be sure, marginalized second-generation children of these Asian immigrants formed and joined gangs (Hong, 2010).

The second wave of Asian refugees (1977–1985) consisted mostly of ethnic Chinese residents in Vietnam and the "boat people" who were predominantly rural Vietnamese farmers. Asian gangs grew in Los Angeles in the 1990s and first decade of the twenty-first century including Filipinos, Koreans, Samoans, and Southeast Asians (Cambodians, Thais, and Vietnamese) (Vigil, 2002; Vigil & Yun, 1990; Yu, 1987). Among the new immigrant groups, the Vietnamese gangs seem to have drawn the most attention, because of their non-territorial style, avoidance of monikers, and fluid structure (incessant changing membership). Other factors are their home invasion crimes, older membership—typically in their mid-teens and early twenties—and the significant cultural gap between the Vietnamese and police (Huff, 1993).

In the 1970s, there were twenty cities in California with populations larger than one hundred thousand people, and nineteen of them reported problems with youth gangs (Miller, 1982/1992). By 1980, gangs were more prevalent in very large California cities than all the other states combined. In fact, by that time, more than half (56 percent) of all U.S. gang problem cities were located in the West (Miller, 1982/1992). After extensive data collection on gang activity from law enforcement authorities in the 1970s, Miller was prompted to observe that "the numbers of cities and towns with gang problems in the extended Los Angeles metropolitan area [were] without precedent in American history" (p. 37). Along with El Paso and Denver, a large number of West Coast cities reported gang activity at that time, including Anaheim, Fresno, Long Beach, Los Angeles, Huntington Beach, Oakland, Riverside, San Diego, Sacramento, San Jose, San Francisco, Santa Ana, Torrance, and Seattle. Gang growth continued there, unabated. In the first decade of the new millennium, California saw a sharp increase in gang homicide outside of Los Angeles, northward toward San Francisco in the ten-year period from 1999 to 2008 (Tita & Abrahamse, 2010). In 2007, the LAPD designated the eleven most notorious gangs in Los Angeles: 18th Street Westside (Southwest Area), 204th Street (Harbor Area), Avenues (Northeast Area), Black P-Stones (Southwest, Wilshire Areas), Canoga Park Alabama (West Valley Area), Grape Street Crips (Southeast Area), La Mirada Locos (Rampart, Northeast Areas), *Mara Salvatrucha* (Rampart, Hollywood, and

Wilshire Areas), Rollin 40s (Southwest Area), Rollin 30s Harlem Crips (Southwest Area), and Rolling 60s (77th St. Area) (LAPD, 2007).

A total of forty-five Western cities with populations greater than one hundred thousand reported persistent violent gang activity during the period 1996–2009 in the National Youth Gang Survey (of which thirty-eight are in the state of California)—each of which reported about 40 percent of total annual homicides as gang related (Howell et al., 2011). The California cities in this group include Long Beach, Los Angeles, Oxnard, Pasadena, Pomona, Riverside, Salinas, San Bernardino, San Diego, San Francisco, San Jose, and Santa Ana, California. In recent years, Long Beach and Oakland, California have emerged as extremely high-rate gang homicide cities along with Los Angeles (Centers for Disease Control, 2012).

In sum, Los Angeles continues to be the Western epicenter of the most serious gang activity, and the accompanying homicides clearly have spread northward in the Western region. From 1996 to 2009, almost nine out of ten (87 percent) of Western gang problem cities with populations greater than fifty thousand were classified as "chronic" gang cities—most of which are in California (Howell & Griffiths, 2016; Howell et al., 2011). Of course, San Diego continues to anchor serious gang violence to the south of Los Angeles. Gangs first formed in San Diego on somewhat parallel tracks, growing out of Chicano and Black traditions (Sanders, 1994). Chicano gangs emerged first, likely before 1970. Sanders found the background for their gang behavior to include economic deprivation, anti-White and anti-establishment sentiment, and cultural themes depicting elements of Mexican culture and Mexican-Americans. During the mid- to late 1970s, Crips and Pirus (Bloods) began showing up in San Diego, and by 1980, the city had a number of Crips and Pirus. Filipino groups began gang activity in San Diego by the late 1980s. Southeast Asian gangs, comprised of the children of Laotian, Khmer (Cambodian), Hmong, and Vietnamese refugees, came into being at the end of the 1980s. Ogden, Utah, and Denver, Colorado independently developed substantial Mexican-American gang activity from racial oppression in society (Durán, 2009, 2012).

GANG EMERGENCE AND EXPANSION IN THE SOUTH REGION

The broad South region emerged much later than other regions as an important gang territory. Several factors account for slow gang emergence therein. First, the South was not engulfed by the two waves of White ethnic immigrants from Europe that came to the East Coast from 1783 to 1860. Even the early European immigrants to Florida—first the Spanish, then the English—never overpopulated the South significantly. Up to the Civil War, only about 5 percent of the Southern states population was foreign born (Dinnerstein &

Reimers, 2009). Second, the South remained an agricultural region until after World War II, when industrial development picked up in the Northern states. The great waves of migration in the nineteenth and early twentieth centuries went north or west.

Third, the South's impending gang problem that might well have errupted from Black-White conflict was moved northward in the "Great Migration" of more than a million Blacks from the rural South between 1910 and 1930—principally from the Mississippi Delta region that spans northeast Louisiana, western Mississippi and southeastern Arkansas. In fact, "up through the 1960s, there were more Black people leaving the South than moving into it" (Thompson, 2013, p. 22). In essence, youth conflicts between Black and both White and Mexican-American youth in the Jim Crow-dominated South were inadvertently reduced with Black migration from the South to the Northeast, Midwest, and to the West regions wherein Black-White racial conflicts became intense and very public in large cities.

Fourth, Southern culture was deeply religious—"the most solidly Protestant population of its size in the Western Hemisphere" (Woodward, 1951, p. 449). "It was the original, often imitated but never duplicated, Bible Belt" (Thompson, 2013, p. 111), which buttressed family control of youth. Fifth, the Southern states largely were bypassed by the Mexicans who migrated mainly to the Midwest and Western regions, as further explained below. Sixth, Southern cities are virtually devoid of public parks where youth conflicts could be staged. Seventh, the construction of large-scale public housing has been somewhat more limited in the South region. Although some of the earliest public housing projects were built in the South (in Atlanta, 1930s; in New Orleans, 1940), gangs were not reported in these public housing projects before the 1970s.

First Period of Gang Emergence in the South Region: 1930s–1960s

As noted earlier, westward migration from Mexico to Los Angeles in the 1920s gave rise to embryo gangs in southwest Texas and its western tip city, El Paso (R. E. Dickerson, cited in Thrasher, 1927/2000, p. 139). Along the migration route from Mexico to Los Angeles, the first gangs in El Paso emerged from the Mexican *palomilla* groups, and others in the region were characterized as "border bandits" (Cummins, 1994; McWilliams, 1948/1990; Moore, 2007). A simultaneous migration route out of Mexico to the Midwest in the 1920s and 1930s followed a path across southwest and west Texas, through Nuevo Laredo, San Antonio, then to Kansas City and onward to Chicago and other cities in that region (McWilliams, 1948/1990). Although most of this phase of Mexican migration northward leapfrogged Texas, embryo gangs likely formed in San Antonio, growing out of the *palomilla* groups, as did gangs in El Paso. For many years, it appears that San Antonio was the only large city in the South that experienced gang activity, but it may have been too isolated geographically to extend its gang influence through the youth subculture (Telles & Ortiz, 2008). San Antonio's gang problem was first identified as a serious one (along with Miami) in Miller's (1975) first multi-city study, and the seriousness of gang violence and drug trafficking in local gangs there has persisted (Valdez, 2007; Valdez, Cepeda, & Kaplan, 2009; Valdez & Sifaneck, 2004).

Other sizeable Southern cities in the early 20th century—New Orleans, Savannah, and Charleston—seemingly had no early gang activity owing to the factors discussed earlier. In short, racial/ethnic tensions were minimal as the Blacks had migrated northward and the Mexicans assimilated easily into the Southern culture (Thompson, 2013), hence White-Black and White-Mexican-American conflicts were minimized in the South region. "In fact, the really interesting thing about Hispanic immigration into the South is not the spectacle of cultures clashing, but the spectacle of cultures assimilating" (p. 33). As for the broader South region, before 1970, "one of the few conclusions accepted without dispute by most students of youth gangs was that the Old South was essentially free of gang problems" (W. Miller, 2001, p. 32). In 1970s, only thirteen gang problem cities were identified in the South (p. 33). This statement is accurate excepting the formation of the Ku Klux Klan, established a century earlier, following the Civil War. It was formed in Pulaski, Tennessee by returning soldiers of Scottish descent who perceived their town and the Southern region generally in a state of extreme economic and social disorganization. More specifically, much like immigrant groups that formed gangs in the Northeast, racist southerners who felt suppressed by the Reconstruction Acts of 1867 (that brought federal troops into the South to enforce the Emancipation Proclamation) started out with but a few goals. "They stood for purity and for preservation of the home and for protection of the orphans of Confederate soldiers. Their 'colors' symbolized these goals— white for purity and red for the blood they were ready to shed in defense of the helpless" (Haskins, 1974, p. 43). In time, the Ku Klux Klan[28] came to act like a street gang, operating in secrecy. "All across the South, the Klansmen roamed, and at their peak they numbered one million, lynching 'uppity [Blacks],' whipping northern school teachers for treating Blacks as equals, threatening and intimidating anyone who dared question the idea of white supremacy" (p. 45). After the Reconstruction Acts were appealed in 1877, the Klan never regained its former size and power.

Second Period of Gang Emergence in the South Region: 1970s–1990s

The Immigration and Nationality Act of 1965 ended national quotas on foreigners and shifted immigration to the United States from European origins to Central and South America and Asia. The next twenty-five years brought in many groups of Latin Americans (Colombians, Cubans, Dominicans, Ecuadorians, Mexicans, Panamanians, and Puerto Ricans); Asians (especially Cambodians, Filipinos, Koreans, Samoans, Thais, and Vietnamese); and other nationalities (W. Miller, 2001). Simultaneous with the movement of Latinos into the Southern region, an immigrant surge occurred during the 1980s that brought large numbers Mexicans, followed by peoples from the Philippines, China, Korea, and Japan into the United States—altogether about 16.6 million people of all nationalities (Pincus & Erlich, 1999, p. 226). Although most of this diverse immigrant group came into New York and California, these receiving states were followed by Texas, Florida, Illinois, and New Jersey. "Almost three-quarters of all newcomers settled in these six states . . . and the rapid changes intensified group tensions" (p. 225).

Given its proximity to Mexico, it comes as a surprise that Houston was not a major gang center in the South before the first decade of the new millennium. By the late 1970s, officials in Houston reported a developing gang problem (Miller, 1982/1992). The Houston Police Department then named sixty to sixty-five groups that were involved in serious criminal activity. But other authorities in the city insisted that these were not bona fide gangs; however, it was only a matter of time before youth gangs would be recognized. From 1996 to 2009, only about 20 percent of homicides in the city were gang related (Howell et al., 2011). Although Miami officials acknowledged a significant gang problem in 1974 (Miller, 1975), few gang-related homicides were reported there in the near term (Miller, 1982/1992). However, Miami has seen considerable growth of gang violence over the past thirty years, so that about 20 percent of homicides in the city were gang related in the period 1996–2009 (Howell et al., 2011). Atlanta and New Orleans have seen more slowly developing—if not underreported—gang activity for many years. Atlanta reported no gang activity before 1980 (Miller, 1982/1992), but 20 percent of homicides in the city were gang related from 1996 to 2009, while New Orleans had twice that rate in the same period (Howell et al., 2011). In 1980, New Orleans agency representatives reported only a relatively serious problem with youth groups; not bona fide gangs (Miller, 1982/1992). In both cities, high-rise public housing projects in which large numbers of poor Black residents were placed appeared to have incubated gangs, though not for some time. Techwood Homes in Atlanta were built in the 1930s, and the Magnolia Projects in New Orleans were built in the 1940s. Officials in Atlanta eventually acknowledged, "With constant exposure to crime and criminals, many children fell into the pit of gangs, drug dealing, stealing and worse" (Atlanta Public Housing Authority, 2010, p. 34).

The South region became a wellspring of gang growth from the 1970s through 1995 as this region led the nation in the number of new gang cities, a 32 percent increase, versus increases of 26 percent in the Midwest, 6 percent in the Northeast, and 3 percent in the West (W. Miller, 2001, p. 32). Several Southern states saw sharp increases in the number of new gang counties between the 1970s and 1995: Florida (23 percent), South Carolina (15 percent), Alabama (12 percent), and Texas (8 percent). Clusters of gang cities also developed as gang activity emerged in multiple cities in a number of Southern counties by 1995, including Dallas County, Texas (eighteen cities); Broward County, Florida (fifteen cities); Palm Beach County, Florida (eleven cities); and Dade County, Florida (eight cities). The latter three Florida counties represented the highest concentration of gang activity across the South at that time. From 1970 to 1995, the South Atlantic cities that reported gang activity increased by 44 percent (W. Miller, 2001, p. 18).[29] Thus Florida and Texas (particularly Dallas County) clearly led the South in gang growth from the 1970s onward.

Accelerated immigration and accompanying racial/ethnic conflict no doubt contributed to gang emergence in the southern states. Notably, the Hispanic population more than tripled in Florida from 1970 to 1990, while the Asian population grew more than twelvefold.[30] Although Cubans came to hold the largest share of the Hispanic population in the state (slightly more than half), about equal proportions are Asians, Koreans, Vietnamese, Indians, Filipinos, Chinese, and the Japanese also were represented. Miami, however, continues to serve as the main center for immigration in Florida. It was one of the first cities in the nation to become a Latino/White "minority-majority." Because of its historically pluralistic population, Miami was insulated from Southern culture and racial conflicts with White youth were nonexistent for many years.[31]

Expansion of Southern Gang Activity to the Present

Serious gang problems were slow to develop in the Southern region for many valid reasons. Having been spared from several obvious contributing factors in other regions—including massive incoming population movements, overwhelming urban social disorganization, and strong racial/ethnic youth conflicts—the South caught up with the other regions over the past thirty years. In time, Houston and the Miami metropolitan area developed intractable gang problems, and numerous other cities across the South soon developed serious gang problems. The growth of the Hispanic population and other ethnic groups contributed to social conflicts and gang emergence in the South region in the new millennium. Nationwide, from 2000 to 2010, most of the growth was accounted for by the Hispanic population (Passel, Cohn, & Lopez, 2011), and, by 2010, nearly half (45 percent) of these people were located in ten U.S. metropolitan areas (Motel & Patton, 2012). Four of the top metropolitan areas were in Southern cities (Houston, Dallas-Fort Worth, San Antonio, and Miami). African-Americans have been moving back to the

South in increasing numbers in recent decades, a social movement commonly identified as "return migration" or "remigration" (Falk, Hunt, & Hunt,
2004). This trend began during the last quarter of the twentieth century and
has been increasing since. In Atlanta, for example, the Black population
more than doubled between 1990 and 2008 (Thompson, 2013, p. 176).

Many Southern cities developed large populations in the late 1980s and
early 1990s, and within those particular cities, serious gang problems were
manifest (W. Miller, 2001; Quinn, Tobolowsky, & Downs, 1994). Miami
officials first recognized gang activity in the mid-1980s (Dade County State
Attorney, 1985, 1988). Within a three-year period (1984–1987), reports of
gang activity by Dade County grand jury witnesses increased sharply, supporting an increase in estimates of active gangs by the Dade County State
Attorney, from thirty-six gangs to more than seventy. Distinguishing features
of Miami gangs also changed significantly, from neighborhood play groups
to gangs with older members that had become involved in more serious and
violent crimes, including drug trafficking, firearm use, and associated violence (Dade County State Attorney, 1988). These developments reflected the
reality that Miami was well established by that time as a major port for the
trafficking of drugs into the United States. Soon, street-based gangs intermin-
gled with organized drug-trafficking groups.

The most significant gangs operating in the Southeast region[32] are said to
be the Crips, Gangster Disciples, Latin Kings, Sureños 13, and United Blood
Nation (FBI, 2009). According to the FBI, the increased migration of Hispanic gangs into the region has contributed significantly to gang growth (p.
20). In the Southwest region (Texas, Oklahoma, New Mexico, Colorado,
Utah, and Arizona), the most significant gangs are Barrio Azteca, Latin
Kings, Mexikanemi, Tango Blast, and Texas Syndicate (FBI, 2009).

From 1996 to 2009, two-thirds of the 116 Southern gang problem cities
with populations greater than fifty thousand achieved the distinction of classification as "chronic" gang cities (Howell & Griffiths, 2016). A total of
twelve Southern cities with populations greater than one hundred thousand
have reported persistent violent gang activity over the past fourteen years in
the National Youth Gang Survey—reporting approximately 40 percent (or
more) of total annual homicides as gang related (Howell et al., 2011). These
cities consist of Huntsville, Alabama; West Palm Beach, Florida; Savanna,
Georgia; New Orleans, Louisiana; Durham and Raleigh, North Carolina;
Oklahoma City and Tulsa, Oklahoma; Killeen and McKinney, Texas; Clarks-
ville, Tennessee; and Chesapeake, Virginia.

Inexplicably, despite its very large population (one of the ten largest cities
in the mid-1970s), Houston was not a major gang center in the South before
the first decade of the new millennium, but that soon changed. The first
gangs to form there likely were barrio gangs much like the Mexican-
American gangs in Los Angeles. As De León (2001) explains, Mexican

immigrants into Houston maintained their barrio/cultural identity for many years. With time, barrio and neighborhood identification intensified, providing the basis for frequent gang fights. Presently, Houston and the surrounding southeast Texas region is home to a number of dangerous street gangs allied with prison gangs, some of which engage in drug trafficking with MDTOs (see chapter 2).

ANOTHER WAVE OF IMMIGRANT GROUPS

The Immigration and Nationality Act of 1965 ended the national quotas on foreigners in the United States. This led to a shift in immigration to the United States, from European origins in the eighteenth and nineteenth centuries, to Central and South America and Asia in the twentieth century (Bankston, 1998). The next twenty-five years brought in many groups of Asians (Cambodians, Filipinos, Koreans, Samoans, Thais, Vietnamese, and others) and Latin Americans (Colombians, Cubans, Dominicans, Ecuadorians, Mexicans, Panamanians, Puerto Ricans, and others) (W. Miller, 2001, p. 43). The new population groups experienced assimilation blockages just as migrating Blacks and Mexicans had in the past, and new Asian and Latino gangs emerged among second-generation youth from Puerto Rico and other Latin American countries. By 1975, the majority of gangs in the United States were no longer White, of various European backgrounds; producing a veritable "rainbow of gangs" (Vigil, 2002).

Asian gangs also were prominent in San Francisco in the early 1970s, and in Los Angeles, New York City, Boston, Toronto, and Vancouver (Huff, 1993; Miller, 1982/1992). By this time, highly organized Chinese gangs had established a notable street presence in New York City's Chinatown as a result of their active involvement in extortion, robbery, debt collection, and protection of Asian-owned vice businesses and they steadily grew into the 1990s (Chin, 2000). "Hong Kong Chinese" drew the most attention on the West Coast, but Filipino, Korean, Japanese, and Thai gangs also drew considerable attention. In the 1970s and 1980s two waves of migrants reached the United States, totaling 6.8 and 7.8 million, respectively (Pincus & Erlich, 1999). By the late 1980s, the children of many American-born or Americanized parents among the new immigrants, dubbed "the new second generation" of the post-1960s immigrant groups (principally Asian and Latin Americans), had reached adolescence or young adulthood (Portes & Rumbaut, 2005; Portes & Zhou, 1993), and many of them joined gangs. Native-American gangs also would emerge much later (Bell & Lim, 2005; Major, Egley, Howell, Mendenhall, & Armstrong, 2004).

Two major changes in the racial/ethnic composition of gangs in the United States have occurred over the past two centuries. Whereas early in

American history, gangs were almost exclusively populated by White European ethnics, by the late 1970s, several multi-city surveys showed that Hispanic/Latino and Black gang members made up about four-fifths of all members (Short, 2002). This proportion has remained somewhat stable since then, with 46 percent Hispanic/Latino, 35 percent Black, 7 percent other race/ethnicity, and Whites making up less than 12 percent of all gang members in law enforcement estimates.[33] Second, a greater proportion of gang members are now multiracial. A recent nine-city U.S. student survey found that multiracial groups were most predominantly represented in young gangs (Esbensen, Brick, Melde, Tusinski, & Taylor, 2008).

NOTES

1. The definition of the term *slum* includes the traditional meaning—that is, housing areas that were once respectable or desirable, but have since deteriorated as the original dwellers have moved to better areas of the cities. Slums have also come to include the vast informal settlements that are quickly becoming the most visible expression of urban poverty in developing world cities, including squatter settlements and illegal subdivisions. The quality of dwellings in such settlements varies from the simplest shack to permanent structures, while access to water, electricity, sanitation and other basic services and infrastructure is usually limited (United Nations, 2003, p. 9). The modern-day term, ghetto, is generally defined as an area in which the overall poverty rate of census tracts is greater than 40 percent (Wacquant, 2007).

2. A leather-covered bludgeon with a short, flexible shaft or strap, used as a hand-held weapon.

3. See Miller (1975) for a description of Philadelphia's gang problem in the early 1970s.

4. Two other riots preceded this one: the anti-Abolitionist riots of 1834 and the Astor Place Theater riot of 1849 (Sante, 1991).

5. Puerto Ricans came to the United States in three periods (Moore & Pinderhughes, 1993). Puerto Rico became a commonwealth of the United States in 1952, after which Puerto Ricans moved back and forth freely. The first group migrated off and on to the United States between 1900 and 1945. The largest movement to the U.S. mainland occurred during the second period (1946–1964), facilitated in part by artificially low fares to New York City. The third period, after 1965 has seen a great deal of "revolving door migration," though a large influx to the United States since 1980 has rivaled the earlier peak, around 1950. Altogether, in 1990 Puerto Ricans represented 12 percent of the twenty-two million Latinos residing in the United States, and 61 percent were Mexican in origin (p. xvii).

6. Hispanic (Spanish-speaking) ethnic groups include Mexicans, Mexican-Americans, Latinos, and Puerto Ricans.

7. Easton, Bethlehem, Allentown, Reading, and Lancaster.

8. A few cities with populations greater than one hundred thousand do not respond annually to the National Youth Gang Survey (NYGS). For example the New York City Police Department first responded in 2010.

9. By several accounts, the seven most serious race riots were those which occurred in Wilmington, NC (1898), Atlanta, GA (1906), Springfield, IL (1908), East St. Louis, IL (1917), Chicago, IL (1919), Tulsa, OK (1921) and Detroit, MI (1943).

10. The *red summer* term was tagged by the early and widely regarded Black Civil Rights advocate, James Weldon Johnson.

11. The locations of numerous riots (and lynchings of Blacks) that occurred from April to November 1919 in seventeen states were mapped by McWhirter. See CameronMcWhirter.com, http://cameronmcwhirter.com/wordpress/redsummerboo/#map. Accessed March 4, 2015.

12. This number may not be exact. Legend has it that student research assistants played a joke on Professor Thrasher in representing 1,313 as the total number of gangs in the study (Short, 2006). This number was the address of a nearby brothel.

13. Thrasher used the term *interstitial* in another way, referring to the ambiguous state of youth in the gap between childhood and adulthood.

14. Zoot suit riots originated in Los Angeles and these are discussed in detail in the third chapter of this volume.

15. Thrasher (1927/2000, p. 80) found only five or six independent female gangs.

16. Chicago Crime Commission's cross-disciplinary seminar on gangs in Chicago, January 27, 2012.

17. University of Illinois, Chicago. "GangResearch.net." Accessed December 16, 2014. http://www.gangresearch.net/.

18. The Great Lakes region of North America includes the eight U.S. states of Illinois, Indiana, Michigan, Minnesota, western New York, Ohio, Pennsylvania, and Wisconsin, as well as parts of several Canadian provinces on the north banks of the Great Lakes.

19. The social, economic, and cultural history of Mexico and Mexican-American's migration into what would come to be known as the Southwest region of the United States is masterfully documented in three volumes that capture historical underpinnings of relevance to gang formation and expansion. Vigil's book, *From Indians to Chicanos: The Dynamics of Mexican-American Culture* (1998) covers Mexican history from the pre-Columbian period to the 1970s. McWilliams (1948/1990) epic book, *North from Mexico: The Spanish-Speaking People of the United States* chronicles northward migration of Mexican peoples. Next, Vigil's (1988) seminal work, *Barrio Gangs: Street Life and Identity in Southern California*, looked closely at the background of Mexican-American gang formation in Los Angeles.

20. Earlier, Chichimecas moved into this area from the far northwest region of what is now the United States. "According to legend, they had migrated from Aztlan, their mythological homeland, which is now either northern Mexico or the southwestern United States" (Vigil, 1998, p. 23).

21. Santa Fe was established in 1610 by Spanish explorers, making it the oldest European settlement west of the Mississippi, and one of the oldest cities in the United States.

22. *El Pueblo de la Reina de Los Angeles* or "The Town of the Queen of the Angels."

23. In Laredo, Texas, Rubel notes that these self-formed friendship associations were called *amigazco*.

24. Chicano is the preferred term for Mexican-American gangs, just as Latino is favored over Hispanic when a generic label is needed (Vigil, 1998). "The term 'Chicano' implies pride in a background of many and mixed heritages" (p. 270), "both ancient and new, made up of Indian, Spanish, Mexican, and Anglo elements" (p. 251). In addition, Chicanos came from different regions of Mexico, and other distinctive cultural variations are seen in earlier immigrants from rural Mexico versus more recent immigrants from urban areas. These multiple sources of social and cultural traditions made assimilation into American society all the more difficult, without solid roots in either Mexican or American society.

25. Meaning *Que Maravilla*! Translated "what a marvel" or "what a wonderful city."

26. For other accounts of Bloods and Crips origins, see Alonso (2013) and Al Valdez (2007).

27. See Alonso's (2004) detailed maps of Black clubs in 1960, and gang territories in 1972 and 1996, vividly showing the growth of Black Los Angeles gangs across three decades.

28. Using the Greek word, *kuklos*, meaning a band or circle, the group decided to split the word, substituting "ux" for "os" in the second half of the word, resulting in Ku Klux.

29. The South Atlantic States, U.S. Census Bureau Region 3, Division 5, consisting of the states of Delaware, Maryland, Virginia, West Virginia, North Carolina, South Carolina, Georgia, Florida, and the District of Columbia.

30. Source: William Leonard, Leon F. Bouvier, and John L. Martin. "Shaping Florida: The Effects of Immigration, 1970–2020." Center for Immigration Studies. 1995. Accessed December 28, 2014. http://www.cis.org/FloridaImmigrants19702020.

31. Personal communication, Javier Camacho, National Gang Center, April 23, 2014.

32. Alabama, Arkansas, Florida, Georgia, Louisiana, Mississippi, North Carolina, South Carolina, and Tennessee.

33. National Gang Center. "National Youth Gang Survey Analysis." Accessed December 16, 2014. http://www.nationalgangcenter.gov/Survey-Analysis/Demographics#anchorregm.

Chapter Two

Development and Transformation of Prison Gangs

This chapter examines the contribution of prison gangs to street gang transformation. Prison gangs first formed to provide protection to inmates from attacks by other racial/ethnic groups. As a last resort, then, the most likely source of personal protection inside prisons is members of one's own racial/ ethnic group. We first define prison gangs and the wider array of "security threat groups" inside U.S. prisons, after which a theory of prison gang development is reviewed. Next, the emergence and expansion of prison gangs in each U.S. region are examined. This chapter concludes with discussion of three issues of widespread concern with respect to prison gangs: violence associated with them, relationships between prison and street gangs, and prison gang ties to Mexican drug trafficking organizations.

DEFINING PRISON GANGS

Unfortunately, prison gangs are not precisely defined, owing to the wide variety of organizational features they displayed in the first major prison gang study (Camp & Camp, 1985). Most of the early prison gangs revealed in that study were seen as counterparts of street gangs—in twenty-six of the thirty-three correctional agencies that reported prison gangs—notably in studies of Illinois (Jacobs, 1977) and California (Irwin, 1980) prison gangs, where the first such gangs developed in the late 1950s and 1960s (Camp & Camp, 1985). A widely recognized prison gang definition is this: "an organization which operates within the prison system as a self-perpetuating criminally oriented entity, consisting of a select group of inmates who have established an organized chain of command and are governed by an established code of conduct" (Lyman, 1989, p. 48).[1]

Many states now include prison gangs in a broader classification of the variety of disruptive groups in prisons, as Security Threat Groups (STG). A STG is typically defined by most prison systems and the FBI as "any group of three or more persons with recurring threatening or disruptive behavior" (Winterdyk & Ruddell, 2010). For the purpose of identifying the variety of disruptive prison groups, the American Correctional Association (ACA) now has three terms or categories for criminal street gangs and other violent groups identified within correctional settings (Santana, 2007b): "Security Threat Groups," "Security Risk Groups," and/or "Disruptive Groups." These groups are collectively defined by the ACA as "two or more inmates, acting together, who pose a threat to the security or safety of staff/inmates, and/or are disruptive to programs and/or to the orderly management of the facility/ system" (Santana, 2007b, p. 1). The important difference in these definitions is that Lyman's (1989) specifically requires ongoing involvement in criminal activity, that is, a *criminally oriented entity*.

The initial study of prison gang organizational structures, conducted in Texas prisons, described the two earliest such gangs, the Texas Syndicate and Mexican Mafia (Buentello, Fong, & Vogel, 1991; Fong, 1990; Fong & Buentello, 1991). Each of these prison gangs was structured similarly, along paramilitary lines, with a president, vice president, and chairman or general who oversees captains, lieutenants, a sergeant of arms, and soldiers (Fong, 1990). Less well-organized prison gangs have an uncomplicated structure, usually with one person designated as the leader who oversees a council of members who make the group's final decisions (Fleisher & Decker, 2001). "The rank and file form a hierarchy, making these groups look more similar to organized crime than their counterparts on the outside" (p. 3).

With the emergence of prison gangs, two serious conditions developed in confinement (Fong, 1990). First, prison officials experienced enormous difficulties in maintaining order and discipline among inmates (Irwin, 1980; Jacobs, 1977). Early efforts to control gangs were relatively unsuccessful, including sequestration of known gang members, transferring gang leaders to other institutions, and aggressive prosecution of all crimes committed by inmates. Second, a rapid increase in violence occurred as prison gangs grew; initially because of the increasing number of violence-prone inmates, later, owing to the prison gangs' involvement in drug trafficking, extortion, homosexual prostitution inside prisons, protection rackets, gambling, and contract murders (Fong, 1990). An early study of prison gang violence revealed that the members accounted for 50 percent or more of all prison problems (Camp & Camp, 1988).

It is intriguing that prison gangs have the capacity to extend their influence on crime in the streets from inside prisons, our nation's most secure correctional institutions. Providing great insight on this matter, (Morales, 2011) aptly phrased the mantra: "he who runs the inside controls the outside." Prison gang leaders are adept at communicating covertly and managing operations both inside and outside prisons (Buentello et al., 1991; Fong, 1990). In addition, released prisoners of both Mexican Mafia and Texas Syndicate gangs are required to stay in close contact with members who remain inside prisons. Moreover, some prison gangs are governed by strict constitutions (See In Focus: Prison Gang Constitutions).

In 1985 the Texas Syndicate declared war on the Mexican Mafia by fatally assaulting four Mexican Mafia members (Fong, 1990). The severity of the war between the Texas Syndicate and the Mexican Mafia was not only felt within the Texas Department of Corrections but also outside Texas prisons and elsewhere. Law enforcement agencies in a number of metropolitan areas identified several recent homicides committed on the streets as being directly related to this war.

IN FOCUS

Prison Gang Constitutions

The Texas Syndicate's constitution consists of eight rules:

1. Be a Texan.
2. Once a member, always a member.
3. The Texas Syndicate comes before anyone and anything.
4. Right or wrong, the Texas Syndicate is right at all times.
5. All members will wear the Texas Syndicate tattoo.
6. Never let a member down.
7. All members will respect each other.
8. Keep all gang information within the group.

The Constitution of the Mexican Mafia of Texas contains twelve rules:

1. Membership is for life—"blood in, blood out."
2. Every member must be prepared to sacrifice his life or take a life at any time when necessary.
3. Every member shall strive to overcome his weakness to achieve discipline within the *Mexikanemi* brotherhood.
4. Never let the *Mexikanemi* (Soldiers of Aztlan, their mythological homeland) down.

5. The sponsoring member is totally responsible for the behavior of the new recruit. If the new recruit turns out to be a traitor, it is the sponsoring member's responsibility to eliminate the recruit.

6. When disrespected by a stranger or a group, all members of the *Mexikanemi* will unite to destroy the person or the other group completely.

7. Always maintain a high level of integrity.

8. Never release *Mexikanemi* business to others.

9. Every member has the right to express opinions, ideas, contradictions, and constructive criticisms.

10. Every member has the right to organize, educate, arm, and defend the *Mexikanemi*.

11. Every member has the right to wear the tattoo of the *Mexikanemi* symbol.

12. The *Mexikanemi* is a criminal organization and therefore will participate in all aspects of criminal interest for monetary benefits.

"For both inmate gangs, the penalty for intentionally or unintentionally violating any of the established rules is death" (Fong, 1990, p. 40).

Source: Fong, 1990.

A THEORY OF PRISON GANG DEVELOPMENT

Just one theory of prison gang development has been proposed to date. This theory was based on extensive study and observations of prison gang formation and operations by a Texas research-practitioner team (Buentello et al., 1991) over a ten-year period. Based on this study, a five-stage process of prison gang development was formulated by Buentello (a Texas Department of Corrections gang specialist) and colleagues (1991, see Table 2.1).

In Stage 1, a convicted offender is sentenced to serve time in prison. Upon arriving there, the inmate is isolated from the traditional support system that he once enjoyed. Finding himself all alone, the inmate realizes that he now lives in a "dog-eat-dog" world, to which he must adjust. Sensing danger, he comes to see that he must cultivate special skills for coping with violence, "a brutal but ever-present aspect of daily prison life" (Buentello et al., 1991, p. 5).

To overcome feeling alone, isolated, and vulnerable, in Stage 2, the inmate begins socializing with other inmates who share common interests and similarly feel the need for survival skills and protection. In time, these associations resemble an informal clique. "As members do not consider them-

Table 2.1.   The Characteristics of Prison Gang Development

Inmate Enters Prison	Feeling fearful of new setting
	Sensing danger
	Feeling isolated
	Feeling lonely
A Clique is Formed	Sense of belonging
	No rules for acceptance
	No commitment to group
	No rules of conduct
	Members can come and go
	No formal or informal leadership exercised
	No involvement in criminal activity
The Clique Changes to a Self Protection Group	Self-identity
	Existence of simple general rules
	Existence recognized by inmates and staff
	No involvement in criminal activity
	Does not initiate violence unless provoked
	Informal leadership based on charisma
	No formal code of conduct
The Self Protection Group Becomes a Predator Group	Discussion of formalizing rules of conduct
	Beginning to realize strength
	Exclusion of "undesirable" or "unwilling" members
	Involvement of inmate/staff intimidation
	Involvement in retaliation and assaults
	Initial entry as a group into illegal activity
	Emergence of strong leadership although informal
	Existence and activity limited to inside penal setting

The Predator Group Becomes a Prison Gang	Formal rules and constitution
	Well-defined goals and philosophy
	Hierarchy of formal leadership with clearly defined authority and responsibility
	Membership for life
	Members wear gang tattoos
	Wholesale involvement in criminal activity both inside and outside the penal setting
	Ongoing criminal enterprise

selves a group, they are free to join or leave the clique anytime they please [and] criminal activity is rarely promoted" (p. 5).

In Stage 3, the clique is transformed into a self-protection group. Though not yet involved in criminal activity, this group associates more regularly but without a code of conduct, and it is recognized by other inmates and staff. Self-identification with the group is common. Leadership is informal, based on charisma, but after receiving recognition from other inmates and drawing attention from prison management, the leaders contemplate leading the group into predatory group activities.

The self-protection group becomes a predator group in Stage 4. First, the group begins to realize its strength, and occasionally is involved in retaliations and assaults with outsiders. Next, the group begins to generate fear among other inmates. "Insiders" and "outsiders" are clearly identified. Individuals who are considered weak or non-cohesive are excluded from the group. Unlike cliques, predator groups are willing to participate actively in criminal activities.

In Stage 5, predator groups that become stronger and more fearful than other like groups elevate themselves into prison gangs. These exclusive groups enjoy their newfound power over other inmates, enabling them to profit from criminal activities. "As part of a prison gang, members see themselves as part of an organized crime syndicate. Involvement in contract murder, extortion, gambling, and homosexual prostitution is required of gang members" (p. 8). Successfully carrying out these criminal activities requires a formal organization, with formal rules (often spelled out in a constitution). Goals, philosophy, and leadership are made explicit. Members must wear gang tattoos. Membership is for life. This hard and fast rule is a major feature of prison gangs that enabled them to expand their crime base to the streets with the help of released gang members.

Having been formed in these stages, the original Texas prison gangs were not extensions of street gangs as in Illinois and California, as explained below. While it is true that many prison gangs have their origins in the streets, such is not the case in Texas, where prison gangs formed and prolife-rated within the prisons. In other words, Texas prison gangs give true meaning to the term "prison gangs." (Buentello et al., 1991, p. 4; see In Focus: Indicators of Prison Gang Development)

IN FOCUS

Indicators of Prison Gang Development

In a unique study, Fong and Buentello (1991) queried high-ranking security staff in the Texas Department of Corrections to determine the most prominent "indicators of prison gang development." Security staff members in separate prisons were asked to assess the frequency of occurrence of each indicator, with the guideline "to the level above and beyond the usual rate" (p. 68). This frequency metric of potential indicators gave intrinsic validity to the study, for "it is the frequency of occurrence that determines whether or not they are [valid] indicators" (p. 68). It should be noted that the timing of Fong and Buentello's study was fortuitous, in the 1980s, during a decade of increasing gang activity in Texas' prisons.
Eleven indicators were used in the study:

1. Inmate requests for protective custody (98 percent) (33 percent)
2. Finding of gang-related tattoos on inmate bodies (97 percent) (65 percent)
3. Inmate disciplinary violations of contraband possession (96 percent) (48 percent)
4. Secret racial groupings of inmates (95 percent) (32 percent)
5. Inmate informants reporting emergence of inmate cliques (93 percent) (33 percent)
6. Inmate physical assaults on other inmates (91 percent) (20 percent)
7. Police agencies reporting gang activities on the streets (91 percent) (18 percent)
8. Inmate requests for inter-unit transfers (85 percent) (13 percent)
9. Inmate families reporting extortion by inmate cliques (85 percent) (11 percent)
10. Verbal threats made to staff by inmates (71 percent) (10 percent)
11. Physical assaults on staff by inmates (71 percent) (12 percent)

The top five indicators in this numerical ordering also were tagged by one-third or more of respondents as frequently occurring (as shown in the second set of parentheses), with much reduced frequency of the remaining items. The five indicators of greatest validity are as follows:

1. Finding of gang-related tattoos on inmate bodies
2. Inmate disciplinary violations of contraband possession
3. Inmate requests for protective custody
4. Inmate informants reporting emergence of inmate cliques
5. Secret racial groupings of inmates

It is noteworthy that none of the assaultive offenses is among either the top five indicators or indicators of greatest validity. These offenses include inmate physical assaults on other inmates, physical assaults on staff by inmates, and verbal threats made to staff by inmates. As Fong and Buentello suggest, in the early stages of gang formation, these gangs hope to avoid drawing disciplinary actions from prison officials, as this could result in the segregation of would-be members. The above five indicators matter more, three of which are common characteristics of gang culture: tattoos, cliques, and secret racial groupings.

Source: Fong and Buentello (1991).

PRISON GANGS IN THE MAJOR U.S. REGIONS

In the overview that follows, we review emergence and development of prison gangs in the chronological order of this process. Prison gangs first developed in the Western region, followed a dozen years later by the Midwest region and the Northeast, and lastly, by the Southern region. Generally speaking, this ordering does not follow closely the pattern of gang emergence. This onset pattern is largely accounted for by the varying racial/ethnic composition of inmate populations, state and regional prison carceral (confinement) trends, and related correctional policies.

Prison Gangs in the West Region

The first acknowledged prison gang, the Gypsy Jokers (a motorcycle club), formed in the 1950s in Washington state prisons (Camp & Camp, 1985). California has been dubbed the "mother" of major prison gangs (Morales, 2011) because six major prison gangs were active in the state's prisons by 1984: Mexican Mafia, *La Nuestra Familia*, Black Guerilla Family, Texas Syndicate, Aryan Brotherhood (a White supremacist group), and CRIPS (Common Revolution in Progress) (Camp & Camp, 1985, p. 23). But the

Mexican Mafia, most generally called *La Eme*, was the first of these to be validated as a prison gang (Camp & Camp, 1985; Morales, 2011).

The future impact of Western prison gangs on the streets grew out of a rivalry that developed in California's prison system between northern and southern gang members that spread across the state in the 1960s (Morales, 2011). Conflict and assaults between northern and southern California gang inmates led to the formation of *Sureños* and *Norteños* networks, a rivalry that produced many gang wars, both in prisons and on the streets (National Alliance of Gang Investigators' Associations, 2009). Rival Southern California Hispanic street gangs were enemies with anyone from Northern California, and vice versa.[2] This rivalry would unite the respective clusters of gangs in jails and state prisons. Northern California street and prison gang members began to use the number fourteen (representing the fourteenth letter, N) to identify with *Norteño* (the Spanish word for northerner) and the prison-based *Nuestra Familia* gang. Smilarly, *Sureños* adopted the number thirteen (representing the thirteenth letter, M, which is the Spanish word *eme*) to identify with *La Eme*, the Southern California based Mexican prison gang.

As the largest and oldest non-White immigrant group in California, Mexican gangs were most prominent, led by the Mexican Mafia. In time, the south-to-north Black migration in the 1950s, 1960s, and 1970s contributed to Black prison gangs populated by imprisoned Crips and Bloods gang members. Without doubt, California provided a springboard for street and prison gang expansion in the Western region. In California, the Street Terrorism Enforcement and Enforcement (STEP) Act of 1988 (California Penal Code § 186.22) mandates an automatic addition of one to three years on prison terms for those who have been convicted of a crime and are members of a gang. Once this law was coupled with the state's indeterminate sentence provision and its "Three Strikes and You're Out" law, confinement of street gang members increased sharply (Schlosser, 1998). Los Angeles Police Chief Gates's war on gangs moved even more of the active gang members into prisons. By the mid-1990s, the California prison system was "full of warring gangs," after members of the street-based Crips and Bloods were added to the mix. At one California state prison, Schlosser (1998) was told that correctional officers had staged "gladiator days" on which members of rival gangs were encouraged to fight, with officers betting on the outcomes. Some inmates reportedly shot one another in the staged combat. Earlier, in unspecified prisons, Toch (1978) also noted the existence of "gladiating arenas" in which aggrieved inmates (some armed with knives) challenge their enemies.

A half century later, the California Department of Corrections and Rehabilitation (California Department of Corrections and Rehabilitation [CDCR], 2012) still recognizes five of the original prison gangs in the state among the top (Level I) "security threat groups" (STG-I) (Mexican Mafia, *Nuestra Familia*, Black Guerilla Family, Texas Syndicate, and Aryan Brotherhood), and the CDCR has added Nazi Low Riders (a White prison gang) and Northern Structure (a spin-off of *La Nuestra Familia*) as STG-I gangs. Both Crips and Bloods, along with *Norteño* and *Sureño*, are recognized as lesser threats as STG-II gangs in the state prison system (CDCR, 2012).

Prison Gangs in the Midwest Region

In the mid-1980s, Illinois had the largest number of gangs and gang members in prison of all U.S. states (Camp & Camp, 1985). Across Illinois, Department of Corrections' officials estimated that some 5,300 inmates were active gang members in eight prison gangs in 1984. The waves of Blacks, Mexican-Americans, and Latinos into Midwest cities, including Chicago and Detroit, in the post–World War II period produced a variety of racial/ethnic Illinois gangs—particularly following the implementation of gang suppression strategies. Chicago Mayor Daley's 1969 gang war had made a direct contribution to prison gang growth for at least the next fifteen years. In fact, Illinois prison officials acknowledged 1969 as the year in which the first prison gangs were formed (Black Disciples and Vice Lords) (p. 20). By the mid-1980s, Illinois had the largest number of gang members in prison of all U.S. states and the largest proportion of gang-involved inmates (34 percent) (p. 19).

The Illinois experience with prison gangs illustrates the symbiotic relationship between confined gang members and other street criminals, and the growth of gangs within correctional systems. Prison administrators inadvertently strengthened the gangs by using them to help maintain order within prisons. Gang leaders thus were able to swell their ranks from inside prison. They soon took control of older inmate organizations by guile and targeted violence, and became the strongest force within the prisons. Some of the gang leaders formed organizational networks both inside and outside prisons that linked inmates with others in jails and on the streets in illegal enterprises, creating what came to be called *webs*, *supergangs*, or *gang nations* (Venkatesh, 2000, p. 134; Hagedorn, 2006; Spergel, 1990). "But significantly, and unlike past inmate groups, the gangs maintained their ties to the streets" (Hagedorn, 2006, p. 203). Once members were freed from prisons, they quickly moved to battle, overpower, and subsume the weaker street corner groups (Cureton, 2009; Short & Strodtbeck, 1965).

Some Illinois prison gangs were "an extension of an identical organization imported from the streets" (Jacobs, 1974, p. 397). By one expert account, the Illinois prison gangs were "reorganized at a level of sophistication that dwarfed the type of structures that had developed in the streets" (Perkins, 1987, p. 17). In the mid-1980s, Black Gangster Disciple Nation and the Latin Disciples formed the Folk alliance. Soon afterward, the Latin Kings and Vice Lords formed the People alliance (Block & Block, 1993). About thirty-one street gangs affiliated with the Folk, and some twenty-seven gangs affiliated with the People, and it has been estimated that more than half of Chicago's recognized street gangs were affiliated with Folk and People coalitions by the mid-1980s (Spergel, 1995). In fact, People and Folk alliances accounted for the major street conflicts that took place in the 1980s (Perkins, 1987).

Next, "the return to the streets of major Black gang leaders had an immediate ripple effect on the reemergence of Black street gangs. The calm before the storm had now turned into a deepening resonance of uncontrolled chaos" (Perkins, 1987, p. 17). Under these coalitions, gang conflicts were far more serious because they involved multiple gangs on occasion. Hence, gang violence (particularly gang-motivated homicides) increased enormously in Chicago in the period between 1965 and 1994, especially in the late 1980s and early 1990s (Block & Block, 1993; Block et al., 1996).

So empowered, street gangs turned to drug trafficking following the return of large numbers of their members from prison. And they were better positioned to run drug distribution operations after having expanded criminal relationships with prisons. "In the late 1970s and early 1980s, members returned to ghetto streets and found few legitimate work opportunities, but increasing opportunities to sell heroin, cocaine, and marijuana, and to join car-theft rings and extortion rackets" (Venkatesh, 2000, p. 133). The Black Disciples gang reigned in the RTH complex and controlled most of the drug market based therein. Another prominent gang, the Sharks, controlled a relatively small section of the drug market in RTH. Consisting of about five hundred members, the Black Disciples gang was comprised of teenagers and young adults, and its sets ranged from fifty to more than two hundred members. But nearly all of the core members were over that age of eighteen because Black Disciples leadership did not trust the "shorties" with responsibility to handle cocaine trafficking. This notorious gang operated in a territory surrounding RTH that it had claimed since the 1970s, and it had ties to a federation of neighborhood Chicago gangs, called Black Gangster Disciples Nation.

Some analysts suggest that militant social organizations in Chicago (the Black Panthers and Young Lords) along with the separatist Nation of Islam may have prepared some Black and Hispanic youth, respectively, for gang membership (Alonso, 2004; Cureton, 2009; Diamond, 2009). A case could also be made that militant philosophy fostered the creation of what came to be called *supergangs* or *gang nations* (Hagedorn, 2006; Venkatesh, 2000). Four gangs rightly earned this designation, two Black gangs (the Black Gangster Disciples Nation and the Vice Lords), and two largely Mexican-American gangs (Latin Kings and Latin Disciples). Together, these four gangs were estimated to have nineteen thousand members in their heyday— constituting about half of all Chicago street gang members in the late 1980s. From 1987 to 1990, the four largest street gangs were also the most criminally active. They accounted for 69 percent of all street gang-motivated crimes and 56 percent of all street gang-motivated homicides in which the street gang affiliation of the offender was known (Block & Block, 1993, p. 3).

The Gangster Disciples had "Institutional Coordinators" in each state prison (Papachristos, 2001) and a corporate-like organizational structure of two separate divisions (prison and street operations) governed by Boards of Directors, with Larry Hoover as Chairman of the Board (p. 35). Although street gangs still align themselves with the People and the Folk at the present time, "law enforcement agencies seem to agree that these alliances mean little" (Chicago Crime Commission, 2006, p. 11).[3] Copycats of People and the Folk, though in name only, are very common across the United States (Federal Bureau of Investigation, 2011).

Prison Gangs in the Northeast Region

In the aforementioned comprehensive prison gang study (Camp & Camp, 1985), Pennsylvania led the way among Northeast cities with fifteen prison gangs, comprising 2,400 members by the mid-1980s, and making up 20 percent of the total prison population. Just one prison gang with three members was reported in Massachusetts, and no prison gangs were identified in New York. But prison gang growth was fueled by a steady stream of immigrant groups into the Northeast that accelerated in the early 1980s. Blacks came in large numbers, and Mexican-American and Latino groups began to succeed Puerto Ricans. Santana (2007a) reports that the Latino Almighty Latin King & Queen Nation (ALKQN) originated in 1986 within New York's Collins Correctional Facility in an effort to combat dominance therein by a Black prison gang. Subsequently, ALKQN strengthened its control in the state's correctional facilities when it joined forces with *Associacion Neta*. Next, in 1993, Santana reports that East Coast Bloods formed within the Rikers Island Correctional Facility. "These rivalries disseminated throughout the tri-state area, gaining control of county and state correctional facilities. Eventually the streets of both urban and suburban America were plagued with the violence and battles of distinction" (p. 1).

In the mid-1990s, Connecticut prison officials documented nearly two thousand inmates as gang members for a major crackdown—almost all of whom were Latino (La Familia, Latin Kings, and the Associacion Ñeta) (Kassel, 1998). Subsequent street-level research in New York City suggested that the Latin Kings and the *Ñeta* were transformed in the early to mid-1990s as they moved from prisons and jails to the streets (Curtis, 2003). But they were no match for the show of force by the New York City police (Hagedorn & Rauch, 2007).

The *Trinitarios* (largely men of Dominican descent) also formed in the late 1980s in the New York correctional system as these inmates banded together for protection from other ethnic groups. *Trinitarios* were first identified on Rikers Island and then expanded into the New York State prison system, and most recently are found in the northeastern states of Delaware, Maryland, Rhode Island, Pennsylvania, Connecticut, Massachusetts, New Hampshire, New York, and in other U.S. regions (National Alliance of Gang Investigators' Associations, 2009).

In addition to the *Trinitarios*, Santana (2007a) reports that East Coast Bloods formed within the New York Rikers Island Correctional Facility in 1993. Some gang sets[4] on Rikers require an individual to "put in work" or "eat food" (cut or slash someone) before they are considered Blood members. In the estimation of some authorities, the East Coast Bloods are said to be the largest street gang in New York City, and it has members in other East Coast cities as well. In the late 1990s, Gangsta Killer Bloods emerged in New York Prisons (Schlosser, 1998). Outside prisons and jails, United Blood Nation is a loose confederation of street gangs, or sets, that once were predominantly African-American. Membership is estimated to be between seven thousand and fifteen thousand along the U.S. eastern corridor (FBI, 2009, p. 27).

Dead Man Inc. is an unusual White prison gang that reportedly was formed in the Maryland Correctional Adjustment Center, known as Supermax. It was founded in the late 1990s by White inmates who desired affiliation with the established Black Guerrilla Family, but the group's request was denied because of its members' race, which conflicted with the BGFs Black membership.[5] Hence, Dead Man Inc. was formed.

Prison Gangs in the Southern Region

Texas and Florida have come to anchor Southern gang activity in the modern era. In 1985, seven states in the region reported prison gangs although these were few in number and relatively small: Arkansas (Ku Klux Klan, Aryan Brotherhood), Kentucky (Aryan Brotherhood), North Carolina (Black Panthers), Oklahoma (Aryan Brotherhood, White Supremacy Family, Black Brotherhood), Texas (Texas Syndicate), Virginia (Pagans), and West Virginia (Avengers) (Camp & Camp, 1985, pp. 23–24). Prison gangs would develop later in Florida.

Texas presents a unique example of how gang members came to organize themselves within the prison control structure. For almost two decades after prison gangs began to emerge in Illinois and California, Texas was virtually free of gang activity (Camp & Camp, 1985). The lag in Texas prison gang emergence is largely explained by a traditional method of controlling security threat groups in Texas prisons that Fong (1990) observed. For many years, prison administrators used "building tenders," carefully chosen inmates who served as informal prison guards, assigned the role of maintaining order. However, this practice was ruled unconstitutional (*Ruiz v. Estelle*,

1980), after which a control vacuum existed in the prisons.[6] As a result, a "state of chaos emerged" in which prison administrators nearly lost control of their prisons for two reasons. First, prison administrators suddenly had a shortage of security staff. Second, they no longer had inmate monitors who served as informants. The control vacuum was quickly filled by prison gangs. "In March, 1983, there was only one prison gang, the Texas Syndicate, with fifty-six members. Two and a half years later, eight inmate gangs . . . formed and the reported membership increased to 1,400" (Fong, 1990, pp. 36–37; see also Beaird, 1986). The Texas Syndicate (a Mexican gang) had emerged in 1975 (Camp & Camp, 1985), formed by members of the parent gang in California that was comprised of inmates who came from Texas (Fong, 1990).

Other prison gangs formed in the 1980s, including Texas Mafia (1982), Aryan Brotherhood of Texas (1983), Texas Mexican Mafia (1984), *Neuestro Carneles* (1984), Mandingo Warriors (1985), Self-Defense Family (1985), and *Hermanos De Pistolero* (1985) according to the Gang Task Force of the Texas Department of Corrections (cited in Fong, 1990, p. 36). The Texas Mexican Mafia, organized in 1984, also known as *Mexikanemi*, became the largest prison gang in the Texas prison system by the mid-1990s (Orlando-Morningstar, 1997). The main factor accounting for its rapid growth was its loosely structured recruiting procedure, granting membership to any Hispanic inmate who met the "homeboy connection" requirement (Fong, 1990). This unique nationalistic prison gang promotes Mexican heritage, insisting that Mexico and the southwestern United States should be returned to native Mexicans. This credo, set forth in a twelve-part constitution, has pushed the *Mexikanemi* into several wars with other prison gangs within both state and federal prisons in the Southwest region (Orlando-Morningstar, 1997). But the most significant gang in the western region of Texas is *Barrio Azteca* (1986) that formed in the El Paso area and spread to other regions of the state (Texas Fusion Center, 2013). This prison gang is said to be one of several that actively smuggles drugs from Mexico into the United States through connections with Mexican Drug Trafficking Organizations along the Southwest border.

During the 1990s, the Texas Department of Criminal Justice (TDCJ) experienced the largest offender population growth in its history. The total inmate population grew from about 50,000 to 128,000 in just five years, 1991–1995. This 153 percent increase from 1991 to 1995 exceeded the nationwide growth in prison populations during the same period (36 percent) by more than 100 percent according to the Sourcebook of Criminal Justice Statistics.[7] In tandem, the TDCJ in general saw a steady increase in overall STG related groups and criminal activity (Texas Fusion Center, 2013). Hence, it is not surprising that Texas prison gangs grew enormously during this period.

Although the exact year in which prison gangs emerged in the Florida state corrections system could not be established in early research (Camp & Camp, 1985), problems with motorcycle/biker gangs were first reported in the mid-1980s (p. 54), along with multiple gangs within federal prisons around the state (p. 213). Prison gangs in Florida appear to have grown significantly along with the increase in the state's prison population in the 1980s and 1990s. For many years, the largest prison gangs in the Florida Department of Corrections were *Associacion Ñeta* and Aryan Brotherhood.[8] The *Ñeta*, a notorious Puerto Rican-American/Hispanic prison gang is said to have originated in 1970 within the Rio Piedras Prison located there. The *Ñeta* see themselves as oppressed people who are unwilling to be governed by the United States, are extremely violent and have ties to street gangs.

In 1992, the Florida Department of Corrections intensified its efforts to assess the levels of gang activity within its inmate/offender population. At that time, racial White (e.g., Aryan Brotherhood) and Black supremacy (e.g., Black Panther Party), and Neo-Nazi groups were predominant in the Florida prison system, along with the Puerto Rican *Associacion Ñeta*. By 2008, the racial/ethnic makeup of Florida prison gangs had changed dramatically, with the growth of traditional prison gangs, especially Latin Kings, Gangster Disciples, and Bloods (Jordan, 2009). "As of June 30, 2012, 8,289 of the Department's 100,527 inmates (8.25 percent) were identified as gang members," and a slight increase was seen from 2011 (Florida Office of the Inspector General, 2013, p. 18). In 2011–2012, the Latin Kings had the most inmates identified as gang members, numbering more than one thousand, followed by Gangster Disciples and Bloods (each with approximately five hundred members). These latter two gangs saw the most growth from 2011 to 2012.

Distinguishing Features of Prison Gangs

In recent years, Texas prison gangs have developed very strong street connections, transforming themselves from strictly prison-based gangs. The Mexican Mafia and Texas Syndicate (predominantly Hispanic, *Syndicato Tejano*) have been the two best known Mexican prison gangs in Texas for decades (Fong, 1990). A third major Texas gang, Tango Blast (*Puro Tango Blast*), formed inside the state prisons during the early 1990s to shield inmates from other prison gangs. Tangos were established by inmates from Houston, Dallas, Fort Worth, and Austin. Hence, these Tango cliques collectively came to be known as the Four Horsemen, and they still band together for protection in the correctional setting (Texas Fusion Center, 2013).

There is some evidence that the relatively young Tango Blast gang may have amassed comparable strength of older established prison gangs in Texas (Tapia, Sparks, & Miller, 2014). The main reason for its transformation is the development of an extensive network of satellite gangs around the state. A unique feature of Tango Blast is its organizational structure, which is structured geographically, by cities, for expansive protection of members once they are released from prison. In fact, the most common translation of Tango is "hometown clique," in specific reference to the Houston-based parent gang, *Houstone Tango Blast* (also called H-Town). Other Tango Blast gangs are located in Austin, Corpus Christi, Dallas, El Paso, Fort Worth, San Antonio, and the Rio Grand Valley. This gang's unusual clique structure also provides networking opportunities for criminal activity locally. Further evidence of the strength of this gang is seen in the security gang threat assessment that follows.

The Texas Fusion Center's (2013) prison gang threat assessment matrix comprises ten well chosen factors that are important in determining the threat posed by each gang. This is a very innovative tool. Aside from permitting classification of these gangs into risk categories (with three "tiers"), several of the criteria suggest a higher likelihood of direct involvement with—or influence upon—local street gangs.[9] The current top (Tier 1) gangs in Texas (see In Focus: Gang Threat Tiers) are Tango Blast and Tango cliques (estimated at ten thousand members); Texas Syndicate (four thousand five hundred members); Texas Mexican Mafia (more than six thousand members); and Barrio Azteca (three thousand five hundred members) (Texas Fusion Center, 2013). "These organizations pose the greatest gang threat to Texas due to their relationships with Mexican cartels, large membership numbers, high levels of transnational criminal activity, and organizational effectiveness" (p. 2). Tier 2 gangs are Latin Kings, *Mara Salvatrucha*, Bloods, and Aryan Brotherhood of Texas. Importantly, Houston Intelligence Support Center (2011) intelligence reveals that

> prison and street gangs are now increasingly working together for financial gain, and the requirement for entrance into some prison gangs has changed, allowing admission of street gang members into at least some factions of prison gangs to order to increase their size and strength. (p. 5)

Presently, street gangs in the Houston area "play an integral role in drug trafficking and closer relationships between street gangs and prison gangs, and some prison gangs and Mexican drug cartels have increased the drug trafficking threat posed by gangs" (p. 3).

IN FOCUS

Prision Gang Threat Tiers

The Texas Fusion Center's prison gang threat assessment matrix incorporates ten factors that are important in determining the threat posed by each gang. Each factor is rated using a weighted point-based system that generates a composite score. This score provides a metric of the overall threat level of each gang. The most threatening gangs are classified as Tier 1, with other significant gangs classified as Tier 2 and Tier 3.

Relationship with Cartels: This factor examines the extent to which a gang is connected to Mexico-based drug cartels. A gang may be assessed as having no relationship, a temporary or short-term association, or a long-term business venture or exclusive relationship.

Transnational Criminal Activity: This factor considers whether a gang has transnational criminal connections, as well as whether the gang's criminal activity has spread into the transnational realm.

Level of Criminal Activity: This factor rates the type and frequency of crimes perpetrated by the gang. Crimes are rated on a scale covering a range of offenses, from misdemeanors to felonies.

Level of Violence: This factor assesses the overall level of violence perpetrated by the gang in its criminal activity. It ranges from generally nonviolent offenses, such as money laundering, to crimes involving extreme violence, such as torture and murder.

Prevalence Throughout Texas: This factor determines the extent to which a gang is active throughout the state. The geographic reach of some gangs is limited to specific cities or regions of Texas, while others are more widespread.

Relationship with Other Gangs: This factor examines the nature of a gang's alliances and influence with other gangs. This may include limited and temporary contact or formal alliances, whereas some gangs exercise direct oversight over other gangs.

Total Strength: This factor assesses the known size of the gang, measured by the number of individuals confirmed by law enforcement and criminal justice agencies to be members of the gang. This number is almost always an underrepresentation of the true size of the gang, as many members are unknown to law enforcement.

Statewide Organizational Effectiveness: This factor examines the gang's effectiveness in organizing members under its leadership across the state.

Juvenile Membership: This factor considers the extent to which the gang recruits juveniles and is active in schools, as gang recruitment of juveniles is considered a unique threat.

<u>Threat to Law Enforcement:</u> This factor considers the extent to which the gang represents a threat to law enforcement. Some gang members may only use violence to resist arrest or to flee from law enforcement, while others may actively target officers.

Source: Texas Fusion Center, 2013, p. 11.

Notably, eleven prison gangs currently are prominent in the Houston area (Houston Intelligence Support Center, 2010, 2011). In the Central Houston area, analysts tag the Houstone Tango Blast as the overall most threatening prison gang, and also Texas Syndicate, Mexican Mafia, and Aryan Brotherhood of Texas as prominent gangs. The Houstone Tango Blast is the overall fastest growing gang in Houston environs, presently extending into twelve of seventeen nearby counties (Houston Intelligence Support Center, 2010).

By way of summary, interactive relationships between prison gangs and affiliated street gangs are readily apparent in the Southern region, thanks to excellent intelligence gathering. Texas security intelligence reports draw attention to several noteworthy trends (Joint Crime Information Center, 2014, p. 26):

- "As a gang grows into a state-wide criminal organization, its structure and focus can change to a business-like model, allowing for greater collaboration between its members and outside forces." Recently, Mexican cartels have begun to ally with various criminal gangs to maximize drug distribution operations. As a result, the gangs appear to continue easing rivalries and generating new illicit business opportunities. "For example, Aryan Brotherhood of Texas (ABT) members operated a drug ring with members of *Houstone Tango Blast*, in association with a Mexican cartel."
- Various Texas gangs have settled long-term differences to further their respective economic goals. "For example, Tango Blast members now have transactional relationships with several gangs, including former rivals." Earlier, the more established criminal groups, such as such as Texas Syndicate, responded to Tango members with aggression as Tangos were growing in strength and extent of criminal activity.
- In Texas, the historically antagonistic relationship between Bloods and Crips has improved recently, as evidenced by cliques from both gangs working together for mutual benefit. The easing of traditional gang rivalries affords gang members greater operational freedom. On occasion, members may maintain connections with friends and associates who, in turn, may also be aligned with other gangs.

IN FOCUS

Prison Gang Organization in Texas

The Texas Department of Public Safety (Texas Fusion Center, 2013, p. 19) has documented four gang organization structures among prison gangs across the state. Each of these gangs has street extensions or counterparts—which are reflected in the gang structures.

Paramilitary models include a hierarchical structure with clear distinction between ranks, which often include military titles such as general, captain, lieutenant, sergeant, and soldier. Senior leaders are able to issue orders to subordinates that are generally carried out as instructed. Gangs using this model include Texas Mexican Mafia and Barrio Azteca.

Regional Cell models are composed of several cells that are part of the same organization, but that act generally independent of one another at an operational level. Each cell may have a strict internal hierarchy similar to a paramilitary model, though between cells there is little coordinated command and control. Texas Syndicate is an example of a Texas gang with a regional cell model.

Cliques of gangs tend to adopt a common culture and identity, but have few tangible connections to one another. Each clique may have a senior member that acts as a leader, and larger cliques may have a more structured hierarchy. In some cases, cliques of the same gang may work in opposition to each other. Examples of clique-based gangs are Bloods, Crips, and *Mara Salvatrucha*.

Loose Affiliation gangs have relaxed membership requirements and little to no detectable leadership hierarchy. This model tends to be the most dynamic, allowing for rapid growth while simultaneously limiting the extent to which groups of members can be effectively managed. Tango Blast is an example of a Texas gang with a loose affiliation model.

The extent of symbiotic relationships among these various Texas gangs is somewhat surprising. In several instances, drug-distribution opportunities have served to unite traditionally opposing gangs. Moreover, inside Texas prisons at least, gangs will tolerate members who do work for another gang so long as that work does not conflict with the activities of the members' gang. This development not only reduces the incidence of inter-gang violence, it also serves to increase collaboration in multi-gang criminal operations.

CENTRAL ISSUES WITH RESPECT TO PRISON GANGS

Three widespread concerns with respect to prison gangs are the violence associated with them, the nature of relationships between prison and street gangs, and the prospect of prison gang ties to Mexican drug trafficking organizations. Each of these issues is addressed in turn.

Violence Associated with Prison Gangs

Understanding gang-related violence in prisons is not a complex matter. Turf wars occur in prison just as on the streets, "where gang members and non-gang members are packed together, leaving few options for retreat to a safe and neutral spot" (Fleisher & Decker, 2001, p. 5). Violence is even more catalytic when profits are at stake, and this certainly is the case when gang control of drug trafficking is widespread. "Motivated by a desire to make money and be at the top of an institution's inmate power structure, prison gangs exploit the inherent weaknesses resulting from overcrowded, under-staffed mega-prisons" (p. 5). Based on interviews with more than five thousand male inmates from 185 state prisons, Huebner (2003) reported that gang membership was a significant predictor of the frequency of assaults on both staff and inmates.

Prison gangs account for a substantial share of violence in prison. In the mid-1980s prison gang members, who represented just 3 percent of all prison inmates were estimated to have caused 50 percent or more of the prison violence (Camp & Camp, 1985). Since then, "estimates of the number of gang-affiliated inmates have increased substantially and prison officials continue to attribute a disproportionate amount of prison violence to gang-affiliated inmates" (Griffin & Hepburn, 2006, p. 423). However, researchers only recently began extensive study of violence associated with prison gangs. Members of prison gangs tend to have extensive personal histories of violence.

> Once in prison, opportunities for involvement in crime abound. Whether by affiliating with members of their own gang, neighborhood or new prison gangs, gang members engage in higher levels of institutional misconduct. This misconduct can take a variety of forms, including but not limited to violence, extortion and the sale of drugs. (Pyrooz, Decker, & Fleisher, 2011, pp. 19–20)

And members of these gangs who are convicted of homicide offenses are "significantly more likely to commit various types of misconduct in prison" (Drury & DeLisi, 2011, p. 142). Racial/ethnic conflicts are universal sources of violence among prison gangs. "The presence of white hate groups in prison exacerbates institutional tensions and conflicts in prison, multiplying the opportunities for misconduct and the longer prison sentences and isolation that accompany such behavior" (Pyrooz et al., 2011, p. 21).

Regional differences in factors associated with external prison gang violence are also important. For example, drug-trafficking enterprises are an extremely important factor in the Southwest, the current main corridor of the flow of drugs from Central America and Mexico into the United States. Nationwide, much of the gang violence in prisons is associated with gang-on-gang fighting instigated by gang leaders over turf control as well as extortion schemes. To be sure, access to contraband also is a major source of violence within prisons—particularly drugs and cell phones.

Relationships Between Prison and Street Gangs

Jacobs's (2001) Illinois study first documented fluid communication between the gang members outside and inside prison. Because he was researching Illinois prison gangs that were extensions of street gangs, Jacobs observed that "criminal schemes are hatched in prison and carried out on the streets and vice versa" (p. vi). Other research on gangs first formed in prisons describes an inside–outside developmental sequence. Notably, Texas prison gangs emerged from predatory groups inside prisons and expanded to develop a street presence with the addition of large memberships that were required to maintain ties after leaving prison (Buentello et al., 1991). Symbiotic relationships between prison gangs, their counterpart street gangs, rival street gangs, and other criminal street groups are common in southwest Texas. For example, some MS-13 gang members were reported by the *Los Angeles Times* to have extensive ties to the notorious *La Eme* prison gang (see chapter 5).

Modern-day prison gangs will allow gangsters on the outside to form alliances with other criminals or provide regular sources for illegal products such as drugs, and the STG also will support and protect others in the gangster's crew when they are incarcerated (Allender & Marcel, 2003). When gang members are released from custody, they often return to their neighborhoods of origin and renew old associations in their original street gang. On release from confinement, street gang members can easily reestablish neighborhood-based ties to gang social networks (Fleisher, 1989; Fleisher & Decker, 2001). Should they resume prior criminal activities, contacts made in the prison system will become more important. Valdez and colleagues (2009) found that Mexican-American prison gangs gradually came to dominate and dissolve the local gangs in a large southwestern city.

Returning gang members also introduce extremely violent prison gang culture into local gangs. The most rapidly increasing factor linked to local gang violence in the National Youth Gang Survey (NYGS) is now gang members returning from confinement (Egley & Howell, 2013). Along with inter-gang conflict and drug trafficking, this factor has become more predominant over the past decade. In fact, the return of gang members from prison to communities is a noticeable problem for more than half of the gang problem jurisdictions nationwide (Figure 2.1; Egley & Howell, 2011).

In the view of law enforcement, returning gang inmates contribute in the following ways, in descending order of importance: violent crime, drug trafficking, property crime, access to weapons, and local gang dress and demeanor (Egley & Howell, 2011). Each year from 2004 to 2011, approximately 700,000 inmates were released from U.S. prisons, and this represents a 40 percent increase from 1996, when almost 500,000 inmates were released (Carson & Golinelli, 2013). Given that an estimated 19 percent of all prison inmates[10] are gang members (Winterdyk & Ruddell, 2010), then one can extrapolate that as many as 133,000 gang involved ex-offenders were returned to communities of origin (in virtually all cases) across the United States each year from 2004 to 2011.

Several conclusions can be drawn from research on elevated crime by returning gang inmates (Pyrooz et al., 2011, p. 21). First, gang members are

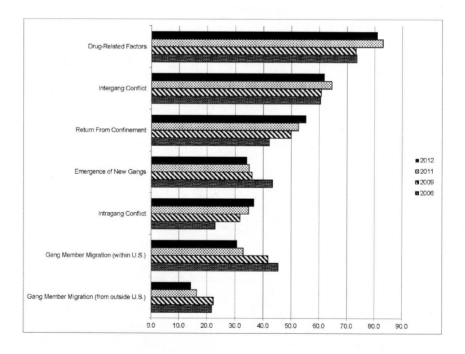

Figure 2.1.   Law Enforcement Views on Factors That Influence Gang Violence in Local Communities (National Youth Gang Survey data: 2006, 2009, 2011, 2012) National Gang Center. National Youth Gang Survey Analysis. http://www.nationalgangcenter.gov/Survey-Analysis. Accessed May 9, 2014.

"hard cases" to manage, often requiring segregation from the larger inmate population. Second, they often are isolated from important educational and employment opportunities that are available to the general prison population. Third, while in prison, gang members often form new alliances with other prison gangs. Fourth, upon leaving prison, gang members often find a changed landscape in their communities, and also in the gangs to which they once belonged. Because of these and other factors, several studies show that gang members as a class are at high risk for committing new crimes in comparison with non-gang inmates (Caudill, 2010; Dooley, Seals, & Skarbek, 2014; Olson, Dooley, & Kane, 2004; Huebner, Varano, & Bynum, 2007; Trulson, Caudill, Haerle, & DeLisi, 2012).

SUMMARY AND IMPLICATIONS

The infrastructure supporting the growth in rates of imprisonment in the United States and the accompanying prison-building binge has been described as a carceral boom (Alexander, 2011; Mauer, 2004; Wacquant, 2009). The American Society of Criminology National Policy Committee's (2001) White Paper, "The Use of Incarceration in the United States," exposed the gross inequities in the uses of imprisonment that was driven by the U.S. "war on drugs" that spanned the presidential terms of Ronald Reagan to William Clinton. The White Paper states, unequivocally, that

> a major reason for the dramatic increase in the U.S. prison population and associated increases in the number of Blacks, Hispanics, and women, has been substantial increases in the numbers of persons sentenced to prison for drug crimes. . . . African Americans and Hispanics are grossly over represented in the prisoner population, and this over representation has increased over the past two decades in concert with the selective enforcement of certain forms of drugs which are associated with race and ethnicity. (p. 15)

Tonry (1994) illustrates how the U.S. "war on drugs" bloated prisons with minor drug offenders, particularly inner city Black males. Until 1990, the majority of admissions to federal and state prisons were White, when the representation of Blacks and Whites reversed. Alexander (2011) termed this phenomenon "the new Jim Crow" in the title of her highly regarded book. This trend, along with extreme racial/ethnic segregation, prompted well respected analysts to frame the process pejoratively as the "colonization" of minorities in American cities (Alexander, 2011; Hawkins, 2011; West, 1993).

The most reliable repeated surveys suggest that 12 percent of all federal and state prison inmates were members of prison gangs in 2003, and this figure grew to 19 percent by 2009, a substantial increase in just seven years

(Winterdyk & Ruddell, 2010). Importantly, only about half of the validated members belonged to a gang prior to confinement, thus half join gangs after entering prison. Given that prison gangs are well institutionalized in the largest state and federal correctional facilities, these are sure to remain strong in the foreseeable future. Although the prison population began declining in 2008, the annual drop each year amounts to only about 1 percent (Glaze & Parks, 2012).

Sharbek (2012) suggests that prison gangs are an increasingly important type of organization operating behind bars and may play a role in controlling and punishing misbehavior. Some gangs, he reports, communicate the standards of appropriate behavior explicitly in written documents. For example, the *Nuestra Familia* prison gang has set forth fourteen principles of behavior for Hispanic inmates in its document, the "Fourteen Bonds" (Fuentes, 2006). Like most prison gangs in California, Fuentes reports that the *Nuestra Familia* maintains an up-to-date record of inmates, known as the "Bad News List," who deserve punishment for misbehavior. The gang designates members in each tier of a correctional facility to identify new inmates, and to act as informal guards in monitoring and regulating inmate behavior.

Prison gang structures vary from one state or region to another. As seen in the In Focus: Gang Organization, Texas prison gang structures vary from "loose affiliation" (Tango Blast) to "paramilitary" organizations (Texas Mexican Mafia and Barrio Azteca). Two forms of prison gang structures between these extremes are "regional cell" models (Texas Syndicate) and "cliques" (*Mara Salvatrucha*, Bloods, and Crips). The varied prison gang structures sharply differ from presumed paramilitary organizations that are prominent in prison gang lore and much of the published literature.

Across all regions, the FBI (2009) considers the following to be the seven major prison gangs in the United States: Mexican Mafia, Aryan Brotherhood, Barrio Azteca, Black Guerrilla Family, *Hermanos de Pistoleros* Latinos, *Mexikanemi*, and *Associacion Ñeta*. Other well-represented street gang members inside prisons in various states nationwide are Latin Kings, *Trinitarios*, Crips, Bloods, Vice Lord Nation, and 18th Street (National Alliance of Gang Investigators' Associations, 2009). Six prison gangs reportedly "aligned with or connected to MDTOs" in the Southwest region are: Barrio Azteca, *Hermanos de Pistoleros* Latinos, Texas Syndicate, La Eme, and Tango Blast (FBI, 2012).

From the accounts of prison gangs described here, three generations of development are apparent. The first generation of prison gangs emerged spontaneously in response to dangers inside prisons. The second generation was for many years extensions of street gangs that grew enormously during the 1980s and 1990s, particularly in large urban centers, as seen in chapter 1—with the exception of Texas prison gangs that formed and proliferated strictly within the prisons. Otherwise, this second generation of prison gangs in major cities extended their influence back to the streets as gang leaders were released. More fully evolved than the second generation, the third generation of prison gangs is extremely active in street-level criminal enterprises in varied forms, often highly structured and well-managed organizations. As a prison gang grows into an established criminal organization, its structure and focus can change to a business-like model. Some prison gangs have settled long-term differences with other prison and street gangs and begun collaborations to further their respective economic goals. This transition has not met with the level of resistance from members that might be expected, for the easing of traditional gang rivalries affords gang members greater operational freedom.

NOTES

1. A looser definition of a *prison gang* is this: "[T]hey have their origin in prison, influence crime in the community, and commit their crimes and exert their influence from within [our] supposedly most secure institutions—prisons and other correctional facilities" (Barker, 2012, p. 117).

2. The north–south geographical dividing line is a grey area in central California, between the cities of Bakersfield and Fresno.

3. The major Folk affiliates are Gangster Disciples, Black Disciples, Black Gangsters, and Maniac Latin Disciples; the major People affiliates are Latin Kings, Black P Stone Nation, Vice Lords, and Four Corner Hustlers (Chicago Crime Commission, 2006).

4. Gang subgroups, sections, or cliques.

5. According to intelligence information compiled by the Gang Identification Task Force. White Prison Gangs: Gang Identification Task Force. "Dead Man Inc." Accessed December 16, 2009. http://whiteprisongangs.blogspot.com/2009/05/dead-man-inc.html.

6. In the case of *Ruiz v. Estelle*, a U.S. District Court in Texas ruled in the plaintiffs' favor citing numerous instances of mistreatment, institutionalized neglect and inadequate resources and facilities. As a consequence, Federal District Judge William Wayne Justice ordered sweeping changes in the state's prison system.

7. Hindelang Criminal Justice Research Center, University at Albany, SUNY. "Sourcebook of Criminal Justice Statistics Online." Accessed December 17, 2014. http://www.albany.edu/sourcebook/pdf/t612011.pdf.

8. Florida Department of Corrections. "Major Prison Gangs." Accessed March 6, 2014. http://www.dc.state.fl.us/pub/gangs/prison.html.

9. The U.S. Bureau of Prisons (Gaes, Wallace, Gilman, Klein-Saffran, & Suppa, 2002) has developed a "threat index" that provides a graphical representation of the threat posed by different prison gang affiliations. In addition, a composite measure of gang misconduct represents the threat that particular gangs pose to prison order.

10. Based on a 2009 survey of Directors of Security in the fifty-three U.S. federal and state prison systems.

Chapter Three

An Historical Analysis of Street Gang Emergence and Transformation

Some gang researchers have suggested four main periods of gang development in the United States: in the late 1800s and around the 1920s, 1960s, and 1980s (Curry, Decker, & Pyrooz, 2014). Rather, as chronicled in this volume, our nation has experienced a remarkably continuous pattern of gang emergence and expansion, marked by periods of increased gang activity from time to time with overlapping periods across the four main geographic regions, beginning with the Northeast, followed by the Midwest, next in the West, and lastly, in the Southern region of the United States. The first gangs were Caucasian, having formed among poor European immigrant youth in the slums, and associated chaos and conflict of major Northeast cities. These gangs formed in the 1820s, and others replaced them in the 1840s, 1860s, 1930s, and 1970s. Almost one-half-century later, gangs formed in Chicago, in the 1860s, and grew in spurts in the 1920s, 1940s, 1960s, and 1970s. In the meantime, gangs had begun to emerge in the West region in the 1930s—particularly in Los Angeles—and grew continuously there until the 1980s with distinctive growth periods. In stark contrast, gangs did not emerge in the Southern region until the 1970s, but expanded rapidly there until the mid-1990s.

In recent years, street gang problems in the United States grew dramatically, reaching a peak in prevalence of gang activity in the mid-1990s. "This growth was manifested by steep increases in the number of cities, counties, and states reporting gang problems" (W. Miller, 2001, p. 42, Figure 4.1, chapter 4). The central question that these reliable statistics raise is this: Why did gang activity proliferate so enormously and so suddenly in the 1980s and 1990s after more than a century of deliberate growth? In seeking to answer this question, in the remainder of this chapter, we turn the spotlight onto gangs themselves and the environments in which they emerged as we examine factors that account for much of their remarkable growth.

The initial emergence and transformation of gangs in the United States can be explained by a series of social and historical events and urban conditions. Figure 3.1 organizes the key developments in five main phases, beginning with the pre-gang era in the United States (at the time of the American Revolution), and extending more than two centuries, to 2012. By and large, these developments account for the main periods of gang emergence and growth in three of the four major U.S. regions, though less so in the Southern region because several of these factors either did not apply or played out less intensively therein.

In Phase 1, social disorganization was an inevitable product of large-scale immigration, clearly seen in immigrant concentration in slums, residential instability, and concentrated disadvantage. In turn, these conditions of social disorganization led to low neighborhood control, family disorganization, youth alienation, and racial ethnic conflicts in Phase 2. Next, in Phase 3, youth gangs formed and attracted alienated youth and others who experienced group conflict and felt unsafe in their neighborhoods and schools. The youth subculture, including influential gangsta rap music, supported gang culture. In Phase 4, several gang violence facilitators led to gang violence, including prison population growth, and gang involvement in drug trafficking. Transformed gangs were the outcome in Phase 5, in the form of street gangs and prison gangs.

PHASE 1. SOCIAL DISORGANIZATION

In the first phase of gang formation, rapid immigration from Europe to the United States following the American Revolution overwhelmed cities of destination. The first gangs were Irish men and adolescents who banded together to forge a wedge of safety and resource accumulation in the social disorder and widespread violence in the slums of New York City. Subsequent waves of immigrants into the United States and concentrations in urban areas were followed by gang formation, but not immediately. In time, gangs continuously developed out of three conditions that large-scale immigration produced: immigrant concentration in slums, residential instability, and "concentrated disadvantage" (extreme poverty). These are the three components of the best substantiated theory of gang violence, social disorganization theory (Papachristos & Kirk, 2006). As these scholars explain, "gangs arise either to take the place of weak social institutions in socially disorganized areas, or because weak social institutions fail to thwart the advent of unconventional value systems that often characterize street gangs" (p. 64). In other words, the newcomers' lives were not organized and stabilized by customs, traditions,

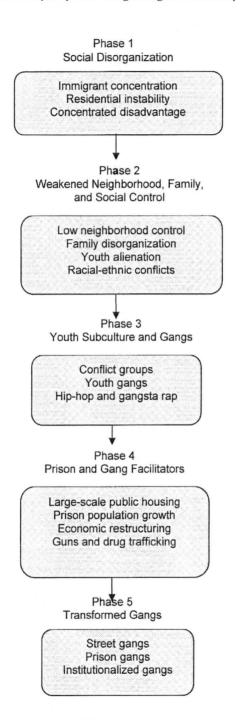

Figure 3.1. An Historical Model of Street Gang Emergence and Transformation

and institutions that nested Americans enjoyed—to which immigrant families did not have access.

The original developers of social disorganization theory, Shaw and McKay (1942/1969), observed from extensive Chicago research that racial/ethnic heterogeneity, low socioeconomic status, and residential mobility reduce the capacity of community residents to control crime. These conditions in communities make it difficult for residents to develop informal social control, mutual trust, and social cohesion, which commonly serve to dampen crime and violence in communities. Shaw and McKay specified three mechanisms by which social disorganization theory accounts for gang existence: neighborhood population mobility, ethnic heterogeneity, and poverty. They viewed mobility and population heterogeneity as disruptive influences on community institutions and networks, but these effects would vary according to, first, the rate of immigration, and second, the similarities between the newly arriving immigrants and the established residents of a neighborhood. As Papachristos and Kirk (2006) explain, these factors disrupt the normative foundation that supports effective social control, thereby contributing to a state of social disorganization. In other words, gangs arise either to fill the void of weak social institutions in socially disorganized areas, or because weak social institutions are thus incapable of thwarting unconventional value systems that often characterize street gangs.

As noted earlier, the continued immigration and expansion of Black and Hispanic populations led to the "hyperghettoization" (Adamson, 1998) of minority populations in large cities across the United States. By the 1950s, it was evident that ethnic succession was a concept that applied only to the European minorities (Hagedorn, 2006). The associated growth of gangs was amply documented in our examination of periods of gang growth in each region in chapter 1.

PHASE 2. WEAKENED NEIGHBORHOOD, FAMILY, AND SOCIAL CONTROL

In the second phase, the context of social disorganization led to family disorganization, low neighborhood control, and youth alienation. In particular, poor family relationships and ineffective schooling impeded child and adolescent social development. Riis (1902/1969) in New York City and Thrasher (1927/2000) in Chicago drew attention to the tensions that family upheaval and relocation in a distant land created. Socialization and control of children and adolescents slipped from the grasp of parents, schools, churches, and other institutions. In time, gangs served as a substitute for residual institutions for youth who had failed to make an adequate social and cultural transition from family, to school, and to work.

For Mexican American and other minority youth, the term *multiple marginality* captures the essence of various obstacles to social adjustment (Vigil, 2002, 2008). Vigil suggests that macrohistorical (racism and repression) and macrostructural (immigration and ghetto/barrio living) forces combine to strain and undermine social control and bonds with the family and school and also diminish respect for law enforcement. As Vigil explains, street subcultures arise to fill the void when family and other social controls do not function as they should. Family stability suffers with the disruptions and stresses from moving frequently and often to unfamiliar neighborhoods. It has long been recognized that low-income and ethnic minorities "have historically suffered negative, damaging experiences in the educational system" (Vigil, 2002, p. 9). Minority youth have far higher dropout and suspension rates. Higher dropout and failure rates are largely attributable to "segregated, underfunded, inferior schools, where they encounter cultural insensitivity and an ethnocentric curriculum" (p. 9). This process, through which young people are left out of mainstream society because of language, education, cultural, and economic barriers, "relegates these urban youths to the margins of society in practically every sense. This positioning leaves them with few options or resources to better their lives. Often, they seek a place where they are not marginalized—and find it in the streets [i.e., in gangs]" (Vigil, 2002, p. 7).

Distinctively for girls, the gang may appear to provide an oasis from problem-prone families. Both Moore's (1991) and J. Miller's (2001) research on girls in gangs described common parental substance use, domestic violence, physical abuse and sexual abuse. Thus, more so than boys, girls feel isolated from their distressed families (Chesney-Lind, 2013). Law enforcement then steps in "as the controlling authority of last resort" (Vigil, 2002, p. 10). Once a Mexican-American youth becomes alienated from schools and families, Vigil explains, street socialization takes over thereafter, and the newly minted street subculture supports the identity of the street youth, the gangs (p. 70). Thus it is the second-generation children[1] of Mexican immigrants that join gangs, under intense marginalization pressures (Telles & Ortiz, 2008; Waters, 1999).

For youth in general, risk factors for gang membership are found in several interacting domains, including individual, family, peer, school, and neighborhood contexts, and the respective domains are more influential at different developmental stages in childhood and adolescence (Howell & Griffiths, 2016). Gang members are distinctively different from ordinary delinquents in that they possess more risk factors and generally experience them in multiple developmental domains during childhood and early adolescence, thereby generating enduring effects (Esbensen, Peterson, Taylor et al., 2010; Gilman, Hill, Hawkins et al., 2014; Hill, Howell, Hawkins et al., 1999; Thornberry, Krohn, et al., 2003).

PHASE 3. YOUTH SUBCULTURE AND GANGS

Much has been written about the socialization gap in American society between childhood and adulthood, commonly called *adolescence*. The youth subculture helps to fill this gap in providing values, customs, behavioral expectations, and the like for youth during the adolescent period. This dynamic is most clearly evident in Mexican-American gangs that grew out of the youth subculture via two traditions in the dominant Mexican culture. The *palomilla* custom of male friendship groups bridged the transition from childhood to adulthood for young males (Rubel, 1965). Youth gangs crystallized from these traditional associations along the migration route from deep in Mexico to the United States—most notably in El Paso. *Palomilla* customs continue to maintain the traditions and strengths of modern-day Chicano gangs. The second tradition comes from difficulties associated with the assimilation of Mexican immigrants into American society. *Cholo* (from the Spanish word solo, alone) refers to "people who never quite anchor themselves in the dominant culture nor totally extricate themselves from the native culture . . . a constant battle in their minds; sometimes Mexican, then Anglo" (Vigil, 1998, p. 216). Vigil calls this adjustment process *choloization*. A new youth subculture evolved to manage this situation, called *cholo*, an ambivalent state of mind, wanting neither to integrate into American culture nor to become Mexican again. Given this mental state, tensions mounted with large-scale Mexican immigration in the 1930s and 1940s. This form of cultural adaptation "was a step, perhaps an unsteady one, towards what later became known as Chicano culture" (p. 211).

Once conflict between Mexican immigrant and American culture grew, second-generation Mexican-American youth embraced the *cholo* style of dress, talk, walk, and a complement of gestures and demeanors that blended parts of cultures. The *cholo* subculture gained prominence in the 1940s, during the zoot-suit period, but the dress styles have varied over the decades. Particularly in the Southwest and West, Chicano gangs have evolved in a unique subculture that is rich in ceremonial ritual and symbolic representations expressed in Mexican language, specific clothing styles, hairstyles, tattoos, and graffiti. Unlike the early gangs composed of White Anglo immigrant youth that faded away, Latino (mostly Mexican) immigrants have continued to pour into and beyond the barrios that generated the first Chicano street gangs. In time, the *cholo* subculture provided the "ought-to" (values) and "blueprints for action" (norms), substitutes for the voids left by conventional social control institutions (Vigil, 2014).

An expert on nuances of the youth subculture in Chicago, Diamond (2009) documents in great detail its omnipresence there over a sixty-year period, from 1908 to 1969, how it proved to be a key influence in the emergence and expansion of gangs. Youth resistance identities first formed in the 1940s and 1950s. It was then that intense inter-group conflicts began, and with these, more intense turf control and expansion (Perkins, 1987). Social turbulence followed in the 1960s, accompanied by aggression and fighting gang subcultures that pitted Blacks, Puerto Ricans, and Mexican-American youth against one another in the constricted spaces allotted to their peoples. To be sure, the racial unrest of that era contributed to rapid gang growth in Chicago (Cureton, 2009; Diamond, 2001; Perkins, 1987). As Diamond (2009) put it, "youth gang subcultures served to magnify racial feelings into sensibilities of injustice, empowerment, and community" (p. 220). In this sense, "gangs were way stations on the path to cultural integration" (Pihos, 2011, p. 466). Because of racial injustices, some politically-oriented gangs formed in the 1960s and 1970s, and the political activism of gangs peaked in the 1980s and 1990s (Hughes & Short, 2006).

Blacks especially bore the brunt of violent victimization from race riots. A "decades-long violent struggle over turf and new generations of gangs spontaneously formed to carry on the fight" (p. 200). Elsewhere, the Civil Rights movement was advocating nonviolence, racial pride, and unity. "But Black students who were having nonviolent demonstrations in the South had little influence on Black street gang members [in Chicago] who were having their own distinctly more violent demonstrations" (Perkins, 1987, p. 29). The rise of the Black Panthers instilled Black pride, and their demise stirred resentment. The Black gangs that were prevalent in Chicago in the 1960s "lived and acted in a world that overlapped with that of other youths [and the gang members] were surely participants in a street culture" that promoted racial empowerment and racial unity (Diamond, 2001, p. 677). In other words, "gang warfare and political activism among Black youth were two sides of the same coin; [that is] gangs used Black Power rhetoric to attract more members, just as Black Power leaders traded on gang imagery to attract followers" (Pihos, 2011, p. 468).

Many Black urban youth were drawn into gangs by gangsta rap music in the decade between the mid-1980s and mid-1990s. The initial version of this musical genre emerged out of East Coast hip-hop party music (Quinn, 2005). Yablonsky (1997) suggests that gangsta rap grew out of a Black gang tradition of "playing the dozens" that Berdie (1947) documented. This game involved a number of youths who engaged in mutual verbal sparring, by creating nasty rhymes such as attacking the opponent's mother. A one-liner that Yablonsky (1997) recalled was "I [had sex with] your Ma in an alleyway, when I got through, she thought she was Cab Calloway" (p. x). Departing from earlier rap forms that were characterized as socially conscious and more politically Afro-centric, gangsta rap quickly gained status as the most controversial type of rap music and rapidly became "the most lucrative subgenre in hip-hop."[2] Source materials used by artists who first developed gangsta rap came from gang traditions: hand signs, vocabulary, gestures, special clothing, and territorial graffiti. "This music struck a responsive chord in portraying the difficulties associated with inner-city life, easily winning converts among neighborhood youth. The gangsta persona [became] a textbook glorification of gang culture . . . the tortured, angry, often poetic rebellion of ghetto youth" (Hagedorn, 2008, p. xxviii). All of this music was marketed outside mainstream music producers, largely because of its violent depiction of urban ghetto life in America, its contentious lyrics that promoted misogynistic (sexual discrimination, denigration of women, violence against women, and sexual objectification of women) and homophobic (prejudice against homosexuals) viewpoints. The gangsta rap music adopted a favorite beverage that helped promote it, 40 oz. malt liquor. "Forty-ounce bottles ('40s') of malt liquor became iconic accessories of gangsta rap, homologous with the focal concerns, activities, and collective self-image of the working-class subculture from which the music sprang" (Quinn, 2005, p. 3). In fact, St. Ides's popular brand of malt liquor was advertized as "ghettocentric," and not by accident. "This term expresses the focus on poor and working-class urban identity, culture and values, which increasingly pervaded Black youth culture in the 1980s and 1990s—in no small part as a result of gangsta rap" (p. 3).

Usually considered the first gangsta rap songs, Schoolly D's 1986 "P. S. K. What Does It Mean?" and "6'n The Mornin'" by Ice-T in 1987, and an early album, *Criminal Minded* by Boggie Down Productions (1987), established gangsta rap's presence on the East Coast of the United States. However, West Coast dominance of gangsta rap quickly emerged, led by N. W. A.'s (Niggaz With Attitude) double platinum album, *Straight Outta Compton* (1988). Compton was a predominately Black working-poor neighborhood in Los Angeles. Two songs on this album were most influential, "Gangsta Gangsta," (from which came the name of the gangsta rap genre) and "F*** tha Police" (which yielded the anti-police manifesto).[3] Among the rappers' targets of hatred, scorn, and murder threats were police—especially the LAPD that had morphed into a "techno-police" department, with helicopter aided surveillance, street barricading, and street sweeps (e.g., in Operation Hammer, that targeted gang members in Chief Daryl Gates's "war on gangs"). Under Chief Gates, the LAPD created a virtual "Fortress LA" from the mid-1980s to early 1990s (Davis, 2006). It developed a reputation for racialized brutality, exemplified in the beating of Rodney King in 1992. In turn, gangsta rappers reflected the rage in their communities over such police abuses as this, often expressed in revenge narratives including direct attacks at police and other institutions of power within the United States.

Self-named "gangsta-funk" (G-funk for short) emerged as a neighborhood- or city-based form of gangsta rap in Southern California in 1992–1996 (Quinn, 2005). In solidifying gangsta rap, G-funk had a "continuing investment of place" (p. 142) in spreading territorial identity of rappers and gangs themselves, beginning with N. W. A.'s *Straight Outta Compton* album that later was featured in a music video. Mapping practices in G-funk rap videos delineated both acclaimed and imagined places. Street gang wars in South Central Los Angeles, Compton, Long Beach, and Oakland—the centralized location of gangsta rap—were featured in this music (Kubrin, 2005; Kubrin & Nielson, 2014). But unlike sets of Los Angeles Crips and Blood gangs that constantly fought, G-funk artists remained united in messaging and representing, creating a profound cultural force (with the benefit of broadcast media) centered on several focal concerns that resonated in the identified places along with hatred of police. These focal concerns were packaged in two overarching behavioral types, the nihilist gangbanger and the enterprising hustler in a ghetto-confined dog-eat-dog world, while stressing "gratuitous, individualist pleasures of the moment" (Quinn, 2005, p. 145). What is most remarkable is that G-funk music became mainstream. Dr. Dre's "Nuthin' but a 'G' thang" arguably was the "hardest rap" to ever rank high (#2) on the Billboard Hot 100 chart (p. 161).

In the course of expansion from the East Coast to the West Coast and into the Southern region of the United States (led by the Geto Boys in Houston) and later in Baton Rouge, Atlanta, and Miami Beach South, gangsta rap became a driving force in adolescent subculture interpretations of social contexts. Its influence became so pervasive that gangsta rap engulfed White youth as well in the course of bridging underground and mainstream music traditions (Quinn, 2005). As an example, Snoop Dog became so popular that he was featured on a *Newsweek* cover (Leland, 1993), personifying the extreme violence associated with gangsta rap. An exhaustive content analysis of lyrics in more than four hundred rap songs revealed that gangsta rap supplied a "code of the street" for gang members and other youth (Kubrin, 2005). Without doubt, gangsta rap strengthened the desire of youth to become part of a gang subculture that was portrayed by the rappers as a glamorous and rewarding lifestyle. "Representing" a neighborhood, a city, or an imagined "gang nation" had a special appeal to disenfranchised inner city minority youth (Quinn, 2005). Gangsta rap was a powerful musical medium in making this prospect seem very real. Alexander (2011) adds that "there is absolutely nothing abnormal or surprising about a severely stigmatized group embracing their stigma . . . a powerful coping strategy" (p. 171).

As W. Miller (2001) observed, gang images have served for many decades as a marketable media product—in movies, novels, news features, and television drama—but the 1990s saw a significant change in how they were presented.

> Language was rough and insistently obscene; women were prostitutes ("bitches," "ho's," and "sluts") to be used, beaten, and thrown away; and extreme violence and cruelty, the gang lifestyle, and craziness or insanity were

glorified. Among the rappers' targets of hatred, scorn, and murder threats were police, especially black police (referred to as "house slaves" and "field hands"); other races and ethnic groups; society as a whole; and members of rival gangs. The target audience for gangsta rap was adolescents at all social levels, with middle-class suburban youth constituting a substantial proportion of the market for rap recordings. The medium had its most direct appeal, however, for children and youth in ghetto and barrio communities, for whom it identified and clarified a set of values, sentiments, and attitudes about life conditions that were familiar to them. The obscene and bitterly iconoclastic gangsta rappers assumed heroic stature for thousands of potential gang members, replacing the drug dealer as a role model for many. (W. Miller, 2001, p. 46)

Thus, gangsta rap gained status as "a culture of resistance" (Lusane, 1993, p. 41). What made gangsta rap especially intimidating was its lyrics that came from the minds and mouths of what many observers considered to be the most violent and threatening segment of America—young angry inner-city Black men (Quinn, 2005). Make no mistake, police and other crime control agencies, and politicians as well, were reminded of the Watts Rebellion of 1965—just twenty-five years earlier. In response, "rappers themselves were frequently the targets of police surveillance and harassment, not only drawing the wary attention of federal law enforcement, but also sparking the creation of hip hop task forces in major police departments across the U.S." (Nielson, 2012, p. 350). In numerous cases, rap lyrics were introduced as evidence of a defendant's guilt (Kubrin & Nielson, 2014).

The top ten gangsta rap artists often include Tupac Shakur (also called 2pac), Eazy E., The Game, Eminem, Ice Cube, 50 Cent, Dr. Dre, Jay Z, Snoop Dogg, and Lil Wayne.[4] Other top artists include Bounty Killa, Goodie Mob, Master P, Notorious B. I. G., Niggaz With Attitudes (N.W.A.), P-Diddy, Ricky Ross, Three 6 Mafia, Trick Daddy, and Young Jeezy (Hagedorn, 2008; Kubrin & Nielson, 2014, Nielson, 2012; Quinn, 2005). Media promotion succeeded to the point that in the early 1990s, rap's East Coast and West Coast stars represented gang-like enemies and a feud that would cost hip-hop some of its most talented stars, namely, Tupac Shakur and Notorious B.I.G. Hagedorn (2008, p. 98) adds that those contrived "wars" turned "real and lethal, a grim reflection of the music industry's amoral capacity to exploit even murder for profit."

Gang culture also was widely diffused by movies including *West Side Story* and *The Warriors* (both about New York City gangs), *Colors* (about Los Angeles's Crips and Bloods), and the 1990s films *Boyz in the Hood*, *South Central*, *New Jack City*, *Blood In, Blood Out*, and *Menace II Society*.[5] As a common theme, these movies transformed gangsters into folk heroes (Huff, 1993; Kubrin, 2005; Ro, 1996). Interestingly, the role model for rags-to-riches success in trafficking drugs in Los Angeles was not a gangster, however. The kingpin was Ricky "Freeway" Ross, whose empire sold as much as $3 million worth of crack cocaine per day at its height (Cockburn & St. Clair, 1998, p. 7).[6] Both Crip and Blood gangs were involved in distribution and sales of crack cocaine.

In sum, gangsta rap contributed significantly to the emergence of more gangs in the late 1980s and early 1990s and, with that, gang membership rolls expanded more than in any period of U.S. history (Howell & Griffiths, 2016; Miller, 2001). Along with the parallel growth of gangs and gang-related violence and drug trafficking, arrests in many cities contributed to substantial growth in imprisonment of young Black men (Nielson, 2012). "Even African Americans with no connection to hip-hop whatsoever increasingly found themselves caught in the 'web of institutional policing,' most evident in the skyrocketing incarceration rates that saw record numbers of Black Americans behind bars" (p. 350). Increased gang involvement in drug trafficking was a contributing factor. The sharpest increase in confinement was from 1989 to 1993 (Blumstein & Beck, 1999), in concert with the popularity of gangsta rap (Quinn, 2005). Without any doubt, youth gangs became more formidable once undergirded by the highly influential youth subculture. The allure of gangs grew stronger because of the widespread glorification of gang culture in rap music. Gang joining became an easier step for alienated youth of all races and ethnicities.

PHASE 4. PRISON AND STREET GANG FACILITATORS[7]

In the fourth phase, both Mexican-American and Black gangs were solidified in public housing projects that not only increased their anti-establishment resolve (as a result of such extreme isolation and resource deprivation), but also provided a distinctive base of operations for gangs and enabled them to increase their span of control. Many of the public housing projects—particularly in Chicago and Los Angeles—literally were contiguous with gang turf. After gang wars erupted in Chicago's high-rise public housing, police deemed some of the buildings too dangerous to enter. Incredibly, in some instances, gangs actually came to serve as *de facto* police. An unusual form of adaptation occurred in Chicago. Because gangs provided some relief to hyperghettoized residents in the form of safety from outsiders, and financial resources for necessities such as building repairs and upkeep, most residents reluctantly tolerated the increased violence associated with gang involvement in drug trafficking (Venkatesh, 1996, 2000). In an uncommon gesture of appreciation, the extremely violent gangs sponsored picnics for residents that were enjoyed by all.

In the 1950s and 1960s, housing policies in many cities were aimed at building highways to speed up the movement of Whites to the suburbs along with manufacturing and other industrial jobs. Indeed, Miller (1982/1992) found in his multi-city survey that slums or ghettos had shifted away from the inner-city to outer-city, ring-city, or suburban areas—often to formerly middle- or working-class neighborhoods. However, this process did not eliminate gangs in inner-city areas; rather, the gangs moved to the suburbs and ring cities with their families or on their own. Special concentration occurred in housing project areas. "The gangs are still in the ghettos, but these are often at some remove from their traditional inner-city locations" (Miller, 1982/1992, p. 76). "That earlier 'White flight' is now reversing itself as Whites 'flee' back to the city to take 'their' land" (Hagedorn, 2008, p. 129)—a "gentrification"[8] process by which lower income households are replaced by higher income households.

Massive imprisonment of gang members increasingly became more widespread as a strategic crime control became a national priority in the 1970s. The "politics of panic" came to dominate crime control policies (Beckett & Sasson, 2003) as "wars" on crime, drugs, gangs, and so-called juvenile "super-predators" hyped crime issues (Howell, 2003). Conservatives viewed the criminal justice system as too lenient; they wanted to see more punishment elements in criminal justice policies. They advocated the just desert principle, a retributive philosophy that holds that offenders should suffer the infliction of deserved pain, commensurate with the severity of the offense. A new breed of lobbyists sponsored by the American Legislative Exchange Council promoted conservative punitive reforms such as mandatory minimums, truth-in-sentencing laws and special provisions that targeted recidivists; for example, "three strikes" laws that carried mandatory life imprisonment sentences. Ready-made bills were carried into lawmakers' offices, and print media promoted more conservative and punitive crime control measures (Beckett & Sasson, 2003; Brownstein, 1996; Reeves & Campbell, 1994).

The resulting increase in prison confinement dwarfed all other periods before leveling off in 2009 (Carson & Golinelli, 2013; Carson & Sabol, 2012; Drucker, 2011; Harrison & Beck, 2006). Remarkably, between the mid-1970s and 2000, the number of state and federal prisoners in the United States grew fivefold (Figure 3.2). This increase has been recognized as "a phenomenon without precedent or comparison in any democratic society, all the more so in that it occurred during a period when the [U.S.] crime rate was stagnant" (Wacquant, 2009, p. 60). By 2007, the American penal system held more than 2.3 million adults, leading both China, with 1.5 million people behind bars, and Russia, with 890,000 inmates (Pew Charitable Trust, 2008). At this point, the United States had achieved the dubious distinction of having one in one hundred adults behind bars. Federal, state and county (jails) confinement rates were highest in states that led the nation in development of prison gangs. By 1993, the states with the highest incarceration rate in the U.S., by region follow: Northeast (New York and Pennsylvania), Midwest

(Illinois, Ohio, Michigan), West (California), and South (Texas and Florida) (Wacquant, 2009, p. 138). Five of these—New York, Illinois, California, Texas, and Florida—were leading states in the development of both street gangs and prison gangs.

The crime control policy of mass confinement contributed in particular to urban gang growth by virtue of returning large numbers of hardened criminals and new gang members to urban areas. Sooner or later, virtually all prison inmates return to their communities of origin, to urban areas (Petersilia, 2003; Travis, 2005) and face considerable obstacles to living crime-free (Visher, Yahner, & La Vigne, 2010) and gang-free lives (Phillips, 2007). Both juvenile (M. Howell & Lassiter, 2011) and adult (Dooley et al., 2014) gang members in confinement are more likely than non-gang offenders to be returned to confinement. Overall, recidivism following confinement is high in the United States: About two-thirds released in the early 1990s were rearrested within three years (Langan & Levin, 2002). This statistic worsened over the next twenty years, as three-fourths were rearrested within five years in the more recent sample (Durose, Cooper, & Snyder, 2014). Prison gang membership boosts recidivism another 6 percent, a quantitatively large effect

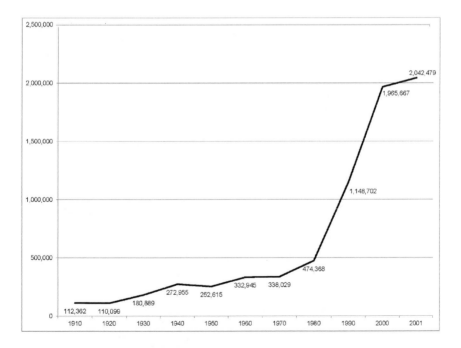

Figure 3.2.   Number of Prison and Jail Inmates, 1910–2000 Source: Justice Policy Institute 2000 analysis of U.S. Department of Justice Data. Reprinted with permission of the Justice Policy Institute.

when taking into account the additional number of life-course gang members on the streets (Dooley et al., 2014).

Travis and Petersilia (2001) observed that prisoners were "less well prepared individually [than in the past] for their return to the community and [were] returning to communities that [were] not well prepared to accept them" (pp. 300–301). Even the most essential services for inmates—basic education and vocational training—in adult prisons are not widely available even today. Only about one-third of inmates currently receive these services while in prison. They return to their communities needing housing and jobs, but their prospects are generally bleak. Beginning in the late 1970s and early 1980s, gang members returning from prison to ghetto streets found few legitimate work opportunities, but plentiful opportunities to sell drugs, including marijuana, cocaine, and heroin (Moore, 1993). Further exacerbating the problem, high levels of social and economic disadvantage often characterize the communities to which prisoners return (Baer et al., 2006). This continuing massive flow of returning inmates remains a major contributor to local gang violence and involvement in drug trafficking has become more prominent in recent years. Most law enforcement agencies nationwide contend that returning inmates is the most predominant influence on local gang violence (Figure 2.1; Egley & Howell, 2013).

Economic restructuring in the United States in the 1980s—that is, the replacement of manufacturing work with services jobs as factories moved outside central cities—served to make gangs more permanent (Moore, 1998; Moore & Pinderhughes, 1993). Until then, gangs were essentially an adolescent phenomenon. Wilson (1987) coined the term *new poverty* to describe severe further urban decay of already impoverished Black Chicago ghettos in the wake of economic restructuring. Most of the new jobs were in low-wage manufacturing and service occupations—jobs easily filled by exploitable immigrants (Moore & Pinderhughes, 1993). In the absence of jobs that supported the transition to adult family-related roles, gang involvement was prolonged as opportunities to mature out of the gang diminished. Drug trafficking opportunities were more readily available. "Gang members in their 20s and 30s, with poor work histories and prison records, had serious difficulty finding jobs; they stayed involved with the gang, and on the streets" (Moore, 2000, p. 15). Generally speaking, when jobs disappeared, families were weakened, and along with this, gangs became stronger "street" agencies of support.

Allowing U.S. residents to own and carry firearms backfired in the gang world. Research shows that beginning in the 1970s, gangs' access to more lethal weapons grew (Block & Block, 1993; Miller, 1975, 1982/1992). While weapons such as brass knuckles and homemade zip guns (single-shot pistols) were predominately used by gangs in the 1930s through the 1950s, by the mid-1990s, gangs possessed a far more deadly variety of weaponry (Bjerregaard & Lizotte, 1995; Sheley & Wright, 1995). Their arsenal then included sawed-off shotguns, handguns of all sizes and types (e.g., .22 cal., .38 cal., .357 cal., .45 cal., and 9 mm. among others) and semi-automatic weapons (e.g., AK-47, Uzi, MAC-10, MAC-11, Colt AR-15). It has been estimated that more than 90 percent of U.S. gang homicides involve firearms (Klein, Weerman, & Thornberry, 2006). Generally speaking, the growing availability of firearms among urban gangs has helped solidify their position in the streets. Studies consistently show that gun availability fuels lethal gang violence (Block & Block, 1993; Cook & Ludwig, 2006; Lizotte, Krohn, Howell, Tobin, & Howard, 2000). Gangs are more likely to recruit youths who own an illegal firearm and gang involvement often promotes the use of these weapons (Bjerregaard & Lizotte, 1994; Lizotte et al., 2000; Lizotte, Tesoriero, Thornberry, & Krohn, 1994). Firearms are readily available on certain streets in virtually all large American cities.[9]

PHASE 5. TRANSFORMED GANGS

In the fifth phase, the gang transformation process was completed, as they became more widespread, solidified, and dangerous in the course of evolving from juvenile or youth gangs to adolescent and adult street and prison gangs. The notion of gang transformation has drawn much attention in recent years, mainly in the context of so-called transnational gangs. International security analysts have formulated stages of gang transformations in terms of degree of threat they represent to established governments (Sullivan, 2006; Sullivan & Bunker, 2002; Sullivan & Elkus, 2008). Viewed through the lens of the present-day global security perspective, the possibility of three "generations" of gang forms have been suggested by Sullivan and colleagues. First-generation gangs are viewed as traditional turf-protecting street gangs. Second-generation gangs, they suggest, sometimes transition from turf protection to market-oriented drug gangs and drug trafficking operations. Third-generation gangs presumably are capable of mixing political and mercenary elements. But international gang experts, particularly Rodgers and Hazen (2014) along with Jones (2014) seriously question the specter of third-generation gangs of such capacity that they could transform themselves into a "new urban insurgency." Rather, Rodgers and Hazen (2014) suggest that knowledge of transformed gangs can be advanced more systematically by adopting the term "gang transformation" to refer to genesis, development, and institutionalization of gangs over time. These scholars make an important point: "Gangs go through a number of transformations. But not all transformations bring gangs to a higher level of organization" (p. 15). Wolf's (2014) review of several recent Central American isthmus studies supports this observation, underscoring that the *maras* primary interest remains territorial control.

The genesis of gangs in the United States is amply documented in the historical accounts of gang emergence in three of the four geographic regions, namely, the Eastern, Midwest, and Western region. Research has not adequately documented the process of gang emergence in the Southern region. The early phases of our historical framework draw attention to community contextual conditions (Phase 1), social disorganization and racism (Phase 2), and the youth subculture (Phase 3), as essential conditions for gang emergence, and these need not be discussed further here. Instead, we move directly into considerations of gang transformations in terms of their development and institutionalization.

Carl Taylor (1990b) identified three distinctive developmental gang forms in Detroit: scavenger, territorial, and corporate. *Scavenger* gangs mainly consist of lower and underclass youths. These are urban survivors who prey on the weak and have no common bond except their impulsive behavior and need to belong. They engage in senseless, spontaneous crimes for fun. Leadership constantly changes (p. 105). *Territorial* gangs, Taylor contends, evolve from scavenger gangs, once they define a territory and become more organized for a specific purpose. Someone assumes a leadership role, which is part of the process of organization. They actively defend their territory, the area of their "business." They become "rulers" of their turf, generally defined as neighborhood and ethnic boundaries, using physical violence as their only enforcement tool against invaders (pp. 107–108). *Corporate* gangs are highly organized for the purpose of engaging in illegal money-making ventures. In Chicago, for a time, street gangs served as "farm teams" for mafia organizations (McKay, 1949; Thrasher, 1927/2000). They took on many of the characteristics of a business organization, motivated only by profit. They operated by rules and military-like discipline.

The gang transformation process that Taylor observed in Detroit is not universal, although several Chicago gangs also achieved the level of corporate gangs (Spergel, 1986, 1995; Venkatesh, 1996, 2002, 2008). Other examples of varied gang forms are plentiful (Ayling, 2011; Hagedorn, 2008; Klein, 1995; Miller, 1966/2011; 1974b, Short, 1990, 1996, 2000; Spergel, 1995). Miller (1974a) carefully dispelled the claims that gangs were radically transformed by civil disorder, political activism, and drug use. Rodgers and Hazen (2014) remind us that

> gangs can follow a number of paths, reaching a number of end points; which path is chosen depends on a set of factors both internal (e.g., leadership, organization) and external (e.g., state response, politics, drugs), and what end state is reached may depend on an entirely different set of factors. (p. 15)

Thus, our attention here is focused on common traits of gangs that may evolve from youth gangs to street gangs.

From Youth Gangs to Street Gangs

Five common traits of serious urban street gangs are evident from the extensive history of gangs chronicled in this volume, regardless of gang locations. First, these street gangs typically claim a turf or territory, and they defend it resolutely. Second, they fight and even kill others over the personal and collective honor of the group. Third, tough, aggressive, fighting postures provide the individual status that is craved by gang members. Fourth, the more criminally active gangs are distinguished by an organizational structure of some sort. Fifth, certain crimes are characteristic of street gangs. We next elaborate these common street gang traits.

First, the claiming and defense of turf or territory is a key characteristic of street gangs in serious gang problem cities. Unlike any other common form of criminal violence, gang violence is established in a specific geographic location. From the point of their origin in the United States, "control over turf has been the basis of street gangs" social honor (Adamson, 1998, p. 60). When the earliest gangs in the United States emerged in the criminal and slum districts of New York City, staking claim to a particular territory in the inner city of New York was a necessary means of survival. In these areas, the gang's very existence sometimes depended upon its capacity to stand its ground and ward off incursions from hostile groups. The gangs fell back on a tributary mode of governance and production with territorial control (Adamson, 1998). In Chicago, "the broad expanse of gangland with its intricate tribal and intertribal relationships is medieval and feudal in its organization rather than modern and urban" and "the hang-out of the gang is its castle and the center of the feudal estate which it guards most jealously" (Thrasher, 1927/2000, p. 1). In "gangland," much like barons of old, gang leaders were alert to invaders and ready to sweep though the territory of rivals and carry off prisoners or inflict punishment upon them.

Adamson (2000) coined the term *defensive localism* to describe a variety of functions that gangs provide in communities that include securing living space, upholding group honor, policing of neighborhoods, and the provision of economic, social, employment, welfare, and recreational services. In fact, defensive localism was the mechanism behind many of the gangs' conflicts; gangs often fought to protect territory, and ethnic gangs would band together if a common enemy was present. The capacity to exact tribute is a feature of the more fearsome street gangs. Indeed, honor is a distinguishing feature of street gangs. To develop the notion of honor, gangs adopted names that "were rooted in feudal, tributary, supernatural, and even regal animal lore—for example, kings, lords, dukes, counts, knights, warriors, outlaws, maniacs, devil's disciples, hell's angels, Satan's choice, eagles, lions, and cobras" (Katz, 1988, p. 162). The turf-demarcating gang graffiti also has been likened to medieval heraldry (Hutchison, 1993). Some gangs developed archaic written constitutions that reflected a medieval attitude of fealty, particularly two Chicago gangs, the Almighty Latin Kings and the Vice Lords (Adamson, 1998). Chicano barrios generally are well-bounded geographically, and gang members will claim it with pride even when facing death, exemplified by "giving it names at all levels—place, cohort, and individual" (Vigil, 2007, p. 70). This and the addition of other signs and symbols made neighborhoods feel like a mini-nation in the narrow worldview of inhabitants.

Owing to assimilation of European ethnics, gradual advancement of these peoples from downtown to suburban areas, and gentrification of central cities, modern-day street gangs are constricted to smaller territories than in the early nineteenth century, yet "gangs [remain] geographically oriented in that they have a strong attachment to the territory, or turf, under their direct control" (Tita & Radil, 2011, p. 525). In addition, a variety of gang behaviors are "associated with the control of territory, such as communicating turf boundaries, regulating activities within turf, and defending turf against rivals, are important elements in the diffusion of violence" (p. 525). These territorial imperatives can produce an enormous volume of crimes once a number of gangs populate a relatively constricted area.

Honor-based conflict is the second key characteristic of early street gangs (Adamson, 1998; Sante, 1991). "Gang ideology is simple. The members of these groups believe that they must respond to insults in kind. In theory, derogation of one of their members affects the collective honor" (Horowitz & Schwartz, 1974, p. 239; see also Vigil, 1988; Decker & Van Winkle, 1996; Hughes & Short, 2005). There is another function of honor at the group or gang level: Collective honor is a function of a group's cohesion and ability to fend off perceived threats (Papachristos, 2009; Short & Strodtbeck, 1963; Kobrin, Puntil, & Peluso, 1967; Decker, 1996). Threat of attack is a perpetual myth against which the gang must constantly demonstrate its cohesive capacity. The most recent information on dispute pretexts among gangs and gang members comes from Hughes and Short's (2005) analysis of more than 2,600 disputes observed in twenty Chicago gangs over a three-year period. This research revealed sixteen types of disputes that were grouped into three broad categories: normative/order violations (50 percent), identity attacks (24 percent), and retaliation (23 percent), with "other" types making up the remainder (3 percent). When outcomes were examined, those that precipitated violence were largely retaliations (55 percent), followed by identity attacks (36 percent), and normative/order violations (31 percent).

Third, tough, aggressive, fighting postures provide the individual status among peers that is craved by gang members. Life in many inner-city neighborhoods is governed by what Anderson (1999) dubbed a *code of the streets*—defined as a set of informal behavioral guides organized around a search for respect that regulates interpersonal interactions. "One of the street code's most pervasive norms is that of *retribution*, a perversion of the 'golden rule' stipulating that personal attacks (verbal or physical) should be avenged" (Papachristos, 2009, p. 79). Showing "toughness" (Miller, 1958) is a particularly important personal attribute, for two reasons (Vigil, 1998). First physical appearance counts in a street world where protective posturing often deters potential aggressors. Second, those who succeed in attaining and maintaining an image of toughness are rewarded with the admiration of fellow gang members and the street community in general. In addition, where there is a scarcity of material resources, a "defiant individualist" personality "leads people to become involved with money-producing economic activities whether legal or not; the trait carries along with it an edge that 'defies' any and all attempts to thwart it" (Sanchez-Jankowski, 2003, p. 201). Thus many gang members display this defiant personality trait. Ethnographic studies in several cities reveal that notions of personal honor are generally associated with acts of hypermasculinity—extreme aggressiveness and the use of violence and fear to protect one's reputation (Anderson, 1999; W. I. Miller, 1993; Papachristos, 2009; Polk, 1999; Stewart, 1994; Tita, 1999; Wilkinson & Fagan, 2006). Recent studies demonstrate that young women similarly experience the threat of violence and, in turn, work "the code" to mediate those threats (N. Jones, 2004, 2008; Ness, 2010).

Fourth, organizational characteristics of gangs are among the common elements in virtually all gang studies. Research shows that well-organized gangs (i.e., have leaders, rules, meetings, and symbols) report more violent gang offenses than do members of less organized gangs—including drug sales and violent victimizations (Decker, Katz, & Webb, 2008). Moreover, national research strongly suggests that the greater the organization of gangs into subgroups based on age, gender, and geographic area or territory, the greater the likelihood of gang-related violence (Egley & Howell, 2010). These researchers found that only 33 percent of localities that acknowledged gang activity reported that none of their gangs had these three sub-group forms. Almost one-third (32 percent) reported one of the three subgroups, 18 percent reported any two of them, and 17 percent reported having all three subgroup forms.

Fifth, certain crimes are characteristic of street gangs. In cities nationwide that first experienced gang problems by 1980 (dubbed *early onset cities*; see Figure 4.3) gangs were far more actively involved in violent crimes than late onset gang jurisdictions, particularly aggravated assault, robbery, and firearm use in assault crimes (Howell, Egley, & Gleason, 2002). In contrast, gangs in the late onset jurisdictions were most likely to be involved in burglary or breaking and entering, and larceny or theft. Gangs in the early onset jurisdictions also were more likely to be involved in control of drug distribution than gangs in the newer gang problem localities. These findings suggest that gangs with earlier onset may be the most suitable candidates for transformation to drug trafficking operations (see Papachristos, in press).

The central importance of these common traits of serious street gangs becomes apparent when we discuss shortly accompanying crescendo of gang violent in the United States. First, however, we pause to consider how prison gangs came to be intertwined with street gangs, an important development that served to strengthen both of these prominent gang forms.

Prison Gangs

Arguably, the growth of prison gangs and their expansion from the 1970s onward gave greater impetus to expansion of gangs in major cities than any other single factor. Experts agree that prison gangs got bigger and more entrenched in the 1980s and 1990s (Camp & Camp, 1985; Jacobs, 2001). In addition, "wars on gangs" led by federal law enforcement put many gang leaders and members in prisons, which contributed to further development of prison gangs, and these steadily became formidable criminal operations once enormous growth in prison populations commenced in the 1960s (Schlosser, 1998). Without doubt, the most important result of Chicago Mayor Daley's "war on gangs" in 1969 was that it moved gang leadership into prisons and inadvertently made gangs stronger, both inside prisons and on the streets. Prison gangs' memberships were expanded enormously by the massive in-carceration of Black males. Nationwide, between the 1970s and the 1990s, the chance that a Black man without a high school education would go to prison by age thirty-five rose from 17 percent to 59 percent (Pihos, 2011, p. 469). By 2007, one in nine Black males between the ages of twenty and thirty-four was behind bars in the United States (Pew Charitable Trusts, 2008; see also Alexander, 2011).

Three generations of prison gang development are apparent. The first generation of these gangs emerged spontaneously in response to dangers inside prisons. As U.S. prison populations began to grow in the 1950s, prison gangs were formed by inmates for protection from gang members who were rivals outside prison. With the growth in numbers of inmates (see Figure 3.2), racial-ethnic conflicts prompted formation of prison gangs. To thwart disruptive behavior and violence inside prisons, for many years the Texas Department of Corrections officially operated a system of deploying "building tenders," carefully chosen inmates who served as informal guards (Fong, 1990). The building tenders effectively maintained order in the state's prisons—often with the use of force—and they also served as an intelligence network for prison officials. "As the 'building tender' system faded away, it left behind a power vacuum" (p. 41), soon to be filled by prison gangs. Prison administrators in Illinois also inadvertently strengthened the gangs by using them to help maintain control of prisons, thus allowing them "to consolidate, form alliances, and grow in number and strength" (Venkatesh, 2000, p. 133). The second generation of prison gang growth saw enormous expansion in the size and number of prison gangs beginning in the 1970s, particularly in large urban centers, along with the U.S. imprisonment binge (Schlosser, 1998). Mass incarceration functioned much like Jim Crow laws in segregating minorities from society (Alexander, 1011). This development and extended periods of confinement gave street gangs the opportunity to recruit more members, realign themselves and strengthen their organizational leadership, and develop more relationships with sophisticated criminal enterprises (Hagedorn, 2006; Sharbek, 2012; Venkatesh, 2000). Some of the gang leaders formed organizational networks both inside and outside prisons that linked inmates with others in jails and on the streets in illegal enterprises, creating what came to be called *alliances, supergangs,* or *gang nations* (Venkatesh, 2000; Hagedorn, 2006, 2008; Olivero, 1991; Spergel, 1990).

It is important to distinguish among these titles. Alliances or coalitions of friendly gangs are formed for the promotion of common interests or protection against common enemies. The best example in gang history is the two enormous gang alliances: Folk and People. These alliances developed in the 1970s in Illinois prisons when the predominantly White Simon City Royals agreed to provide narcotics in exchange for protection of inmates belonging to the Black Disciples, soon to be known as the "Folk" alliance (Spergel, 1990). In response to this development, members of the Latin Kings (manly a Hispanic gang comprised of Mexican-Americans and Puerto Ricans) aligned with the Vice Lords, forming the "People" alliance. Until recent years, these alliances were respectfully maintained on Chicago's streets and the People and the Folk were strong rivals. "Now, although street gangs still align themselves with the People and the Folk, law enforcement agencies [in Chicago] all seem to agree that these alliances mean little" (Chicago Crime Commission, 2006, p. 11). Similarly, an alliance of *Sureños* and *Norteños* developed in California's state prisons. This equally formidable alliance, discussed in the next section, spawned gangs by the same name across the state and elsewhere and remains influential in gang culture to the present time. Law enforcement agencies find that numerous local gangs still name themselves after Chicago-based People and the Folk gangs and also use the California-based *Sureños* and *Norteños* name tags (FBI, 2009, 2011; National Alliance of Gang Investigators' Associations, 2009) although these acclaimed affiliations are now less common.

The third generation of prison gangs are now active in street-level criminal enterprises that sometimes are carried out in collaboration with organized crime[10] groups that often are highly structured and well managed organizations—particularly in drug trafficking. This generation of prison gangs in major cities extended their influence back to the streets upon release of gang leaders who had been schooled in more sophisticated criminal enterprises while in prison and also had expanded their contacts with other criminal organizations (Texas Fusion Center, 2013). In addition, many prison gangs are now connected directly to their counterpart street gangs. Modern-day prison gangs also will allow gangsters on the outside to form alliances with other criminals or provide regular sources for illegal products such as drugs, and the STGs also will support and protect others in the gangster's crew when they are incarcerated (Allender & Marcel, 2003). In some cases, local gangs took on some of the features of organized crime groups, particularly when successfully involved in drug trafficking (Taylor, 1990a, 1990b; Venkatesh, 2008). But street gangs could not achieve the operational status of "organized crime" because they do not have the necessary access to banks to launder money, or strong political support. Thus, in organized drug crime, they could not operate as drug cartels, only as drug distribution networks and, more often in street-level drug sales (Eddy, Sabogal, & Walden, 1988).

The pathway to prison gang membership begins in juvenile detention and correctional facilities (M. Howell & Lassiter, 2011) that serve as entry portals to long-term gang careers.[11] Confinement in a juvenile correctional facility is one of the strongest predictors of adult prison gang membership (Ralph, Hunter, Marquart, Cuvelier, & Merianos, 1996). The Chicago Vice Lords originated in the St. Charles Illinois State Training School for Boys when several residents decided to form a new gang by pooling their affiliations with other gangs, with dreams of forming the toughest gang in Chicago (Dawley, 1992; Keiser, 1969). When gang members are released from custody, they generally return to their neighborhoods of origin and renew old associations in their original street gang. Having done time and handled it successfully, they earned "rep" on the streets, particularly from fellow gang members and antagonists. If they resume prior criminal activity, the contacts made in the prison system will become more important. This amounts to a vicious cycle. More confinement of gang members increases the strength of prison gangs. This, in turn, expands prison gangs' influence on local gang violence, thereby generating more arrests, starting the cycle again.

INSTITUTIONALIZED STREET GANGS

Although gangs have been transformed into street gangs and prison gangs by economic, political, social, and cultural forces, this does not mean that youth gangs have disappeared. The transformation process is continuous within neighborhoods, communities, and cities. Children and adolescents form "starter gangs" to introduce themselves to gang culture (i.e., distinctive attitudes, jargon, rituals, and symbols) (Howell, 2010). These starter gangs—with members approximately ages 10 to 13—are formed in small groups of rejected, alienated, and aggressive children (Craig, Vitaro, Gagnon, & Tremblay, 2002). A recent French study (Debarbieux & Baya, 2008) found that twice as many students are gang members in poorly organized schools that contain larger groups of highly rebellious pupils. Yet most starter gangs do not survive. In a recent survey of middle school students in nine cities with known gang problems, 25 percent of all gangs the students identified had been in existence for less than one year, and only 10 percent were said to have existed for eleven years or more (Esbensen et al., 2008). Determining gang membership can also be difficult. Based on a large-scale study (Esbensen et al., 2010), a single-item self-identification definition of gang membership ("Are you now in a gang?" proved to be a highly reliable indicator. These researchers underscore that the *gang* term "connotes something unique and distinguishable" (p. 78). "The vast majority (89 percent) of youths who indicated that they were currently in a gang also indicated that their gang was involved in delinquent activity" (p. 78).

Various definitions may capture gangs with varying degrees of structure, permanence, and seriousness. Three examples follow. The Eurogang Network definition is this: "A youth gang, or troublesome youth group, is any durable, street-oriented youth group whose involvement in illegal activity is part of its group identity" (Esbensen et al., 2008, p. 117). This very broad definition seriously over-classified American gangs in a multi-city U.S. study, in which only 38 percent of the youth classified as gang members using a more rigorous methodology considered their group to be a gang (Esbensen et al., 2008). Definitions that include specific gang criteria have proven to be more reliable for classifying youth in early adolescence, ages thirteen to fifteen: somewhat organized (i.e., had initiation rites, established leaders, and symbols or colors) (Esbensen, Winfree, He, et al., 2001; Huizinga & Esbensen, 1993). Based on this research, the *youth gang* definition that follows should identify more bona fide gangs populated by youth between late childhood and early adulthood (Howell, 2013b):

- The group has at least five members, generally aged eleven to twenty-four.
- Members share an identity, typically linked to a name.
- Members view themselves as a gang, and are recognized by others as a gang.
- The group has some permanence (at least six months).
- The group has a degree of organization (e.g., initiation rites, established leaders, symbols).
- The group is involved in an elevated level of criminal activity.

For the identification of urban street gangs with older members—in late adolescence and adulthood—Miller's (1982/1992) gang definition may be most suitable: "a self-formed association of peers, united by mutual interests, with identifiable leadership and internal organization, who act collectively or as individuals to achieve specific purposes, including the conduct of illegal activity and control of a particular territory, facility, or enterprise" (p. 21). This gang definition places more emphasis on strategic and organized criminal activity. Decker (2007) outlines specific requirements for ongoing gang operations as follow: First, gangs must have an organizational structure with a hierarchy of leaders, role, and rules. Second, gangs must have group goals that are widely shared by members. Third, gangs must promote stronger allegiance to the larger organization than to subgroups within it. Finally, gangs must possess the means to control and discipline their members to produce compliance with group goals. (p. 392).

Although no gang can be considered fully institutionalized in a formal way, say, like Boy Scouts, gangs have three features that distinguish them as being far less transitory than other youth groups (Moore, 1998): self-definition, street socialization, and the potential to become quasi-institutionalized in a specific territory. *Self-definition* implies not only that group members define themselves as a gang, but also that the group has a social structure and group-determined norms that are not controlled by others in any way. *Street socialization* means that unsupervised young people are socialized by each other (and by older peers in some cases) far more effectively than by conventional socializing agents such as families and schools. To achieve quasi-institutionalization, gangs must develop the *capacity for reproduction*— meaning that they must recruit continuously, provide age-graded cliques in the gang for younger members, and extend respect and solidarity toward older members. Moore further suggests that in order for youth groups with these characteristics to become established, certain conditions must be met. First, conventional socializing agents, such as families, schools, and social services, must be ineffective and alienating (which often is the case where gangs exist). Under these conditions, conventional adult supervision is largely missing, inconsistent, and irrelevant. Second, the adolescents must have a great deal of free time that is not consumed by other roles, permitting ample time to hang out. Third, for the gang to become at least partly institutionalized, members must have limited access to appealing conventional career lines (i.e., good adult jobs).

As Ayling (2011, p. 7) put it, once a gang "evolves into a fixture in a community, it can be regarded as institutionalized." Hagedorn (2008) proposed five indicators of gang institutionalization: (1) the gang persists despite changes in leadership, (2) its organizational structure is sufficiently flexible to sustain multiple roles of its members (including accommodations for women and children), (3) adaptations to a changing environment can be made (e.g., police suppression), (4) it fulfills certain community needs (e.g., economic, security, services), and (5) it provides a distinct worldview for its members (minimally, symbols, rituals, and traditions; perhaps more generally, a subculture).

While these are validated indicators to be sure, a renowned Harvard University sociologist, Talcott Parsons, developed a broader framework for assessing whether social groups have reached the threshold for classification as a social "organization" that enjoys stability and permanence. Parsons (1951, 1967) constructed a set of attributes of organizations and societies that give them permanence. His "AGIL" paradigm identifies four functional pre-requisites of any permanent social organization: 1) *Adaptation* to the physical and social environment, 2) *Goal attainment*, the need to define primary goals and enlist individuals to strive to attain these goals, 3) *Integration*, the coordination of the society or group as a cohesive whole, and 4) *Latent pattern maintenance*, maintaining the motivation of individuals to perform their roles according to expectations of the organization or group. This framework offers a straightforward heuristic method in assessing the extent of gang "institutionalization," that is, indications of functional attributes that give permanence to organizations. We next examine the historical evolution of gangs through the lens of Parsons' framework.

The conventional *adaptation* process began once European White ethnics arrived in the United States, in their struggles to "maintain a toehold" in urban social systems (Moore, 1998). Gangs emerged as a group that facilitated the social adaptation of adolescents and young adults to conditions of extreme poverty and the weakening of social controls, that is, social disorganization. But those early European White ethnic gangs did not become fully institutionalized anywhere (Miller, 1982/1992; Thrasher, 1927/2000). Most White immigrant gang youth matured out of gangs as their families moved out of downtown in Northeast and Midwest cities, into areas of second settlement, and assimilated into mainstream American society and into the adult labor force.

The adaptation experience was not so rapid for Black and Mexican-American families.[12] Having been sequestered in highly segregated areas of major cities, and sometimes constrained in neighborhood and public housing projects, these groups were blocked from enjoying the relatively rapid assimilation pace for European White ethnic groups. Adamson (1998) used the term *hyperghetto* to describe extremely ghettoized neighborhoods that formed in many U.S. cities. In New York, Chicago, and Los Angeles, minority peoples were restrained territorially to the ghettos, in restrictive covenants, and further constrained once they were moved into high-rise public housing. When they attempted to advance into better neighborhoods, clashes with White youth led to gang formation. Unlike the European White ethnics, they were not afforded ample opportunity to move out, assimilate, and acculturate into mainstream American society. Gangs emerged and provided protection in these hostile environments.

In fact, racial conflicts across America served to expand gangs' role to the protection of minority groups to which they belonged. In the period 1900–1949, gang-involved adolescents and young adults championed the cause of disenfranchised minorities—Black, Mexican-American, and Puerto Rican—in self-defense against White-induced race riots and unjust and discriminatory criminal justice system practices in several U.S. cities, most amply documented in New York City (Adamson, 1998; Haskins, 1974), Chicago (Cureton, 2009; Perkins, 1987), and Los Angeles (Alonso, 2004; McWilliams 1948/1990). But two race riots stand out for the special impetus they yielded for gang growth. The bloody Chicago riot of 1919 was precipitated by a White fellow's fatal assault of a Black youth who had been swimming in Lake Michigan (Tuttle, 1996; Voogd, 2008). This tragic event was one of many violent attacks that led to Black gang formation in the Windy City as Black males united to confront hostile White gangs who were terrorizing the Black community (Cureton, 2009; Perkins, 1987). A quarter century later, the original zoot suit riot in Los Angeles in which Mexican-American youth suffered repeated public attacks, compounded by injustice in the operation of the criminal justice system, had far greater impact in solidifying and expanding Mexican-American gangs in the West and Southwest (McWilliams, 1948/1990). The negative effects of these discriminatory policies linger to the present time. Each of the riots and racial/ethnic attacks served to solidify the adaptive role of gangs as a social mechanism for adjustment to hostile reactions of Whites to attempted assimilation by minorities.

Goal attainment aims are straightforward for most gangs. "At their most basic level, gangs are social networks of individuals who come together in time and space, engage in collective activities, and produce a collective identity" (Papachristos et al., 2013, p. 418). Their longer-term goals may include providing safety, social, and economic benefits to their members and the neighborhoods and communities surrounding them (Thrasher, 1927/2000; Suttles, 1968; Vigil, 1988; Whyte, 1943a 1943b). Economic benefits come from criminal activity such as drug trafficking and assorted other crimes. Providing safety proved to be a tall order for the first gangs in America. In the early nineteenth century, they struggled to secure a wedge of safety on turbulent streets of Eastern cites that were teeming with waves of poor immigrants. They succeeded only occasionally in protecting their White European ethnic members. Better organized gangs in Chicago, such as Ragen's Colts, a fighting gang of Irish youth with strong political connections were more successful under their mantra: "Hit me and you hit a thousand," advertising their *de facto* policing service for the community (Adamson, 2000, p. 278). Modern-day gangs that are far better armed with weapons of greater lethality typically have no shortcomings in retaliatory violence.

For Chicano gangs, a large measure of *integration* comes from the tradition of linking the gang name with neighborhood or barrio of residence—with *mi barrio* (my neighborhood) becoming synonymous with my gang (Vigil, 1993). In Chicago, Mexican[13] street gangs clearly were integrated in the everyday life of many communities. These discourses were often narratives of familiarity that came from living with the reality of gangs as contenders for many of the same urban spaces that migrants and their children commonly inhabited or traversed. The everyday struggle over space was manifested in many ways that served to unite gangs with neighborhood residents, in graffiti, street-side gatherings, verbal pronouncements, hand signs, pictographic symbols, and distinctive clothing (De Genova, 2008).

Female gangs also have been well integrated in neighborhoods of large cities for decades, particularly in chronic gang problem cities such as Boston (Miller, 1973, 1980), Chicago (Horowitz, 1983), Los Angeles (Moore, 1991), New York (Campbell, 1984/1991), Philadelphia (Brown, 1977), Los Angeles (Bowker, 1978), and in St. Louis (J. Miller, 2002). At the outset, however, females functioned as auxiliaries to male gangs, particularly in battles with other gangs. But female Chicano gangs existed in Los Angeles (in Boyle Heights and Maravilla) as early as 1935 and some of them still operated forty-five years later (Moore, 1991). The gangs that began to emerge in barrios there in the 1930s and 1940s attracted both boys and girls because the gangs started as friendship groups of adolescents, who shared common interests, with a more or less clearly defined territory in which most of the members lived. "They were committed to defending one another, the barrio, the families, and the gang name in the status-setting fights that occurred in school and on the streets" (p. 31).

Latent pattern maintenance refers to gang perpetuation. Once gangs become pervasive features of neighborhood and barrio environments, youth must reckon with gangs and adapt to them (Vigil, 1988, 1993). This process of pattern maintenance begins with clique formation by youngsters about ages twelve to fourteen in middle school. By the time the clique is fully developed and well established in the streets in terms of organized gang activities, about ages fourteen to eighteen, it has become an influential model for the members of a younger cohort to pattern themselves after. In turn, the younger clique will serve as a model for the elementary school youth to emulate, thus perpetuating gang pattern maintenance. By age eighteen, most original cliques peak in gang violence and begin to dissolve, as its members marry and get jobs or continue gangbanging in and out of correctional institutions. Many older members establish gang family households. Their children are thus virtually preselected to associate with other troubled barrio youths in emergent cliques, often at far younger ages (see also Coughlin & Venkatesh, 2003, on gang features).

Chicano gangs are maintained continuously in the barrios of East Los Angeles through four distinct processes: kinship, alliance in fights, extensions of barrio boundaries, and forming branches (Moore, Vigil, & Garcia, 1983). First, gang membership is readily extended to relatives who live outside the barrio. For Chicano gang boys, a *homeboy* (fellow gang member) is the equivalent of a *carnal* (blood) brother. In the time-honored Mexican cultural norm, the gang takes on kin-like characteristics, especially mutual obligations among gang members. Second, because fighting is the defining characteristic of barrio gangs—particularly with another gang—boys from other barrios often become allies in fights. Third, gang boundaries may extend into several barrios when members of multiple gangs live within them. Expansion typically works as follows: Once a gang recruits one or two boys who live a block or so outside one of its boundaries, it becomes more difficult for a rival gang to defend that area. Thus, the gang begins to claim that area as its turf. In time, the rival gang ceases to claim its original turf and the successful recruiting gang has expanded into the area. Last, extension from the home barrio by forming branches can mean designation of *klikas* in noncontiguous areas. This typically happens when new Chicanos move into the general area. In addition, age-graded gang structures in Chicano gangs ensure that there is a place for everyone, even the youngest members. It allows for gang regeneration with the inclusion of each new generation; and it additionally provides the social arena for youngsters to learn and demonstrate important gang customs among themselves (Vigil, 1993).

The White Fence, *Cuatro Flats*, and various cliques of *Marvilla* gangs have been maintained for approximately eighty years through these traditions (Moore, 1991; Vigil, 2007). This unusual longevity is also attributable to Mexican nationalism, cultural tradition, close-knit family relationships, attachment of gangs to *barrios*, and strong loyalties to both *barrios* and gangs. These attributes, along with the process by which gangs expand territories, ensure perpetual gang propagation and extended pattern maintenance.

TRANSFORMED GANG MEMBERS

How have gang history and the transformed gangs affected gang members? Members themselves have been transformed as well, particularly in large cities with earlier onset of gang activity, and both more accelerated and intense gang transformation into more violent and destructive gangs. This transformation has been associated with distinctive psychological features, particularly in Vigil's (1988, 1990, 2002, 2007, 2014) pioneering gang research. In addition, several psychologists, including Yablonsky, Goldstein, and Glick, have suggested unique psychological features of gang members in general. Quinn (2005) amply documented in gangsta culture the widely acclaimed and exalted sociopathic characteristics of gang members. We first draw upon Vigil's Chicano gang research to illustrate individual-level transformations. Next, we consider other research that suggests psychological transformations among gang members in general.

The Chicano Experience

Vigil (2014) describes in some detail the psychological dynamics associated with Chicano gang member transformation. His documentation and that of other scholars (especially McWilliams, 1948/1990; Moore et al., 1983) suggests that this process has been ongoing for almost one hundred years, with continuing large-scale immigration from Mexico and Central America, virtually ensuring that a sizeable portion of the new population will be marginalized. These migrating families had major difficulties coping with pressures of poverty and social discrimination in employment, public services, housing, and other amenities and necessities of life. As a result, a substantial second-generation youth cohort had social control voids, many of whom were socialized in the streets. Youths from such backgrounds established the basic patterns of Chicano gang behavior, including violence, in the *cholo* subculture beginning in the 1930s (Vigil, 2014).

Vigil contends that key personality characteristics of Chicano gang members can be traced directly to street socialization. Gangs generate through the process of street socialization the assumption that one must act crazy on occasion in order to survive (Vigil, 2014). Once a person early in life has been socialized in the streets, the setting of last resort when home, school, and other caretakers fail, many youngsters feel the necessity of taking on a crazy persona as an actor. *Locura* is a state of mind where various quasi-controlled actions denoting a type of craziness or wildness occur: "a mind-set complex that values crazy or unpredictable thinking and acting" (Vigil, 1988, p. 178). A person who is a *loco* demonstrates this state of mind by alternately displaying fearlessness, toughness, daring, and other unpredictable forms of destructive behavior, such as getting *loco* on drugs and alcohol or excelling in gangbanging. A person who is loco adds an important dimension to the group. This is especially the case where the barrio is beleaguered by other barrio gangs and must show a stronger force of resistance to outside challenges and pressures. While the "loco" is a prized member of the group, he can sometimes act as a deterrent to stave off confrontations. On other occasions, however, the "loco" can be a hindrance or detriment to the group when his unbridled actions cause unnecessary and unwanted trouble.

These activities can be understood as an altered type of "storm and stress" response during adolescence when daring, excitement, courage, and adventure are valued by peers; indeed, it is doing these "gang" things that earn you respect and recognition as a dependable gang member (Vigil & Howell,

2012a). Striking fear into the hearts of others is in part a defensive action, much like beating someone to the punch. For many gang members who are small in stature or weak in physical strength, the gang is a crucial haven; being able to act *loco* is even more important to them. Acting tough affords them status and prestige, with the assurance of being backed by the gang if trouble arises. Not fighting back or sticking up for your rights (e.g., space) is tantamount to giving up and inviting even more physical and mental testing. Gang participation came to have both public (e.g., drive-bys, stabbings, other criminal acts) and private (e.g., the ingestion and abuse of alcohol and drugs, suicidal behavior) consequences. Variations in *locura* behavior are common among individuals within a barrio and between barrios (Moore, 1993). But this volatile, out-of-control experience appears to be common in that area of Los Angeles and in other cities where immigrant youths have had to adapt and adjust to the street gang style.

Experiences of Gang Members in General

Lewis Yablonsky (1997) constructed in similar fashion the psychological dynamics associated with gang member transformation in various racial/ethnic groups. However, he identifies three historical factors that undergird the psychological stressors associated with Black gang member transformation. First, ghetto conditions (characterized in this volume as hyperghettos) that served to create the violent gang provided a setting in which young persons "can achieve a sense of personal power, and it serves as a vehicle through which they can act out their rage about the hopeless experience in their neighborhood" (p. 79). Second, the Black gangster's rage is fueled by "the very real prejudice and discrimination they experience in American society," particularly unfair targeting of them by police (p. 79). Third, Yablonsky suggests that the "breakdown of the Black family" produced a disproportionate number of Black youth who grew up without their fathers, a condition associated with the enormous increases in the confinement of Black men from the 1970s through the 1990s.

From wide-ranging interviews with gang members and providing therapy to many of them in several southern California hospitals, Yablonsky (1997) distinguishes sociopathic gang members from sociopathic gang behavior. Although other experts caution that most gang violence does not have sociopathic roots (Goldstein & Glick, 1994), it is apparent that much of the recent gang-related violence can safely be classified as such. Goldstein and Glick summarize the common features of sociopaths:

• Is aggressive, reckless, cruel to others, impulsive, manipulative, superficial, callous, irresponsible, cunning, and self-assured

- Fails to learn by experience, is unable to form meaningful relationships, is chronically antisocial, and is unresponsive to punishment
- Is unable to experience guilt, is self-centered, and lacks a moral sense
- Is unreliable, untruthful, shameless, shows poor judgment, and is highly egocentric
- Is unable to show empathy or genuine concern for others, manipulates others
- Is loveless and guiltless (p. 20)

Similarly, Yablonsky (1997) describes the characteristics that most, if not all, sociopaths have:

- A limited social conscience
- Egocentrism dominating most interactions, including the "instrumental manipulation" of others for self-advantage
- An inability to forego immediate pleasure for future goals
- A habit of pathological lying to achieve personal advantage (p. 105)

Yablonsky (1997) describes sociopathic gang behavior as consisting of: "the dehumanization of other people, especially enemy gangs, and the necessity 'to murder them before they murder us'; the ruthless behavior of robbery, carjacking, and burglary; the use and distribution of deadly drugs; and murder through drive-bys" (pp. 101–102). Generally speaking, Yablonsky suggests, the more sociopathic youths are core gang members, almost completely committed to sociopathic gang activity, whereas the less sociopathically disturbed youth is more likely to become a "marginal gangster." Marginals tend to join gangs largely to satisfy a desire for some form of community or family for regular companionship. In contrast, the core gang member has shallow emotional relationships, fleeting ones that are self-satisfying of his own egocentric desires. He is "a highly impulsive and explosive youth for whom the moment is a segment of time detached from all other" (p. 111). In addition, he is unable to appreciate the pain of violence that he inflicts on a rival gang member.

The sociopathic character and personalities of active urban gang members found in gangsta culture and rap music are illuminated in great detail in Quinn's (2005) exhaustive research. Three themes were melded in the sociopathic personality: the nihilist gangbanger, the enterprising hustler in a ghetto-confined dog-eat-dog world, and "gratuitous, individualist pleasures of the moment" (p. 145). Remarkably, judged by music sales and prolonged popularity, this gangsta persona had nationwide appeal among youth of all races and ethnicities.

Unfortunately, little research has tested gang members for sociopathic traits. In a San Antonio study, just 4 percent of the sample of members of twenty-six gangs (all males, ages fourteen to twenty-five) was classified as sociopaths (Valdez, Kaplan, & Codina, 2000). Nevertheless, 20 percent were assessed as possibly having serious psychological problems with the potential for a sociopathic diagnosis. A larger proportion of embedded gang members are diagnosed as sociopathic. For example, among a sample of convicted serious and violent juvenile offenders ages fourteen to seventeen in Philadelphia and Phoenix, researchers (Dmitrieva, Gibson, Steinberg, Piquero, & Fagan, 2014) commonly found sociopathic traits among gang leaders. Also, in a British study, very high incidence of serious psychiatric problems was found among older gang members, ages eighteen to thirty-four, particularly among those who had experienced violence (Coid, Ullrich, Keers, Bebbington, & DeStavola, 2013). Overall, one in four gang members suffered from psychosis, 60 percent had high anxiety, 85 percent were diagnosed with an antisocial personality disorder, and more than half were dependent on drugs or alcohol. Violent ruminative[14] thinking, violent victimization, and fear of further victimization accounted for the high levels of psychosis and anxiety disorders in gang members. In sum, sparse research to date on the prevalence of sociopathic personalities among gang members suggests that a larger proportion of sociopaths are found among older and more long-term gang members of all racial/ethnic origins where exposure to violence is greater in modern-day street gangs.

NOTES

1. Born in the United States.
2. Gangster City. "Rap history: Gangster Rap History." Accessed December 17, 2014. http://bestgangstermoviesever.yolasite.com.
3. Gangster City. "Rap history: Gangster Rap History." Accessed December 17, 2014. http://bestgangstermoviesever.yolasite.com.
4. Gangster City. "Rap history: Gangster Rap History." Accessed December 17, 2014. http://bestgangstermoviesever.yolasite.com.
5. Gangster City. "Rap history: Gangster Rap History." Accessed December 17, 2014. http://bestgangstermoviesever.yolasite.com.
6. Ricky "Freeway" Ross was at the center of a highly controversial matter, the source of crack cocaine that suddenly appeared on the streets Los Angeles in 1985, enabling him to establish a lucrative operation. The source of the improbable huge cocaine shipments was the subject of Gary Webb's (1999) controversial investigative reports first published in the *San Jose Mercury News*—under the title, "Dark Alliance." Segments were subtitled "America's Crack Plague Has Roots in Nicaragua," and "The Story Behind the Crack Explosion." Webb's investigative journalism documented that Nicaraguan Democratic Forces (the Contras) partly financed their 1980s war against the Sandinista regime in Nicaragua through a cocaine pipeline that originated in Colombia, traveled to the San Francisco Bay area, then to the streets of Los Angeles, where crack cocaine and guns were supplied to the Crips and the Bloods gangs for local marketing. The opening paragraph in Webb's account reads as follows: "For the better part of a decade, a San Francisco Bay Area drug ring sold tons of cocaine to the Crips and Bloods street gangs of Los Angeles and funneled millions in drug profits to a Latin American guerrilla army run by the CIA" (quoted in Cockburn & St. Clair, 1998, p. 2). Gary Webb was both exalted for his courage and outstanding investigative journalism, and also castigated for

his controversial account (see Bratich, 2004 for endless attempts to discredit Webb's discovery and issues surrounding its presentation). In 2004, Gary Webb was found dead, having died somewhat mysteriously from two gunshot wounds to his head, judged a suicide by the coroner. A suicide note was found nearby. U.S. Sen. Barbara Boxer (D-Calif.) and Rep. Maxine Waters (D-Calif., representing South Central Los Angeles) have repeatedly called for a full federal investigation of the Contra–crack cocaine connections (see Waters, 1998).

7. I am indebted to my colleague, Elizabeth Griffiths, for the concept of facilitators in this context.

8. This term has been explicitly defined as "a temporal and spatial churning process of higher income households, directly and indirectly displacing lower income households changing the character and composition of a neighborhood" (Smith, 2014, p. 571). Smith (2014) identifies three types of gentrification: (1) private economic investment, gentrification that assesses property potential based on neighborhood demographics (e.g., more coffee shops); (2) forced state intervention, a more controversial type of gentrification that turns over public lands to private investors under the guise of urban revitalization (e.g., public housing demolition); and (3) changing demographic composition, the in-migration of particular residents and their resources into previously poorer neighborhoods.

9. The most reliable estimate of the total number of guns (both licit and illicit) currently held by civilians in the United States is 270 million to 310 million, of which up to 114 million are handguns, according to GunPolicy.org. Accessed December 6, 2014. http://www.gunpolicy.org/firearms/region/united-states.

10. A straightforward definition of *organized crime* is "a hierarchical organizational structure, restricted membership, a criminal subculture, use of violence or threats of violence, a drive for profits from traffic in illicit goods and services in public demand, and immunity from law enforcement through political corruption and intimidation" (Johnson, 1990, p. 113).

11. Statewide North Carolina data showed that youth gang members represent 7 percent of all juveniles on whom delinquent complaints are filed, 13 percent of juveniles adjudicated, 21 percent of juveniles admitted to short-term detention, and 38 percent of juveniles committed to secure residential facilities.

12. Though researched much less, other Latino youth had similar assimilation experiences (see Bourgois, 2003).

13. De Genova (2008) insists that persons of Mexican heritage in Chicago virtually never use the terms *Mexican-American* or *Chicano* to describe themselves, and prefer instead, *mexicana* or *mexicano* in Spanish, or Mexican in English.

14. The capacity to turn a matter over and over in the mind.

Chapter Four

Nationwide Gang Growth and Expansion

Walter Miller (2001) combined data on nearly 1,500 cities that reported gang problems at any time between the 1970s, 1980s, and the late-1990s to examine nation trends across these three decades (Figure 4.1). In the space of just twenty-five years (1970–1995), the proportion of cities that reported gang problems increased more than sevenfold, from 201 to 1,487, "reaching unprecedented levels" (p. 42). The following are key findings of Miller's analysis covering the twenty-eight-year period from 1970 to 1998:

- In the 1970s, only nineteen states reported youth gang problems. By the late 1990s, all fifty states and the District of Columbia had reported gang problems.
- The number of cities reporting youth gang problems rose from 270 in the 1970s to 2,547 in 1998—an increase of 843 percent.
- The number of counties reporting gang problems rose from 101 in the 1970s to 1,152 in 1998—an increase of more than 1,000 percent.
- The regional location of gang cities changed substantially from the 1970s to the 1990s. In the 1970s, the West led the Nation, while the South ranked lowest. By 1998, the South had risen to second place, with a thirty-three-fold increase, while the number of gang cities in the West had increased only by a factor of four.

A CRESCENDO OF GANG VIOLENCE

Owing to sustained growth in gang activity from the 1970s onward, gang violence in the United States reached a crescendo in the period from the mid-

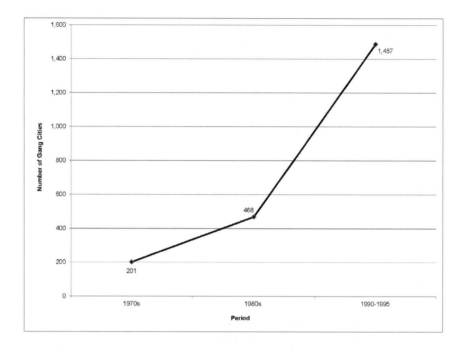

Figure 4.1.   Cumulative Numbers of Gang Cities in the United States, 1970–1995, by Decade Source: W. B. Miller. (2001). The growth of youth gang problems in the United States: 1970–1998. Washington, DC: U.S. Department of Justice, Office of Juvenile Justice and Delinquency Prevention.

1980s to the mid-1990s (see figure 4.1). The growing availability of automobiles, coupled with the use of more lethal weapons, fueled the growth of drive-by shootings, a tactic that previously took the form of on-foot, hit-and-run forays. Gangs of this era seem to have both younger and older members than before, and more members with prison records or ties to prison inmates. A key development of the 1970s was a substantial increase in the availability, lethality, and use of firearms as instruments of gang violence (Miller, 1982/ 1992). Gang fights previously fought with blunt objects, fists, or brass knuckles increasingly involved high-caliber, automatic, or semiautomatic weapons (Block & Block, 1993). Nationwide, larger cities clearly demonstrated more rapid onset of gang activity, consistent with diffusion of the gang culture outward from springboard cities in each major region of the United States as shown earlier in this volume. Yet, compared with those in later-onset jurisdictions, gangs in the very large early onset cities (with populations of one hundred thousand or more) had older members, were of a more homogeneous racial/ethnic mixture, more involved in drug trafficking, and more involved in violent crimes, including homicides (Howell et al., 2002).

We feature Chicago and Los Angeles here in describing the crescendo of gang violence that occurred in the United States during the fifteen-year period between the mid-1980s and around 2000. The apex of gang violence in these gang capitals—albeit writ large—is illustrative of patterns of increased levels of violent gang activity in very large cities across the United States (Howell et al., 2011). The number of gang homicides increased sharply in the late 1980s and early 1990s in both Chicago and Los Angeles (Howell, 1999; Maxson, 1999), growing to the level that these two cities accounted for half of all gang homicides reported in the United States by 2001 (Egley, Howell, & Major, 2006). These cities continue to lead the nation in gang homicides.

The annual number of street gang–motivated homicides in Chicago increased almost fivefold between 1987 and 1994 (Block et al., 1996). Drive-by shootings also increased enormously in the 1980s and 1990s, replacing fair fights, also called *rumbles* or *gangbangs*. This development was disturbing, not only because of the lethality and impersonality of drive-bys, but more important, for the fact that innocent bystanders—non-gang youth, children, and older persons—were sometimes wounded or killed. Senseless homicides became common in Chicago and Los Angeles in the early 1990s. In 1991, there were 771 gang-related homicides throughout Los Angeles County, one-third of which were secondary to drive-by shootings (Hutson, Anglin, Mallon, et al., 1994). From 1989 through 1993, there were 6,327 drive-by shootings (accounting for 33 percent of all Los Angeles gang-related homicides in that period), an astounding 590 homicides (Hutson, Anglin, & Eckstein, 1996).[1]

Studies also showed that an increasingly larger proportion of homicides in both Chicago and Los Angeles were gang related in the recent past in comparison with a decade earlier. In Los Angeles County, 15 percent of all homicides in 1984 were gang related, compared to nearly half (45 percent) in 1995 (Maxson, 1999),[2] reaching an epidemic level by the standards of public health science (Hutson et al., 1995). Research that examined gang homicide participants and settings in Los Angeles revealed characteristic features of modern-day street gangs compared with non-gang homicides (Klein & Maxson, 1989; Maxson, Gordon, & Klein, 1985). Not only did gang homicides involve a larger number of participants; they were also more likely to take place in public settings, particularly on the street; were somewhat more likely to involve automobiles, and shooting out of them; were more likely to involve weapons, particularly guns, in the incident; were more likely to result in more injuries; and generally involved a larger number of other violent offenses. Gang homicides were also more likely to involve younger participants and minority youth. On average, gang homicide suspects were about nineteen years of age, and victims averaged nearly twenty-four years of age in Los Angeles (Klein & Maxson, 1989).

In Chicago, Block and Block (1993) spatially located offenses within the boundaries of gang turfs based on maps drawn by street gang officers in Chicago's twenty-six districts. Analyses focused on the city's four largest and most criminally active street gangs during 1987–1990: the Black Gangster Disciples Nation, the Latin Disciples, the Latin Kings, and the Vice Lords. The Chicago Police Department estimates that membership in these four gangs numbered about nineteen thousand at that time. From 1987 to 1990, the four gangs accounted for 69 percent of all street gang–motivated crimes and for 56 percent of all street gang–motivated homicides in the city, although they represented only about 10 percent of the "major" Chicago youth gangs. Each of these gangs still exists.[3] Another analysis of gang-motivated drug-business homicides in Chicago from 1987 to 1994 revealed two street gang drug market wars (Block et al. 1996). The first set of episodes involved two "brother" gangs, the Black Gangster Disciples and the Black Disciples, whose clashes resulted in forty-five homicides. The second set accounted for sixty-one homicides, which were associated with an attempt by the Black P Stones to reestablish themselves in the drug market. In 1996—at the height of gang violence in Chicago, Block's (2000) study showed that multiple-gang activity was observed in just 5 percent of the more than twenty-five thousand grid squares citywide; however, "these squares accounted for 23.0 percent of the assaults and 44.3 percent of all drug-related incidents" (p. 379).

Crescendos in gang violence are episodic (Block & Block, 1993; Decker, 1996; Miller, 1974b; Moore, 1993). Cohesive gangs challenge more rival gangs and, in turn, are more frequently challenged themselves, a process that often accounts for observed gang violence spurts—episodic gang conflicts that wax and wane and sometimes extend over a number of years. Similarly, Decker (1996) observed in St. Louis a "cycle of violence" process that begins with a loosely organized gang. Members have loose bonds to the gang. The collective identification of threat from a rival gang (through rumors, symbolic shows of force, cruising, and mythic violence) reinforces the centrality of violence that expands the number of participants and increases cohesion. Next, a mobilizing event occurs, possibly, but not necessarily, violence. This escalates cohesive gang activity and the group becomes more alert and cohesive. A violent incident against the threatening group occurs, followed by rapid deescalation. Later, violent retaliation by the opposing gang occurs. "Whatever the 'purpose' of violence, it often leads to retaliation and revenge creating a feedback loop where each killing requires a new killing" (Decker & Van Winkle 1996, p. 186), often "spreading from one neighborhood to another and outliving the initial source of the problem" (Decker, 2007, p. 398). Papachristos's (2009) extensive Chicago research revealed that "gang members come and go, but their patterns of behavior create a network structure that persists and may very well provide the conduit through which gang values, norms, and culture are transmitted to future generations" (p. 119). Stated more emphatically, Papachristos's (2009) finds "that gangs are not groups of murderers per se, but rather embedded social networks in which violence ricochets back and forth . . . [and] what begins as a single murder soon generates a dozen more as it diffuses through these murder networks" (p. 76). These events become, in effect, "dominance contests" in which "violence spreads through a process of social contagion that is fueled by normative and behavioral precepts of the code of the street" (p. 81).

California researchers led by George Tita mapped the locations of thirteen of the twenty-nine active criminal street gangs in the East Los Angeles area where Chicano gangs first formed. Gang-involved violence in this area accounts for 75 percent of all lethal violence (Tita et al., 2003). In the first analysis, focused on a thirty-month period between 2000 and 2002, the research team found that police arrests in more than one thousand violent crimes (assault with a deadly weapon, attempted homicide, and homicide) were recorded in the relatively small study area, an average of slightly more than ten violent gang crimes per census block over the study period. A second analysis, using data on 563 between-gang shootings, involving thirteen rival street gangs in the same area, showed that violence mainly clusters along the boundaries between gangs. Two of the four gangs that were involved in more than fifty events each, White Fence and Cuatro Flats (Brantingham et al., 2012), were gangs that formed in the 1930s and 1940s, respectively (Vigil, 2007).

Cuatro Flats was one of the "classic" East Los Angeles gangs (Vigil, 2007). Mexican families first migrated there in the 1920s, settling in rundown shacks that were hastily constructed from discarded building materials. Formed in the early 1940s, shortly after the Pico Gardens housing project was built in 1942, claiming 4th Street as its domain, *Cuatro Flats* provided "an alternative set of social norms, conventions, rituals, and enforcement mechanisms that, in effect, serve as a surrogate family" (p. 132). Its members grew up in the streets, products of marginalized families. Gang life in more established gangs such as *Cuatro Flats* was governed by a clear set of values and norms. For example, (1) protection is valued, thus watching one another's backs is essential; (2) gang loyalty is demanded and this was linked to turf protection; (3) respect is essential, particularly toward older members; and (4) emotional support is expected, as if gang members are family members (p. 61). From the 1940s onward, *Cuatro Flats* grew to comprise fourteen cliques or *klikas*, typically starting with thirteen- and fourteen-year-old members and often lasting until they are twenty or twenty-one years old (Vigil, 2007, p. 65). At first, the gang was preoccupied by just hanging around and partying, but by the 1950s, fights (more so rumbles than shootings) were a common occurrence among the *Cuatro Flats* and other gangs in Pico Gardens and in the broader Boyle Heights area. Gang violence escalated in the

1950s and 1960s. Still, guns were rarely used. "The key figure in these disputes was the gang's toughest leader, who was considered . . . the baddest dude of the gang and the person who best understood the gang's place in the larger context of the barrio" (p. 43).

But the 1980s were a "difficult and disruptive era for *Cuatro Flats*" (Vigil, 2007, p. 45). The combination of fewer young dedicated recruits and the lure of drug use and trafficking crack cocaine on occasion rendered the gang vulnerable. In fact, the new flood of guns and drugs would determine its future character. Younger members ceased following the leadership of the OGs, the street term for *original gangsters*, and no longer sought tutelage from them. Instead, young gang members commenced establishing their own rules. At the same time, many of the *veterano* leaders had become relatively inactive, some of whom were in jail or prison, and others had died or became drug addicts. "Bad role models, guns, and drugs made a volatile combination" (p. 45). *Cuatro Flats* became splintered over PCP (Phencyclidine[4]) and crack cocaine drug trafficking. Gang members began fighting with other young adults inside the barrio, an act that further alienated potential recruits. "*Cuatro Flats'* influence diminished, and its internal structure had become irreversibly fragmented" (p. 46).

Battles with adults involved in drug enterprises further alienated potential recruits. Drive-by shootings became commonplace. Street gangs expanded and violence exploded. The *Cuatro Flats* gang transformed into something entirely different, a major gang in the area that vied with the most dangerous Black gangs in the 1970s and 1980s. As of 2007, there were eight major gangs and dozens of disorganized ones operating in the broader Pico-Aliso area, and the LAPD estimated that the number of gangs located there is "unequaled anywhere" (p. 49). Transformed from a barrio gang to a multineighborhood gang with enormous capacity for firearm violence, *Cuatro Flats* persisted as one of the most violent gangs in that area since the 1980s (Brantingham et al., 2012).

Vigil (2007) observed that *Cuatro Flats* somehow survived a metamorphism, an alteration of its structure. This gang lost its community orientation and commitment to traditional gang values and norms. In particular, the absence and disrespect of *veterano* leaders diminished gang loyalty and weakened the gang structure, a loss of continuity in the gang's status hierarchy. Protection of members lost primacy as a goal, giving way to money making via drug trafficking. In the meantime, immigrants continued to pour into Pico-Aliso. Additional small gangs were formed. Violence was no longer managed by the *Cuatro Flats* gang. Over a three-year period, from 1999 to 2002, police attributed seventy-one violent crimes to this gang; just three gangs totaled more crimes (White Fence, State Street, and the Krazy Ass Mexicans gangs) (Brantingham et al., 2012).

In short, *Cuatro Flats* transformed itself from a classic barrio gang to a modern-day street gang, preoccupied with competition with rival gangs for physical space in a highly constricted ghetto area. Overall, more than one thousand particularly violent crimes (assault with a deadly weapon, attempted homicide, and homicide) were recorded on twenty-nine street gangs in a three-year period in the Hollenbeck policing district located on the eastern edge of the city of Los Angeles, a relatively small area covering about fifteen square miles.

In sum, the onset of gang problems in many cities during 1980–2000 appears to reflect the somewhat rapid institutionalization of gangs and the influence of key socio-historical events that contributed to long-term perpetuation of gangs: particularly the youth subculture and gangsta rap, drug trafficking, access to more lethal weapons, public housing projects, and the growth of prison gangs (Figure 3.1). Three features of gangs themselves characterize those gangs that are most violent: the number of gangs, size of gang membership, and extent of gang organization and structure (Howell & Griffiths, 2016).

NATIONWIDE GANG EXPANSION

Following the end-point of Miller's data collection (mid-1990s), the National Youth Gang Survey (NYGS) has charted gang activity throughout the United States (shown in Figure 4.2).[5] The first year of data collection in this nationally representative survey of law enforcement (1996) has stood up as the single year with the most widespread reported gang activity, an apex that also was observed in Miller's data (shown in Figure 4.1).[6] Except for a sharp drop in prevalence from 1996 to 2001, reported gang activity has remained fairly stable since 2002 (Figure 4.2, Egley, Howell, & Harris, 2014).

The National Gang Center uses three indicators to gauge the overall magnitude of the U.S. gang problem: the numbers of gangs, gang members, and gang-related homicides. Despite a small decrease (about 5 percent) in reported gang activity across the United States in 2009–2012 (Figure 4.2), the three gang problem magnitude indicators increased sharply from 2007 to 2012. Compared with the previous five-year average, the number of gangs, gang members, and gang homicides increased 8 percent, 11 percent, and 20 percent, respectively, nationwide in 2012 (Egley, et al., 2014). Other trends follow.

- By 2012, 16 percent of all homicides reported in the United States were gang-related (Egley, et al., 2014). And from 2007 to 2012, the gang homicide rate remained virtually unchanged in very large cities (populations of

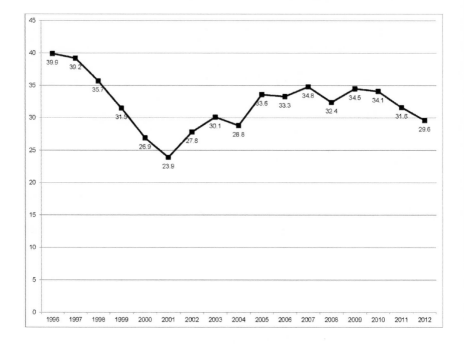

Figure 4.2.   Percentage of Law Enforcement Agencies Reporting Youth Gang Problems, 1996–2012 Source: National Gang Center, accessed December 20, 2014. https://www.nationalgangcenter.gov/Survey-Analysis/Prevalence-of-Gang-Problems#prevalenceyouthgang.

more than one hundred thousand), wherein annually, one in four homicides in 2009 were associated with gang activity (Howell et al., 2011).

- Reflecting the increasing concentration of gang activity in large cities, 56 percent of gangs, 75 percent of gang members, and 87 percent of gang homicides are located in metropolitan areas[7] (Egley & Howell, 2013).
- Gang problems are also serious in most large cities in the United States. Nearly seven out of ten large cities (with populations greater than fifty thousand that reported gang activity between 1996 and 2009 also reported a chronic gang problem (every year) across the fourteen year period; conversely, almost one-third had an intermittent gang problem (Howell et al., 2011).
- Based on these findings, National Gang Center analysts concluded that gang activity is becoming concentrated more and more in very large cities, while declining in outlying areas (Egley et al., 2014).

In contrast, overall violent crime and property crime arrest rates have declined dramatically nationwide over the past two decades (FBI, 2013). Total firearm homicides in 2011 dropped 39 percent from a high in 1993 (Planty & Truman, 2013), while the rate of violent crime victimization decreased by 72 percent (Truman & Planty, 2012). This contrasting trend between overall violence and gang-related violence suggests that gang crimes in very large cities are largely unaffected by, if not independent from, other crime trends. Gang violence has its own dynamics, related to local situations and conditions.

Year of Gang Problem Onset

The year of gang problem onset varies among cities of different sizes. Figure 4.3 shows the year of gang problem onset in cities that reported gang activity in the National Youth Gang Survey (grouped by city size from top to bottom). The emergence of gang activity in the very large cities (Group 1, with populations of more than one hundred thousand persons) began to unfold in the mid-1970s (Howell, Egley, & Gleason, 2002). In the space of just 25 years (1975–2000), the proportion of these very large cities that had gang problems increased more than eightfold, from less than 10 percent to 93 percent. The sharpest increase occurred between the mid-1980s and mid-1990s, when reported gang activity tripled in just fifteen years. Group 2 cities (with populations from fifty thousand to one hundred thousand persons) increased from 2 percent to 66 percent in the twenty-five-year period. The average year of onset across population groups was 1985 for Group 1 cities, 1988 for Group 2 cities, 1990 for Group 3 cities, and 1992 for those in Group 4 (cities, towns, and villages with populations of less than twenty-five thousand).

Gangs that formed in large U.S. cities before 1985 became more permanent with the passage of time. These cities reported five times more homicides than cities with fewer than one hundred thousand persons from 2007 to 2011.[8] In general, gang problems in the larger cities with earlier onset (prior to the 1990s) were far more serious (Howell et al., 2002). Gangs in these cities were much more likely than the later onset jurisdictions (during the 1990s) to be involved in violent crimes (homicide, aggravated assault, robbery, and use of firearms) and drug trafficking. Overall, gang homicides are more likely to be reported in areas with larger populations, with longstanding and persistent gang problems. The later onset jurisdictions, characterized by far less involvement in violent crime, were most likely to be in rural counties, smaller cities, and suburban counties with populations of less than fifty thousand.

Cities with populations in excess of one hundred thousand persons are now home to the overwhelming majority of dangerous gangs representing the bulk of gang members in the entire country, particularly older, more violent gangs with mainly young adult participants (Howell et al., 2011). These

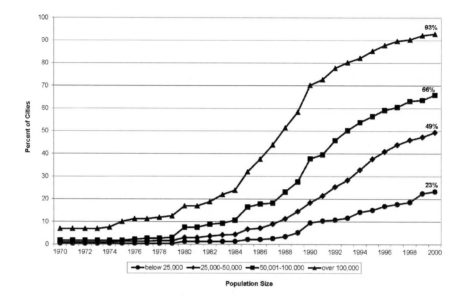

Figure 4.3.   Year of Gang Problem Onset Source: Egley, A., Jr., Howell, J. C., & Major, A. K. (2006). National Youth Gang Survey: 1999–2001. Washington, DC: U.S. Department of Justice, Office of Juvenile Justice and Delinquency Prevention.

cities consistently experience large numbers of gang-related homicides and other gang-related violence, mayhem, intimidation, and pervasive fear. As expected, very large cities have larger gangs and more of them (Egley, 2005):

- Cities with populations between fifty thousand and one hundred thousand typically report about ten gangs with about one hundred fifty total members, an average of about fifteen per gang.
- Cities with populations between one hundred thousand and two hundred fifty thousand typically have up to thirty gangs, and a total of about five hundred members, an average of about twenty per gang.
- Cities with populations greater than two hundred fifty thousand typically report more than thirty gangs and a total of one thousand or more members, an average of more than thirty per gang.

Factors that Account for Early Onset

Several factors have been suggested as contributors to the nationwide upturn in violent gang activity in the late 1980s and early 1990s (W. Miller, 2001). Gang involvement in drug trafficking is the predominant one. As reports of gang activity increased in certain cities, broadcast media and some federal government sources speculated that gangs were migrating across the United States and setting up lucrative drug-trafficking operations in conjunction with a presumed crack cocaine "epidemic" (i.e., usage well above normal consumption). The sharp increase in adolescent and young adult homicides was tied to drug-trafficking by Los Angeles Bloods and Crips gangs that presumably profited from the so-called epidemic. Imprisoned members of several gangs convinced several respected researchers that they were expanding their drug-trafficking operations to other cities across the United States (Skolnick, 1989; Skolnick, Correl, Navarro, & Rabb, 1990). The myth quickly gained traction. Along with broadcast media, a few observers in all levels of government began promoting the assumption of Bloods and Crips gang migration across the United States (Bryant, 1989; California Council on Criminal Justice, 1989; Clark, 1991; Drug Enforcement Administration, 1988; Hayeslip, 1989; McKinney, 1988; U.S. Government Accounting Office, 1989, 1996). The National Drug Intelligence Center (NDIC, 1994) surveyed law enforcement agencies in 237 U.S. cities, and a total of 115 cities reported Bloods/Crips gang activity in their jurisdiction (See Map 1, p. 6A of the NDIC report). In addition, a 1996 survey of 301 local law enforcement agencies (NDIC, 1996) asserted that Chicago-based gangs such as the Black Gangster Disciples, Vice Lords, and Almighty Latin Kings were reported in 110 jurisdictions in thirty-five states. These reports prompted U.S. President William Clinton to declare a "war on gangs" in his 1997 State of the Union address, albeit to no avail.

Because the growth in gang violence in the period from the mid-1980s to the early 1990s coincided with the so-called crack cocaine epidemic, a couple of researchers built a case that these two developments were directly related (Blumstein, 1995a, 1995b; Blumstein & Rosenfeld, 1999). Blumstein and Rosenfeld insisted,

> As the crack epidemic spread in the mid- and late-1980s, so did the danger around inner city drug markets, driving up the incentive for more kids to arm themselves in an increasingly threatening environment. That environment also became a prime recruiting ground for urban street gangs. (1999, p. 162)

To date, no one has presented convincing empirical evidence of a *nationwide* crack cocaine epidemic (for evidence to the contrary, see Hartman & Golub, 1999; Reeves & Campbell, 1994). Only a few cities appear to have experienced such widespread crack cocaine distribution to qualify as an "epidemic." In the best effort to document a large number of crack-infiltrated cities (Cork, 1999; Grogger & Willis, 1998; Golub & Johnson, 1997), the evidence was not convincing because these studies had several important methodological limitations.[9] In reality, crack cocaine was extensively marketed in but a few very large cities, principally in Chicago, Detroit, Los Angeles, Miami, Oakland, New York City, St. Louis, and Washington, DC (Reeves & Campbell, 1994, p. 160; Steinberg, 1996), and studies in only a few of these connected gangs to crack distribution (Gordon, Rowe, Pardini et al., 2014; Levitt & Venkatesh, 2000; Venkatesh, 2000). The most authoritative sources are in agreement that the so-called crack cocaine epidemic was an instrumental part of the Reagan Administration's "war on drugs" (Brownstein, 1996; Reeves & Campbell, 1994; Steinberg, 1996).

Another issue, whether or not street gangs have the capacity to manage drug distribution enterprises, is less easily resolved. In Phase 4 of the transformation of gangs, drug trafficking along with growing availability of firearms were important contributing factors. But two issues can be raised with respect to the widespread influence of gang involvement in drug distribution enterprises. First, there are important differences between street gangs and drug gangs (Decker, 2007; Klein, 1995). Street gangs are versatile in their criminal activities ("cafeteria-style" crime), have larger structures, are less cohesive, and have looser leadership. In contrast, drug trafficking groups are strictly focused on the drug business, have smaller structures, are more cohesive, and have more centralized leadership. However, the distinctions are not so clear in the case of drug "crews" and "posses" that closely resemble street gangs. Of course, some street gangs have developed viable organizations for street-level sales (Block & Block, 1993; Cohen & Tita, 1999; Levitt & Venkatesh, 2000; Venkatesh, 2008). In Chicago, Venkatesh (2000) described in great detail how the Black Disciples street gang reigned in the RTH complex and controlled most of the drug market therein. In Detroit, "scavenger" gangs of the 1950s–1970s were transformed into "corporate" gangs involved in illegal money-making ventures, including drug trafficking (Taylor, 1990a, 1990b, 1993). The drug economy turned gangs into businesses that operated both within Detroit and with some out-of-state operations.

Although a few street gangs have evolved into highly organized, entrepreneurial adult criminal organizations, to be sure, few street gangs could meet the essential criteria for classification as "organized crime" (Decker, Bynum, & Weisel, 1998; Klein, 1995). Moreover, studies showed that the gangs' involvement in cocaine drug trafficking in Los Angeles was overstated (Klein, Maxson, & Cunningham, 1991; Maxson, 1998; Maxson, Woods, & Klein, 1996). Moreover, the prospect of gangs—made up largely of adolescents—migrating across the United States and managing drug-trafficking operations without substantial financial backing and extensive criminal networks that organized crime operatives enjoy raised doubts among many observers in the gang research community (Howell & Decker, 1999; Huff, 2007; Klein, 1995, 2004; Maxson et al., 1985). "Organized crime groups such as drug cartels must have strong leadership, codes of loyalty, severe sanctions for failure to abide by these codes, and a level of entrepreneurial expertise that enables them to accumulate and invest proceeds from drug sales" (Klein, 2004, pp. 57–59). Most drug-trafficking operations are managed by adult drug cartels or syndicates (Eddy et al., 1988; Gugliotta & Leen, 1989). However, gang members are extensively involved in street-level drug sales (Bjerregaard, 2010).

The prospect of extensive migrating of gangs themselves has been called into question. Findings from a 1992–1993 University of Southern California (USC) survey of law enforcement agencies did not find gang migration as a main explanation for enormous gang proliferation at that time. Covering sixty cities with a population of between ten thousand and one hundred thousand (Maxson, 1998), "this study provides evidence that gang member migration, although widespread, should not be viewed as the major culprit in the nationwide proliferation of gangs" (p. 8). In most cases, localities that experienced gang migration already had a gang problem. In large part, the USC study findings agree with earlier studies, finding that gang formation was only minimally buttressed by the infusion of gang members from other cities: Decker and Van Winkle (1996), Hagedorn (1988), Huff (1989), Rosenbaum and Grant (1983), Waldorf (1993), and Zevitz and Takata (1992). Street gangs themselves rarely migrate—though drug-trafficking groups do so more often (Starbuck et al., 2001)—and most gang-related migration involves individual members, most of whom relocate for social reasons, such as visiting relatives and family moves (Maxson, 1998). Almost without exception, street gangs are affiliated with a specific geographic location.

Thus, the predominant explanation of similar names found in distant cities is copycatting the names of big city gangs. Of course, there are exceptions. Fleisher (1995) found that some Compton and Hoover Crips in Los Angeles moved north to Seattle, Washington, and set up drug-trafficking gangs there. The National Alliance of Gang Investigators' Associations (2005) contends that a few gangs do have the capacity to expand into other regions. However, W. Miller (2001) insists that most gang member migration occurred in conjunction with the enormous U.S. population shift during the 1980s and 1990s from metropolitan to suburban and rural areas. As seen in Figure 2.1, law enforcement agencies nationwide do not view gang member migration as an important influence on local gang violence, and the perceived importance of this factor has declined sharply since 2006.

Gang problems in the United States as a whole appear to occur in spurts or cycles, and the length of the upswings and downturns cannot be predicted. Indeed, variations from one geographic area to another are common—even within the same city—depending on the existence of recurring gang conflicts that create peaks and valleys in gang crimes (Alonso, 2004; Block & Block, 1993; Decker & Van Winkle, 1996; Moore, 1993). As Moore explains, gang dynamics account for variable periods of gang violence. Moore reports that, in East Lost Angeles, the escalating violence (undergirded by *locura*) in the

1970s occurred as new cliques strove to outdo their predecessor cliques by increasing the rate and intensity of violence with more guns and more drive-by shootings in rival gang neighborhoods. At the same time, in South Central Lost Angeles, gang violence escalated as the constellation of Crips gangs grew, in large part out of racialization in the 1960s (Alonso, 2004). In Alonso's view, sensational media coverage was a key catalyst, prompting other youths to join. With the combined escalation in both Mexican American and Black communities, a literal epidemic of violence was documented citywide in Los Angeles—to the level that two-thirds of all child and adolescent homicides were gang related by the end of the period from 1979 to 1994 (Hutson et al., 1995).

City Trajectories of Gang Homicide Histories

Researchers recently applied trajectory modeling to group serious gang problem cities on the dimension of violent crime involvement over multiple years—an examination of cities' violent gang histories. Trajectory models are used here to group jurisdictions that share similar trends in the outcome of interest (gang homicide in this instance) and to graphically illustrate those patterns over a fourteen-year period.[10] This trajectory analysis presented in

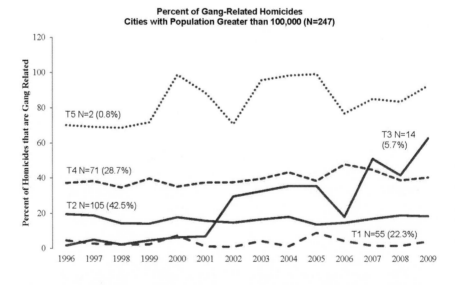

Figure 4.4. Trajectory Model: Percentage of Gang-Related Homicides (Populations Greater Than 100,000, N=247). Source: Howell, J. C., Egley, A., Jr., Tita, G., & Griffiths, E. (2011). U.S. gang problem trends and seriousness. Tallahassee, FL: Institute for Intergovernmental Research, National Gang Center. Reprinted with permission of the Institute for Intergovernmental Research.

Figure 4.4 examines trends in the proportion of all homicides in cities of interest that are gang related nationwide.[11] The analysis presented here is limited to 247 very large cities, those with populations in excess of one hundred thousand persons.

This analysis can be summarized with four observations. First, three groups of cities (T1, T2, and T4) evidence a relatively stable gang homicide rate over the fourteen-year period, with a few peaks and valleys. Second, almost two-thirds reported between 20 percent and 40 percent of all homicides were gang related between 1996 and 2009 (T1 and T2). Third, a very small proportion of the cities, 6 percent (T3 and T5) experienced sharp increases in the gang homicide rate over the fourteen-year period. Fourth, the higher-rate cities (T2, T3, and T5), cluster mainly in five U.S. regions: the Los Angeles Basin, the Bay Area of California, the Great Lakes Region, the Northeast Region, and Florida's Atlantic Coast—from Miami northward (Howell et al., 2011). Each of the 247 very large cities experiencing these

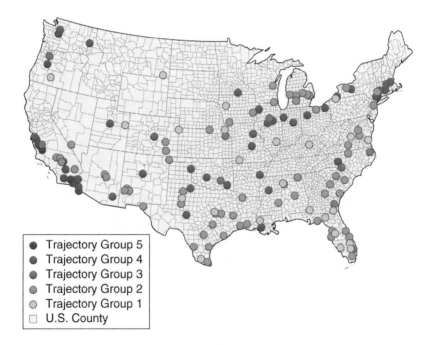

- Trajectory Group 5
- Trajectory Group 4
- Trajectory Group 3
- Trajectory Group 2
- Trajectory Group 1
- U.S. County

Figure 4.5. Map of Trajectories Reflecting Gang-Related Homicide Trends (Counties with Cities Having Populations Greater Than 100,000). Source: Howell, J. C., Egley, A., Jr., Tita, G., & Griffiths, E. (2011). U.S. gang problem trends and seriousness. Tallahassee, FL: Institute for Intergovernmental Research, National Gang Center. Reprinted with permission of the Institute for Intergovernmental Research.

varied levels and trends in the proportion of all homicides that are gang related are mapped in Figure 4.5 (Howell & Griffiths, 2015). The T4 cities, or places where approximately 40 percent of all homicides are gang related over the period, are more typical in major urban centers located in the West, the Northeast, and parts of the Midwest. Cities characterized by T1 (around 10 percent of all homicides were gang related), T2 (20 percent), or T3 (30 percent) trends appear more evenly spread across the United States, while the two T5 (50 percent or more) cities are located only in the West (California, more specifically).

It is readily apparent that very large cities with consistently high levels of gang homicides are widely dispersed across the United States. Although visual inspection of the map, alone, cannot confirm specific regional patterns, five clusters of relatively high-rate gang (20 percent to 40 percent) homicide cities are evident (e.g., the Bay Area of California, Los Angeles Basin, Great Lakes Region, Northeast, and Florida's Atlantic Coast) (Howell et al., 2011). Some regional clustering is visible in the Northeast (including New York City, Boston, and Philadelphia); the Midwest (including Chicago, Detroit, Columbus, St. Louis, and Milwaukee), the West (particularly Los Angeles, Inglewood, Salinas, and San Francisco), and South (Miami and northward along the Atlantic Coast). But does the expanded gang activity in the United States extend to other countries? This is the topic of the chapter that follows.

NOTES

1. Sanders (1994) offered several explanations for the popularity of drive-by shootings in Southern California. The expansive geographical region is not well suited for treks by a large number of youths to a gang fight. Police could easily spot large groups engaged in fighting. In addition, the drive-by shooting tactic enabled gangs to cope with the spread-out city and survive retaliation. Another characteristic of Southern California has rendered the area well suited for drive-bys, an excellent highway system (Miller, 1982/1992).

2. It is important to keep in mind that use of the more restricted, gang-motivated definition used in Chicago at that time diminished both the total number of gang homicides and the relative proportion, compared to Los Angeles.

3. The University of Illinois at Chicago. "Index of /orgs." Accessed March 4, 2015. http://www.uic.edu/orgs/.

4. Commonly initialized as PCP, Phencyclidine is known colloquially as Angel Dust and is a recreational dissociative drug.

5. The NYGS is the first gang survey in any country that annually contacts a nationally representative sample of authoritative respondents in their respective jurisdictions regarding the prevalence and characteristics of gang activity using the same methodology each year. The current sample consists of the following respondents:

All police departments serving cities with populations of 50,000 or more (n=624);
All suburban county police and sheriffs' departments (n=739);
A randomly selected sample of police departments serving cities with populations between 2,500 and 49,999 (n=543);
A randomly selected sample of rural county police and sheriffs' departments (n=492).

6. Independent evaluations have confirmed and demonstrated the validity and reliability of the NYGS data (Decker & Pyrooz, 2010; Katz, Fox, Britt, & Stevenson, 2012; Pyrooz, 2012).

7. Police departments serving cities with populations greater than one hundred thousand and suburban county sheriffs' and police departments.

8. National Gang Center. Accessed December 20, 2014. https://www.nationalgangcenter. gov/Survey-Analysis/Measuring-the-Extent-of-Gang-Problems#homicidesnumber.

9. Law enforcement agencies did not maintain statistics on crack cocaine arrests, and national survey data on crack cocaine use were not available at that time. Valiant efforts to substantiate Blumstein's and Rosenfeld's assumption were made by Golub and Johnson (1997) and Cork (1999), in an effort to identify cities that experienced a crack cocaine "epidemic." But their data were based on urine analysis among arrested persons (Drug Use Forecasting data) that were not representative of either the general population or drug users. Nevertheless, in 1999, Cork concluded that the crack markets–gun availability connection is "highly plausible." Blumstein (2000) wrote more definitively, in saying that "Cork (1999) has shown the connection between the rise in handgun homicides and the recruitment of juveniles in the crack markets" (p. 38). Another serious limitation is that neither study took into account the massive "war on drugs" waged by the Reagan administration in the 1980s that was continued by the Clinton administration, and both Bush administrations (Ousey & Lee, 2004; Reeves & Campbell, 1994; Tonry, 1994). The "politics of panic" had begun to dominate U.S. crime control policies (Beckett & Sasson, 2003) as "wars" on crime, drugs, and gangs hyped crime issues. Thus, through the lens of panic, and sporadic reports of a crack cocaine "epidemic" in certain cities, generalizations were temping, though lacking evidence linking those to rising juvenile and young adult homicide rates. For example, Hagan and Foster (2000) found juvenile homicide rates also increased sharply in the mid- to late 1980s in Canada in concert with the United States increase, but without the presence of any crack cocaine epidemic.

10. In this case, the trajectory procedure was used to examine trends in gang presence, and gang homicide as a proportion of total homicide within U.S. policing jurisdictions between 1996 and 2009. Trajectory models essentially group jurisdictions sharing similar trends in the outcome of interest and graphically illustrate those patterns over the period. For example, some jurisdictions may report a consistent presence of gangs while others could experience no gang activity over time, rapid increases over time, rapid decreases, fluctuating presence of gang activity, or other kinds of more complex trends between 1996 and 2009. This methodology does not require that researchers specify the number of groups or the shape of the trajectories in advance.

11. Proportional homicide rates—along which cities' patterns are aligned here—were determined by dividing the total number of gang homicides reported in the NYGS annually by the total number of homicides reported for the city in the Federal Bureau of Investigation Uniform Crime Report (UCR), multiplied by one hundred. This procedure provides the percentage of all homicides that are gang related at each year for each jurisdiction.

Chapter Five

Transnational Gangs

Widespread media and national security attention is now given to so-called "transnational" gangs. By and large, these are assumed to be uniquely American products, street gangs that presumably extend internationally. There is an important barrier in assessing this prospect, however: the absence of a widely accepted definition of a transnational gang. Franco (2010), a security analyst in the U.S. Congressional Research Service, provides the various characteristics often attributed to transnational gangs:

- These gangs are criminally active and operational in more than one country.
- Criminal activities that gang members commit in one country are planned, directed, and controlled by gang leaders in another country.
- These gangs tend to be mobile and to adapt to new areas.
- The criminal activities of such gangs tend to be sophisticated and to transcend borders.

For a gang to be considered transnational, Franco insists that it should have more than one of the preceding characteristics; however, this rule is not followed in much of the literature and media coverage, which characterizes gangs as transnational merely because they are present in more than one country.

Los Angeles gang culture produced two gangs that have been dubbed transnational groups, the 18th Street gang (*Mara Dieciocho*) and *Mara Salvatrucha* (MS-13), a Salvadoran gang.[1] These gangs emerged in the United States, and their gang culture was diffused across the Mesoamerican cultural region (Vigil, 1998). The 18th Street Mexican-American gang formed in the Pico-Union neighborhood just west of downtown Los Angeles in the 1960s

(Vigil, 2002). Having been rejected by this gang that accepted only Mexican-American youth at that time, the Salvadoran youth formed MS-13[2] for protection in the dangerous Pico-Union area that had multiple gangs by the 1980s. The MS-13 gang was composed of Salvadoran youth who had come there with their families that fled El Salvador as civil war refugees. For more than a decade (1981–1992), a civil war was waged in El Salvador between the government and the leftist guerrilla forces of the Salvadoran National Liberation Front. With deaths numbering as many as one hundred thousand, approximately one million natives fled the country, about ten thousand of which landed in MacArthur Park, in the heart of the Pico-Union neighborhood in Los Angeles (Zilberg, 2011). The expanding population of Salvadorians in Los Angles grew from approximately ninety-four thousand in 1980 to around five hundred thousand by the mid-1980s (Vigil, 2002). Originally an Anglo neighborhood that housed residents in numerous four-story apartment buildings along with single-family homes, by the 1990s, a majority of the population of Pico-Union was Latino—"predominantly of Mexican, Salvadoran, and Guatemalan origin, in that order" (p. 130).

But Los Angeles proved to be less than an inviting refuge. "Youth coming from a characteristically violent homeland confronted a new environment of violence [particularly in Pico-Union], and together these experiences of violence seem to have converged to facilitate [even more] violent behavior" (Vigil, 2002, p. 140). With roots in a non-territorial stoner gang (Ward, 2013), the MS-13 was formed by Salvadorian youth for protection against harassment and attacks from 18th Street and some thirty other gangs in the area, and this gang grew rapidly in numbers along with the continuing arrival of immigrant youth from El Salvador. In the meantime, 18th Street also was fast growing once Salvadoran immigrant youth were permitted to join and more and more age-graded cliques were formed that claimed specific territories of their own. Co-existing in the Pico-Union neighborhood of some eight square miles, the Salvadoran MS-13 gang eventually came into conflict with a clique of the 18th Street gang, and by 1992, these gangs locked an all-out war with one another. "With both MS and 18th Street in Pico-Union, it became the gang hotspot of Los Angeles in the mid-1990s" (Vigil, 2002, p. 142). To make matters worse, some of the MS-13 gang members had begun to affiliate with a prison gang, *La Eme* (the Mexican Mafia), in the course of drug trafficking in Pico-Union, and MS-13 and *La Eme* began operating criminal and drug-sale rings (Vigil, 2002).

By the mid-1980s, the Pico-Union and surrounding area was engulfed by growing gang violence and drug trafficking. In response, the LAPD Chief Daryl F. Gates [3] formed the Community Resources Against Street Hoodlums (CRASH) unit in its Ramparts Area that included Pico-Union. CRASH officers were given wide latitude to fight gangs (i.e., "hoodlums"). "In some sections, road blocks erected by the police to curb drug trafficking gave the neighborhood the appearance of a war zone" (Vigil, 2002, p. 145). Operation Hammer, the most notorious gang sweep, carried out in 1988 brought infamy to LAPD gang suppression tactics. Deploying a force of a thousand police officers in street sweeps on two consecutive nights, CRASH unit officers arrested gang members and others on a wide variety of charges, including existing warrants, new traffic citations, curfew violations, illegal gang-related behaviors, and observed criminal activities (Klein, 1995). Altogether, 1,453 people were arrested and taken to a mobile booking operation adjacent to the Los Angeles Memorial Coliseum. Most of the arrested youths were released without charges. Slightly more than half were gang members. There were only sixty felony arrests, and charges were filed on just thirty-two of them.

Nevertheless, Rampart CRASH was immediately deemed successful by the LAPD, as measured by the sheer number of arrests, and drug, and weapons seizures, but the ensuing scandal deeply tarnished the reputation of the LAPD (Zilberg, 2011). An investigation for police corruption led to overturning more than one hundred prior convictions that came from the CRASH operations, and settlements in more than 140 lawsuits amounting to approximately $125 million (p. 42). Officer Rafael Perez, who worked in the LAPD CRASH unit and admitted framing innocent gang members, for which he was sentenced to five years in prison, offered this explanation: "The lines between right and wrong became fuzzy and indistinct. The us-against-them ethos of the overzealous cop began to consume me, and the ends seemed to justify the means" (Deutsch, 2000, p. 6).

Other deterrent measures targeting Los Angeles gangs followed the disbanding of CRASH units in 2001, including gang injunctions that placed restrictions on free association between gang members. These restrictions followed the Street Terrorism Enforcement and Prevention (STEP) Act of 1988 (California Penal Code § 186.22) that banned all forms of communication between gang members. In 2002, William Bratton, former Chief of the New York City Police Department, was named LAPD Chief. He brought with him a widely reputed "zero tolerance" anti-crime strategy.[4] Chief Bratton immediately conflated gang activity with terrorism under the term "homeland terrorism" (Zilberg, 2011, p. 44). This unfortunate linkage suggested the prospect of transnational terrorist gangs in the absence of any substantiation.

Members of both the MS-13 and 18th Street gangs were deported to Central America after a riot that followed a controversial not-guilty verdict in 1992 that exonerated the LAPD of excessive use of force. A video camera had captured the police beating a Black driver, Rodney King, following a car chase, with more than fifty blows to his body. A spontaneous multi-ethnic riot broke out that engulfed all residents of Pico-Union and surrounding neighborhoods of Central and South Los Angeles—Mexicans, Central

Americans, and others—"caught in the midst of the riots as innocent victims and peace brokers, looters and thugs. But it [was] the figure of the Latino as looter that [dominated] local media coverage" (Zilberg, 2011, p. 31). The riots lasted five days, and gang members were active participants.[5] Altogether, police arrested seventeen thousand Latino immigrants, "most purportedly for looting, and at least one thousand [were] deported before the ACLU or immigrant rights groups [could] intervene" (p. 31).[6] Police targeted many Salvadorian youth for deportation. Eight teams of federal immigration agents were recruited to work with the LAPD Gang Task Force in identifying and deporting gang members (Vigil, 2002). More deportations of Latino gang members followed later in the same year, after the civil war in El Salvador was ended 1992 with the Salvadoran Peace Accords. Members of both MS-13 and 18th Street gangs who were deported to Central American countries carried with them their respective gang cultures and gang identities, yet these gangs remained strong in Pico-Union even though the total number deported reached at least 780 (Vigil, 2002).

Within two years after the Civil War ended, 375,000 Salvadorans voluntarily returned home, and in a three-year period during the mid-1990s, another 200,000 Central Americans were deported to Central American countries (Jütersonke, Muggah, & Rodgers, 2009). Further deportations were made under the U.S. Illegal Immigration Reform and Immigrant Responsibility Act of 1996 (P.L. 104-208, Division C). In February 2005, the U.S. Immigration and Customs Enforcement (ICE) agency launched Operation Community Shield, a federal, state, and local law enforcement operation, with the expressed purpose of apprehending and deporting members of MS-13. In July of that same year, its operation was extended to include 18th Street and other Latino gangs. "By September 24, 2007, ICE claims to have arrested 7,655 gang members and associates, representing over 700 different gangs, but MS-13 remains the poster child of the operation" (Zilberg, 2011, p. 47). By the end of 2006, ICE had deported 10,588 Salvadorians, and a year later, the figure climbed to 20,045 (p. 49). The number of gang members in these figures is unknown, though relatively small.

This "reverse migration" of Los Angeles MS-13 and 18th Street gang members diffused U.S.-style hard-boiled gang culture to existing *maras* (less-structured, territorial cliques or gangs) in the Central American isthmus (principally El Salvador, Honduras, and Guatemala). The MS-13 returned with a stronger identity, bolstered by hand signs for communication, norms, values, and awareness of who the enemy is (Cruz, 2014). Local Salvadorian cliques were renamed MS-13 or 18th Street, depending on which gang happened to be in control of the neighborhood or community where the *mara* member lived. Cloaked in Los Angeles gang culture, local El Salvadorian gangs took on the appearance of Los Angeles MS-13 and 18th Street gangs, even though they had never been out of El Salvador (Cruz, 2014). In other words, the gangs to which the El Salvadorian youth belonged were neither transplanted nor expanded American MS-13 and 18th Street gangs; rather, Cruz notes, native Salvadorian youth belonged to hybrid versions of their own *maras* that had been "transformed" in appearance, at least, by exposure to U.S. MS-13 and 18th Street gangs. Cruz reports that by 1996, 84 percent of surveyed young people in gangs in the country's capital, San Salvador, said they belonged to either the MS-13 or 18th Street gangs; however, in a recent survey of imprisoned gang members in El Salvador, only 7 percent said they were members of these gangs in the United States. Thus Cruz (2014) insists that

> it would be a mistake to ascribe the expansion of gang membership and the emergence of the "gang problem" in the 1990s to the constant influx of depor-tees and returnees of the postwar years. The majority of gang members joined the cliques and barrios on Salvadorian soil and had never been out of the country. (p. 126)

Although other gang cultures were diffused from Los Angeles to the Central American region, most local youth mimicked the MS-13 and 18th Street gangs, particularly in El Salvador, Guatemala, and Honduras (Hazen & Rodgers, 2014). In addition, Cruz (2014) identifies three dynamics that transformed the hybrid El Salvadorian MS-13 and 18th Street gangs. First, earlier loose *mara* affiliations were crystallized in either MS-13 or 18th Street identities. Cruz is incredulous that members of these gangs resolutely fought one another over the U.S.-born custom of intense personal identifica-tion with a gang name—strictly over personal identity, not territory! Second, Cruz asserts that the more important impetus for growth and increased vi-ciousness of the El Salvadorian gangs was the enactment of the 2003 Mano Dura Act, known as *Ley Antimaras*. This El Salvadorian law permitted the detention and prosecution of suspected gang members under the newly clas-sified felony of "illicit association." The new law backfired. "By overpopu-lating the prisons, the crackdowns provided the opportunity for gang organ-ization and strengthening" (p. 133). Once in prisons, the youth gangs began to organize themselves into hierarchical structures, elect leaders, and elicit support from other violent groups and organizations. Third, the massive po-lice and military crackdown also opened the door to abuses perpetrated by state agents and actors associated with them, violating fundamental human rights. "In response, gangs prepared for an all-out war against the state and its agents" (p. 135).

A leading international security analyst suggests that hypothetical third-generation gangs conceivably could transform themselves into a "new urban insurgency," that "third-generation gangs inevitably begin to control ungov-erned territory within a nation-state and/or begin to acquire political power in poorly governed space" (Manwaring, 2007, p. 6). Manwaring goes further in suggesting that some third generation gangs might act as mercenaries for larger organized criminal groups, as they expand their geographical and commercial parameters. "Then as gangs operate and evolve, they generate more and more violence and instability over wider and wider sections of the political map and generate subnational, national, and regional instability and insecurity" (p. 4). Manwaring also suggests that "most gangs stay firmly within [the] first generation of development, but more than a few have evolved into and beyond the second generation" (p. 4). The prospect of highly evolved gangs suggested by Manwaring (2005, 2007) and others (Sullivan & Bunker, 2002; Wilson & Sullivan, 2007) seemed plausible at first glance. When viewed through a post-9/11 terrorist threat lens, it seemed feasible for a time that if gangs joined forces with other insurgents, these groups could possibly represent a potential "new urban insurgency," perhaps one that that might have the capacity to depose or control incumbent governments in Central America (Manwaring, 2007). But Rodgers and Hazen (2014) insist that neither MS-13 and 18th Street "is a federal structure, much less a transnational one, with a federated nature more imagined and symbolic of a particular historical origin than demonstrative of any real unity, be it of leadership or action" (p. 3). And Jones (2008) cautions, "circumspect assessments cast doubt on the veracity of the gang-terrorist claims, and view the state response to the 'gang threat' more generally as overreaction. Studies reveal that youth gangs rarely venture outside their territory, within which they act as the local 'authority' " (p. 346).

U.S. officials remain steadfast in having designated MS-13 as a as a major Transnational Criminal Organization (TCO), as recent as 2012 (Seelke, 2014).[7] Yet some international gang analysts contend that transnational collaboration is not common for the MS-13, and that neither this gang nor 18th Street meet criteria for "transnational" status (see Rodgers & Hazen, 2014 for supporting information). Importantly, these analysts maintain that even though the MS-13 and M-18th street *maras* can be seen as hybrid gangs that combine certain practices of U.S. gangs, "the transnational nature of the *maras* is more imagined than real, at least in the present" (p. 4). Other observers link *maras* with insurgents, organized crime, drug cartels, or international terrorist groups. But most international security experts suggest that caution is the order of the day. "Groups that appear similar at first glance may be quite different on closer inspection" (p. 5). Other authoritative sources question the very existence of truly transnational street gangs (McGuire, 2007; United Nations Office on Drugs and Crime, 2007; Washington Office on Latin America, 2010).

The issue of the extent of MS-13 gang presence in the United States outside the West–Southwest region remains unresolved. It is worth noting that, although Los Angeles was the main destination of Salvadorian refugees, a number of other U.S. cities received significant numbers, including Chicago, Dallas, Houston, Miami, New Orleans, New York City, Phoenix, San Francisco, and Washington, DC (Zilberg, 2011, p. 133). Several of these cities have been tagged by the FBI as locations in which MS-13 gangs have been documented, including the Atlanta, Dallas, Los Angeles, Washington, DC, and New York metropolitan areas (FBI, 2009). McGuire (2007) found only small cliques of MS-13 in Washington, DC. Across the United States, only about 14 percent of law enforcement agencies presently consider gang member migration from outside the United States to be an important influence on local gang violence, and this figure has declined substantially in recent years (Figure 2.1).

Nevertheless, the intermingling of local gangs with Mexican Drug Trafficking Organizations (MDTOs), and TCOs that does occur in the Mexico and Central America corridor is a serious matter (Seele, Arnson, & Olson, 2013; Seelke, 2014; U.S. Agency for International Development, 2006). With the growth and criminal sophistication of prison gangs, their ties to Mexican drug-trafficking organizations (MDTOs) recently became a matter of security concerns. FBI sources assert that "MDTOs use street and prison gang members in Mexico, Texas, and California to protect smuggling routes, collect debts, transport illicit goods, including drugs and weapons, and execute rival traffickers" (FBI, 2011, p. 27). According to the Texas Fusion Center (2013), each of the Tier 1 and Tier 2 security threat gangs in Texas has established connections with MDTOs. These prison gang experts tag four of the major gangs in Texas as traditional prison gangs: Mexican Mafia, Texas Syndicate, Tango Blast, and Barrio Azteca. Each of these four gangs has multiple relationships with MDTOs. Even though contacts frequently occur, relationships are in a constant state of flux, according to Texas Fusion Center analysts. These firsthand sources also underscore that MS-13 and 18th Street gangs are involved in cross-border criminal activities, but the prospect that these gangs enjoy special relationships with particular MDTOs is another matter. The most prominent MDTOs offer ready opportunities for collusion with American prison and street gangs along the U.S.–Mexico border.[8]

But the extent of U.S. gang involvement with DTOs or TCOs is unresolved (Hazen & Rodgers, 2014). The extent of collusion among U.S. gangs and other criminal organizations along the U.S.–Mexico border has long been "very murky" (Burton & West, 2009). Indeed, "some studies maintain that ties between Central American gangs and organized criminal groups have increased; others have downplayed the connection" (Seelke, 2014, p. 7). The United Nations Office on Drugs and Crime in 2007 concluded that "while some drug trafficking may involve gang members, the backbone of the flow seems to be in the hands of more sophisticated organized crime operations" (p. 17). Also, as Seelke (2014) has noted, "press reports and some Central American officials have blamed MS-13 and other gangs for a large percentage of violent crimes committed in those countries, but some analysts assert that those claims may be exaggerated" (p. 4) and "the lines between transnational gang activity and organized crime are increasingly blurry" (p. 2). The more pressing matter of concern to U.S. security interests is possible street gang involvement in drug trafficking and associated criminal activity along our nation's border with Mexico.

NOTES

1. The name, *La Mara Salvatrucha* has many possible meanings (Zilberg, 2011, n. 3, p. 268), aside from the certainty that *mara* means a group of people, including a gang, and generally across Central America. *Salva* is drawn directly from Salvadorian. *Trucha* means "trout" but is also a slang term for "shrewd Salvadoran." Among the various translations of *Salvatrucha*, Zilberg (2011) notes that *Trucha* references a trout fish that has to swim upstream against the current in order to reproduce. Along with this translation, *Trucha* also stands for a streetwise or alert person, or simply slang for "watch out" (Vigil, 2002, p. 142).

2. This gang came to be called MS-13 once it became aligned to the Mexican Mafia prison gang and thus became Sureños, adopting the number thirteen into their iconography (for the letter "M," the thirteenth letter of the alphabet). As a result, *Mara Salvatrucha* is often known as MS-13. But MS is its true shorthand name (Zilberg, 2011).

3. The enormous growth of gangs and related violence in Los Angles in the mid- to late 1980s prompted Police Chief Daryl Gates to declare "war on gangs" and to form the nation's first gang unit (Davis, 2006). He served as Chief of the LAPD from 1978 through 1992 when he resigned in the wake of the turmoil from the 1991 police beating of Rodney King and the riots that followed.

4. In collaboration with New York City Mayor Rudolph Giuliani, NYC Police Chief William Bratton implemented the "broken windows" strategy to clean up crime in NYC. This punitive policing strategy, more broadly called "zero tolerance," was based on deterrence notions, that punishing minor crimes quickly and severely would reduce future crimes. Assessments of outcomes were complicated by a number of lawsuits alleging police misconduct and abuse of force (Greene, 1999).

5. These riots in the spring of 1992 left more than fifty people dead, and more than 2,000 injured. More than 9,800 California National Guard troops were dispatched to restore order. The rioting destroyed or damaged over 1,000 buildings in the Los Angeles area. The estimated cost of the damages was over $1 billion (CNN Library, 2014).

6. An Amnesty International (1992) report, *United States of America: Torture, Ill Treatment and Excessive Force by Police in Los Angeles, California*, "found a disturbing number of cases where police officers and Sheriff's deputies have used unjustified force" including the Rodney King incident (p. 2). The victims in the examined cases included Whites, Blacks, Latinos, and other races, with Blacks and Latinos together accounting for some two-thirds of the total. "Amnesty International received reports that Black and Latino males were regularly harassed and humiliated by police as well as subjected to unjustified stops and searches purely on account of their race. This routinely happened, Amnesty International was told, during police sweeps of certain neighborhoods, or if a Black male, for example, was seen outside his 'area,' in a white middle class neighborhood" (p. 2). The Christopher Commission (1991), an Independent Commission on the Los Angeles Police Department, made similar findings. On June 15, 2001, the City of Los Angeles agreed to a Consent Decree with the U.S. Department of Justice that subjected the LAPD to federal oversight.

7. The U.S. Government also considers two other street gangs to be transnational: Florencia 13 and Latin Kings (U.S. Government Accountability Office, 2010). In addition, this federal source identifies six prison gangs as transnational: Barrio Azteca, Hermanos de Pistoleros Latinos, Mexican Mafia, Mexikanemi, Surenos, and Texas Syndicate. Each of these prison

gangs—along with Florencia 13 and Latin Kings—is reputed to have transnational connections in criminal enterprises in Mexico or Central America, mainly drug trafficking (U.S. Government Accountability Office, 2010). However, Franco's (2010) criteria for classification of gangs as transnational were not applied in these designations; only the single criterion, gangs with members who are either present or criminally active (or both) in more than one country.

8. Ethnographic research is underway on gangs along the southern New Mexico–Texas border, led by Robert J. Durán at New Mexico State University (Durán, 2008). This research presently is focused on gang activity in three border cities (Las Cruces, NM; Anthony, NM; and El Paso, TX), that are populated by a numerical majority of Mexican and Spanish descents. This research bears close watch.

Epilogue

The United States is presently experiencing its fourth massive immigration wave that appears to be as large in scope as the first one in its history, during the 1880s to 1920s. Once again, the effects of immigration on gang composition could intensify over the next two decades. The common perception is that the brunt of the present wave is not expected to be as dramatic as observed in the initial wave, owing largely to more families of middle-class status in the current wave than in the past. If this were the case, then assimilation should occur more rapidly. However, the full picture is not so rosy. The U.S. immigrant population (legal and illegal) hit a record 41.3 million in July 2013, an increase of 10.2 million since 2000 (Zeigler & Camarota, 2014). The ethnic diversity of recent immigrants is noteworthy, with the largest growth since 2010 in Asian, Caribbean, and Middle Eastern immigrant populations. In addition, although the poverty rate of immigrants from a number of regions has declined in recent years, the composition of the U.S. immigrant population by country of origin has shifted decisively toward countries that send immigrants who are more likely to be poor (Jimenez, 2011). It is unlikely that these disadvantaged people will assimilate quickly or smoothly, possibly contributing more gang members in time.

Moreover, racial and ethnic minorities accounted for 92 percent of the nation's population growth from 2000 to 2010, and more than half (56 percent) of the increase in this period was accounted for by the Hispanic population (Passel et al., 2011). In 1980, 75 percent of U.S. children were White. But by 2030, the percentage of Whites is predicted to drop to 46 percent, while Hispanics are projected to account for 31 percent of all children in the United States; an estimated 13 percent will be Black; and 9 percent, Asian or Hawaiian or other Pacific Islander (Hernandez, Denton, & Blanchard, 2011). In fact, the U.S. Census Bureau projects that by 2023, Whites will be a numerical minority. The United States can expect to see a greater multiracial and multiethnic mixture among gang members in successive generations of immigrants if social policies and programs fail to interrupt gang joining among second-generation children.

To be sure, immigration contributes to gang involvement in the United States. However, this relationship is indirect, conditioned on failed assimilation of racial/ethnic groups. Gang participation begins with second-generation children of immigrants. The delayed pattern is attributable to instigating conditions described as "multiple marginality"—a result of language, education, cultural, and economic barriers (Vigil, 2008, 2010). Gang formation and participation are elevated, in turn, with racial/ethnic "churning" and conflicts. Immigrant concentration appears to be less important than proximity to other hostile immigrant groups and conflict with dominant local groups (Griffiths & Chavez, 2004). Continued immigration and within-U.S. population shifts are inevitable, and so is the racial/ethnic divide in the United States (Alexander, 2011; Telles & Ortiz, 2008), sounding a clarion for solutions (Vigil & Howell, 2012b).

EFFECTIVE PROGRAMS

Gang problems in the United States are here to stay now that gangs are rooted in the youth subculture and gangs themselves are institutionalized in nearly two hundred very large cities across this country and many smaller cities as well. The ready availability of firearms, drugs, and alcohol; persistent conditions of social disorganization and social isolation; a steady stream of returning gang member inmates; and continuous generations of new recruits ensure their permanence. As noted in chapter 4, over a five-year period leading up to 2012, the reported number of gangs, gang members, and gang related homicides increased—while overall violent crime was dropping sharply across the United States. Notwithstanding the long history of gang problems in this country and high odds of perpetual violence in most very large cities, effective programs and strategies are available that can significantly reduce the severity of gang violence.

It is no longer constructive for researchers, practitioners, and policymakers to argue about whether gang programs "work," as if that were a question that could be answered with a simple "yes" or "no." As a generality, some programs clearly work. We must get on with the business of developing and identifying the programs that will be most effective and providing these to jurisdictions with gang problems. Given that gangs are rooted in fissures within the social fabric of American society, one would be naive to expect large impacts. At least a dozen programs have shown evidence of effectiveness in reducing gang crime, and several non-gang programs have also shown good potential for preventing or reducing gang-related activity (Howell & Griffiths, 2016).

Hodgkinson and colleagues' (2009) systematic review of comprehensive gang programs suggests that the key features of effective programs are (1) case management (an intervention team), (2) community involvement in the planning and delivery of interventions, and (3) expertise sharing among involved agencies. The higher quality programs that produced positive effects included one or more of the following mechanisms of change:

- A case management strategy for service provision that was personalized to individual offenders;
- Community involvement in the planning and delivery of interventions;
- Expertise sharing between agencies;
- Provision of incentives to gang members to change their offending behavior, including educational opportunities, tattoo removal, and financial assistance (pp. 2–3).

One of the effective programs identified in Hodgkinson and colleagues rigorous review is the Comprehensive Gang Prevention, Intervention, and Suppression Model (called the Comprehensive Gang Program Model, or CGPM, for short) that has demonstrated effectiveness in several cities. In 1992, a fuller version of the CGPM was implemented in the Little Village neighborhood of Chicago. This program targeted more than two hundred of the most active members and influential leaders of two particularly violent gangs. The project produced reductions in serious violence (homicide, aggravated assault, aggravated battery, and robbery), reductions in property crimes, and reductions in the frequency of various types of offenses including robbery, gang intimidations, and drive-by shootings (Spergel, 2007). In the mid-1990s, additional cities that implemented the CGPM demonstrated evidence of effectiveness, including Los Angeles and Riverside, California, and Mesa, Arizona (Cahill & Hayeslip, 2010; Spergel, Wa, & Sosa, 2006). In Chicago, Riverside, and Mesa, there were statistically significant reductions in gang violence, and in two of these sites, there were statistically significant reductions in drug-related offenses when compared with the control groups of youth and neighborhoods. Gang programs are no exception to the rule that is firmly established for all treatment programs: outcomes vary from one site to another, even with the same intervention (Lipsey & Cullen, 2007).

The CGPM is a *program structure*, an organizational framework that guides users through a systematic data gathering, analysis, and strategic planning process, and supports an organized community initiative that becomes a permanent component of local governance. Thus, successful implementation depends on community stakeholders' (1) acknowledgment that they possibly or actually have a gang problem and (2) a willingness to work together in solving it. A more formal organizational framework will be needed to execute a long-term plan to control and dissolve institutionalized gangs that have transformed themselves into sophisticated criminal enterprises, in particular, within very large cities that have multiple such gangs. The first step is a systematic and thorough gang problem assessment, a foundation for long-term strategies that engage all sectors of the community or city.

Wyrick (2006) organizes the CGPM continuum in four levels. *Primary prevention* (also called *universal* prevention) targets the entire population (all youth and families and other members) in communities. A key resource might be a one-stop community center that makes services accessible and visible to the entire community, including prenatal and infant care, after-school activities, truancy and dropout prevention, and job training programs. *Secondary prevention* identifies young children (ages seven to fourteen) at high risk and—drawing on the resources of schools, community-based organizations, and faith-based groups—intervenes with appropriate services before early problem behaviors turn into serious delinquency and gang involvement. *Intervention* targets active gang members and their close associates, and involves establishing an intervention team that provides case management coupled with intensive outreach services. Support services for gang-involved youth and their families help youth make positive choices. *Suppression* focuses on identifying the most dangerous gangs and weakens them by removing the most criminally active and influential gang members from gangs and from the community. (For evidence-based programs that should be considered in building a full continuum, see Howell & Griffiths, 2016.) Prevention and intervention before a pattern of violence continues or retaliation occurs is sure to be the most cost effective.

Several prevention strategies fit nicely with the public health model, that is, insulating youth from risk factors and increasing protective factors in multiple developmental domains of youths' lives (Simon, Ritter, & Mahendra, 2013). A practical school-based anti-gang curriculum, Gang Resistance Education and Training (GREAT), is tailored to elementary and middle school students and taught by uniformed law enforcement officers in thirteen classroom sessions. GREAT has proven effective (Esbensen, Osgood, Peterson, et al., 2013; Esbensen, Peterson, Taylor, et al., 2012). In a four-year follow-up period, GREAT reduced the odds of gang joining among racially/ethnically diverse groups of youth by 24 percent across thirty-one schools in seven cities. This program produces large cost-benefits because schools are not required to remunerate school resource officers (the classroom instructers) who typically would be on school premises in the absence of GREAT. Thus, from a practical viewpoint, the GREAT curriculum has very high transportability potential. In addition to many U.S. school systems over the past decade, the GREAT program has been implemented successfully within schools in El Salvador, Guatemala, Nicaragua, Costa Rica, Panama, Belize, and Honduras. There is much to be said for very early prevention that reaches children in elementary school because most youth who join gangs do so between the ages eleven and fifteen, with ages fourteen to sixteen the peak for gang involvement (Howell & Griffiths, 2016).

The effectiveness of the CGPM can be enhanced with the integration of it with juvenile and criminal justice agencies. Intervention Teams deployed in the CGPM provide a natural interface. Selection criteria for Intervention Team clients should always include documented gang membership. Intervention Teams should be able to rely on juvenile and criminal justice systems to control and rehabilitate gang members. Juvenile justice system offender management tools are more refined than those used in the adult system. Seven administrative tools empower juvenile justice systems to protect the public with graduated sanctions and reduce recidivism with evidence-based services (Howell, Lipsey, & Wilson, 2014). First, valid risk assessment instruments can sort offenders into distinguishable risk categories for assignment to supervision levels to protect the public and themselves. Second, comprehensive assessments of treatment needs guide the selection of services most likely to reduce recidivism. These assessments should identify and prioritize services to address circumstances that contribute to delinquency in the developmentally relevant family, school, peer, individual, and/or community domains. Third, graduated assessments (increasingly in-depth) will be required for some offenders, particularly those with substance abuse and mental health problems, to obtain a more accurate assessment of presenting problems. Fourth, disposition matrices serve the dual goals of assigning offenders to appropriate supervision levels to protect the public and also facilitate matching offenders with developmentally appropriate services at the respective supervision levels. Fifth, comprehensive case plans integrate supervision strategies with treatment services. Sixth, quality assurance procedures must be established to ensure that case management plans are implemented with fidelity. Seventh, a management information system is needed to track clients and service delivery, and evaluate outcomes. Juvenile justice risk assessment tools should include gang involvement as a predictor of recidivism, and juvenile justice treatment need assessment instruments should screen for gang associations. These best practices should be promulgated widely.

It also is important to target gangs with violence reduction strategies. Cure Violence approaches gang homicide as a social disease in applying the public health model. Its program director, Dr. Gary Slutkin, Executive Director and Professor of Epidemiology and International Health at the University of Illinois at Chicago, explains, "Violence behaves like an infectious disease—one fight leads to another; one killing leads to another. In order to reverse the epidemic, we need to interrupt transmission, identify and re-direct those at highest risk, and change behavioral norms" (quoted in Haegerich,

Mercy, & Weiss, 2013, p. 41). Cure Violence focuses on street-level outreach, conflict mediation, and changing community norms to reduce violence, particularly shootings. The program relies on highly trained "violence interrupters" (mostly former gang members) who work alone or in pairs mediating conflicts between gangs and high-risk individuals on the streets and in hospital emergency rooms. With reality therapy, they interject themselves into on-the-spot decision making by individuals at risk of shooting others, helping potential shooters weigh the likely long-term negative outcomes such as lifetime imprisonment against perceived short-term gains. Long-term change agents (outreach workers) serve as positive role models for young people, steering them to resources such as jobs or educational training and needed services. Cure Violence first proved effective in Chicago, and has been replicated in six Illinois cities outside Chicago, and in neighborhoods in Baltimore, Maryland; Kansas City, Missouri; New Orleans, Louisiana; New York City and other neighborhoods in New York; Philadelphia, Pennsylvania; and Puerto Rico (Howell & Young, 2013).

The Group Violence Reduction Strategy (VRS), targeted selected Chicago gang factions or sets using a focused-deterrence strategy. This unique strategy set out to change the street dynamics among certain gangs in Chicago that were involved in ongoing conflicts (Papachristos, Wildeman, & Roberto, 2015). Altogether, 18 call-ins were strategically organized, targeting 149 gang factions and 438 individual gang members who were affiliated with gang factions currently involved in shootings—either as victims or offenders. The strategy balanced services with punitive sanctions. Representatives from local, state, and federal law enforcement explained how their respective agencies might be deployed against the various factions in the event of the next shooting. The services consisted of a range of health, mental health, housing, drug treatment, education and employment services, all of which were made available free of charge to those who participated in community call-ins. The program evaluation showed that those gang factions whose members attended a VRS call-in experienced a 23 percent reduction in overall shooting behavior and a 32 percent reduction in gunshot victimization in the year following treatment as compared to equivalent factions involved in similar disputes (Papachristos & Kirk, in press).

Operation Ceasefire is a police problem-oriented deterrence project that instituted a zero-tolerance policy for any law-breaking activity on the part of identified individuals, with the aim of reducing homicide. In Boston, high-rate violent offenders with histories of gang-related crimes (identified through a review of police arrest records in a problem analysis) were rounded up and notified in a community meeting that they were subject to long prison sentences for any subsequent law, probation, or parole violations. Successful subsequent convictions of continuing offenders drew long federal sentences that were widely publicized in the community to deter others. In various

Ceasefire sites, a menu of "sticks" (a range of federal sanctions) and "carrots" (job training and development, substance abuse treatment, and tattoo removal) were offered to offenders (Braga & Hureau, 2012). A large reduction in the annual number of youth homicides was reported in Boston and significant decreases were noted in other cities, including Indianapolis, Indiana; Los Angeles, California; Lowell, Massachusetts; Cincinnati, Ohio; and Stockton, California (Braga & Weisburd, 2012).

Helping adolescent gang members desist from gang activity also is a viable yet challenging strategy, particularly in chronic gang problem cities. Homeboy Industries (HBI) serves high-risk, active gang-involved men and women in the Boyle Heights area of East Los Angeles (the birthplace of the City's gangs) with a continuum of free services and programs, and HBI also operates several economic enterprises that serve as job-training sites, including the Homeboy Bakery, Homeboy Diner, and a Homegirl Cafe. Evaluation findings suggest that participation in HBI appears to lead to a significant decrease in criminal activity (Leap, Franke, Christie, & Bonis, 2010). Four services were strongly associated with positive outcomes on several HBI client goals: (1) alcohol and drug rehabilitation, (2) anger management and domestic violence, (3) mental health services, and (4) tattoo removal. From the viewpoints of youth who voluntarily came to HBI for help in getting out of gang life and succeeded in making this transition, five key services were deemed most critical to their success: (1) ending gang-banging and replacing it with positive activities, including jobs; (2), establishing a new identity; (3) improved parenting and family relationships; (4) overcoming drug and alcohol addiction; and (5) establishing plans for a future. In the viewpoint of HBI's founder, Father Greg Boyle (2011), addressing trauma, mental illness, and hopelessness with services and employment are critical to individuals' success in changing their life-course. The program's mantra is "Nothing stops a bullet like a job."

But few career-track jobs are presently available in the United States for disconnected adolescents between sixteen and twenty-four years of age, many of whom are not in school and chronically out of work, and involved in street gangs (Patterson, 2015). Street schooling of children for gang careers begins much earlier, in "distressed" communities wherein extremely harmful conditions such as severe, chronic abuse are repetitive and/or prolonged. Over the long term, such conditions can be physiologically "toxic" for children; that is, compromise their capacity to cope (Rivara, 2012). In particular, those who experience toxic stress "are the children who grow up in poverty, live in dangerous neighborhoods, are exposed to violence both inside and outside the home, and face personal and familial substance abuse and a peer group of similarly associated individuals" (p. 160). A continuum of cradle-to-career supports, including developmentally appropriate family and child social services, high quality education, and gang awareness training, can buffer children from toxic conditions and reduce gang joining and gang crime over the long term (Howell & Camacho, 2015). Gang interventions can be most effective if they provide youth with means of building social capital, such as employment, and improved relationships with their families, prosocial peer networks, school officials, and community leaders.

References

Adamson, C. (1998). Tribute, turf, honor and the American street gang: Patterns of continuity and change since 1820. *Theoretical Criminology*, 2, 57–84.

Adamson, C. (2000). Defensive localism in White and Black: A comparative history of European-American and African-American youth gangs. *Ethnic and Racial Studies*, 23, 272–298.

Alexander, M. (2011). *The new Jim Crow: Mass incarceration in an age of colorblindness* (rev. ed.). New York: New Press.

Allender, D. M., & Marcell, F. (2003). Career criminals, security threat groups, and prison gangs. *FBI Law Enforcement Bulletin*, June, 8–12.

Alonso, A. A. (2004). Racialized identities and the formation of Black gangs in Los Angeles. *Urban Geography*, 25, 658–674.

Alonso, A. A. (2013). Black street gangs in Los Angeles: A history. In Alonso, A. A., *Territoriality among African-American street gangs in Los Angeles*. Los Angeles: University of Southern California. Streetgangs.com, Black Street Gangs. Accessed October 22, 2014, http://www.streetgangs.com/crips/Blackstreetgangs.

American Society of Criminology National Policy Committee. (2001). The use of incarceration in the United States. *The Criminologist*, 26(3), 14–16.

Amnesty International. (1992). *United States of America: Torture, Ill Treatment and Excessive Force by Police in Los Angeles, California*. New York: Author.

Anbinder, T. (2001). *Five Points*. New York: Free Press.

Anderson, E. (1999). *Code of the street: Decency, violence, and the moral life of the inner city*. New York: W. W. Norton.

Arredondo, G. F. (2004). Navigating ethno-racial currents: Mexicans in Chicago, 1919–1939. *Journal of Urban History*, 30, 399–427.

Arredondo, G. F. (2008). *Mexican Chicago: Race, identity, and nation, 1916–39*. Chicago: University of Illinois Press.

Asbury, H. (1927). *Gangs of New York: An informal history of the underworld*. New York: Knopf.

Atlanta Public Housing Authority. (2010). *Atlanta Housing Authority 15 year progress report: 1995–2010*. Atlanta: Atlanta Public Housing Authority.

Ayling, J. (2011). Gang change and evolutionary theory. *Criminal Law and Social Change*, 56, 1–26.

Baer, D., Bhati, A., Brooks, L., Castro, J., La Vigne, N., & et al. (2006). *Understanding the challenges of prisoner reentry*. Washington, DC: Urban Institute.

Bankston, C. L. (1998). Youth gangs and the new second generation: A review essay. *Aggression and Violent Behavior*, 3, 33–45.

Barker, T. Ed. (2012). *North American criminal gangs.* Durham, NC: Carolina Academic Press.

Beaird, L. H. (1986). Prison gangs: Texas. *Corrections Today,* July, pp. 12, 18, 22.

Beckett, K., & Sasson, T. (2003). *The politics of injustice: Crime and punishment in America.* Thousand Oaks, CA: Sage.

Bell, J., & Lim, N. (2005). Young once, Indian forever: Youth gangs in Indian Country. *The American Indian Quarterly,* 29, 626–650.

Berdie, R. F. (1947). Playing the dozens. *The Journal of Abnormal and Social Psychology,* 42, 120–121.

Berkin, C., Miller, C., & Cherney, R. W. (2011). *Making America: A history of the United States* (6th ed.). Boston: Wadsworth.

Bjerregaard, B. (2010). Gang membership and drug involvement: Untangling the complex relationship. *Crime and Delinquency,* 56, 3–34.

Bjerregaard, B., & Lizotte, A. J. (1995). Gun ownership and gang membership. *Journal of Criminal Law and Criminology,* 86, 37–58.

Block, C. R., & Block, R. (1993). Street gang crime in Chicago. *Research in Brief.* Washington, DC: U.S. Department of Justice, National Institute of Justice.

Block, C. R., Christakos, A., Jacob, A., & Przybylski, R. (1996). *Street gangs and crime: Patterns and trends in Chicago.* Chicago: Illinois Criminal Justice Information Authority.

Block, R. (2000). Gang activity and overall levels of crime: A new mapping tool for defining areas of gang activity using police records. *Journal of Quantitative Criminology,* 16, 369–383.

Blumstein, A. (2000). Disaggregating the Violence Trends. In A. Blumstein & J. Wallman (Eds.) *The Crime Drop in America* (pp. 13–41). Cambridge , UK: Cambridge University Press.

Blumstein, A. (1995a). Violence by young people: Why the deadly nexus? *National Institute of Justice Journal*(August), 1–9.

Blumstein, A. (1995b). Youth violence, guns, and the illicit-drug industry. *Journal of Criminal Law and Criminology,* 86, 10–36.

Blumstein, A., & Beck, A. (1999). Population growth in U.S. prisons, 1980–1996. In M. Tonry & J. Petersilia (Eds.), *Crime and justice: A review of research* (vol. 26, pp. 17–61). Chicago: University of Chicago Press.

Blumstein, A., & Rosenfeld, R. (1999). Trends in rates of violence in the U.S.A. *Studies on Crime and Prevention,* 8, 139–167.

Boskin, J. (1969). The revolt of the urban ghettos: 1964–1967. *The Annals of the American Academy of Political and Social Science,* 382, 1–14.

Boskin, J. (1976). *Urban racial violence in the twentieth century.* Boston: Glencoe-Macmillan.

Bourgois, P. (2003). *In search of respect: Selling crack in El Barrio* (2nd ed.). New York: Cambridge University Press.

Bowker, L. H. (Ed.). (1978). *Women, crime and the criminal justice system.* Lexington, MA: Lexington Books.

Boyle, G. (2011). *Tattoos on the heart: The power of boundless compassion.* New York: Free Press.

Braga, A. A., & Hureau, D. M. (2012). Strategic problem analysis to guide comprehensive gang violence reduction strategies. In E. Gebo & B. J. Bond (Eds.), *Beyond suppression: Community strategies to reduce gang violence* (pp. 129–151). Lanham, MD: Lexington Books.

Braga, A. A., & Weisburd, D. L. (2012). The effects of focused deterrence strategies on crime: A systematic review and meta-analysis of the empirical evidence. *Journal of Research in Crime and Delinquency,* 49, 323–358.

Brantingham, P. J., Tita, G. E., Short, M. B., & Reid, S. (2012). The ecology of gang territorial boundaries. *Criminology,* 50, 851–885.

Bratich, J. Z. (2004). Trust no one (on the Internet): The CIA-crack-contra conspiracy theory and professional journalism. *Television & New Media,* 5, 109–139.

Brown, W. K. (1977). Black female gangs in Philadelphia. *International Journal of Offender Therapy and Comparative Criminology,* 21, 221–228.

Brownstein, H. (1996). *The rise and fall of a violent crime wave: Crack cocaine and the social construction of a crime problem.* Guilderland, NY: Harrow and Heston.

Bryant, D. (1989). Communitywide responses crucial for dealing with youth gangs. *Juvenile Justice Bulletin.* Washington, DC: U.S. Department of Justice, Office of Juvenile Justice and Delinquency Prevention.

Buentello, S., Fong, R. S., & Vogel, R. E. (1991). Prison gang development: A theoretical model. *The Prison Journal*, 71, 3–14.

Burton, F., & West, B. (2009). *When the Mexican drug trade hits the border.* Stratfor Global Intelligence. Accessed July 16, 2014, http://www.stratfor.com/weekly/20090415_when_mexican_drug_trade_hits_border.

Cahill, M., & Hayeslip, D. (2010). *Findings from the Evaluation of OJJDP's Gang Reduction Program* (Juvenile Justice Bulletin). Washington, DC: U.S. Department of Justice, Office of Juvenile Justice and Delinquency Prevention.

California Council on Criminal Justice. (1989). *Task force report on gangs and drugs.* Sacramento: California Council on Criminal Justice.

California Department of Corrections and Rehabilitation. (2012). *Security threat group prevention, identification and management strategy.* Sacramento: California Department of Corrections and Rehabilitation.

Camp, C. G., & Camp, G. M. (1988). *Management strategies for combating prison gang violence.* South Salem, NY: Criminal Justice Institute.

Camp, G. M, & C. G. Camp (Eds.). (1985). *Prison gangs: Their extent, nature and impact on prisons.* Washington, DC: U.S. Department of Justice.

Campa, A. (1993). *Hispanic culture in the Southwest.* Norman: University of Oklahoma Press.

Campbell, A. (1984/1991). *The girls in the gang: A report from New York City.* New York: Basil Blackwell.

Carson, E. A., & Golinelli, D. (2013). Prisoners in 2012: Trends in admissions and releases, 1991–2012. *Bulletin.* Washington, DC: U.S. Department of Justice, Bureau of Justice Statistics.

Carson, E. A., & Sabol, W. J. (2012). Prisoners in 2011. *Bulletin.* Washington, DC: U.S. Department of Justice, Bureau of Justice Statistics.

Castells, M. (1983). *From city to grassroots.* Berkeley: University of California Press.

Caudill, J. W. (2010). Back on the swagger: Institutional release and recidivism timing among gang affiliates. *Youth Violence and Juvenile Justice*, 8, 58–70.

Centers for Disease Control. (2012, January 27). Gang homicides—Five U.S. cities, 2003–2008, *Morbidity and Mortality Weekly Report*, 61(3), 46–51.

Chesney-Lind, M. (2013). How can we prevent girls from joining gangs? In T.R. Simon, N.M. Ritter, & R.R. Mahendra (Eds.). *Changing Course: Preventing Gang Membership* (pp. 121–133). Washington, DC: U.S. Department of Justice, U.S. Department of Health and Human Services.

Chicago Commission on Race Relations. (1922). *The Negro in Chicago: A study of race relations and a race riot.* Chicago: University of Chicago Press.

Chicago Crime Commission. (1995). *Gangs: Public enemy number one, 75 years of fighting crime in Chicagoland.* Chicago: Author.

Chicago Crime Commission. (2006). *The Chicago Crime Commission gang book.* Chicago: Author.

Chicago Police Department. (2012). *Murder analysis in Chicago: 2011.* Chicago: Author.

Chin, K. (2000). *Chinatown gangs: Extortion, enterprise and ethnicity.* New York: Oxford University Press.

Clark, C. S. (1991). Youth gangs. *Congressional Quarterly Research*, 22, 755–771.

CNN Library. Cable News Network. *Los Angeles riots fast facts.* Accessed May 3, 2014, http://www.cnn.com/2013/09/18/us/los-angeles-riots-fast-facts/.

Cockburn, A., & St. Clair, J. (1998). *Whiteout: The CIA, drugs and the press.* London: Verso.

Cohen, J., & Tita, G. E. (1999). Spatial diffusion in homicide: Exploring a general method of detecting spatial diffusion processes. *Journal of Quantitative Criminology*, 15, 451–493.

Coid, J. W., Ullrich, S., Keers, R., Bebbington, P., & DeStavola, B. L. (2013). Gang membership, violence, and psychiatric morbidity. *American Journal of Psychiatry*, 170, 985–993.

Cook, P. J., & Ludwig, J. (2006). The social costs of gun ownership. *Journal of Public Economics*, 90, 379–391.

Cork, D. (1999). Examining space-time interaction in city-level homicide data: Crack markets and the diffusion of guns among youth. *Journal of Quantitative Criminology*, 15, 379–406.

Coughlin, B. C., & Venkatesh, S. A. (2003). The urban street gang after 1970. *Annual Review of Sociology*, 29, 41–64.

Craig, W. M., Vitaro, F., Gagnon, C., & Tremblay, R. E. (2002). The road to gang membership: Characteristics of male gang and non-gang members from ages 10 to 14. *Social Development*, 11, 53–68.

Cruz, J. M. (2014). *Maras* and the politics of violence in El Salvador. In J. M. Hazen & D. Rodgers (Eds.), *Global gangs: Street violence across the world* (pp. 123–146). Minneapolis: University of Minnesota Press.

Cureton, S. R. (2002). Introducing Hoover: I'll ride for you, Gangsta'. In C. R. Huff (Ed.), *Gangs in America III* (pp. 83–100). Thousand Oaks, CA: Sage.

Cureton, S. R. (2008). *Hoover Gangster Crips: When Cripin' becomes a way of life*. Lanham, MD: University Press of America.

Cureton, S. R. (2009). Something wicked this way comes: A historical account of Black gangsterism offers wisdom and warning for African American leadership. *Journal of Black Studies*, 40, 347–361.

Curry, G. D., Decker, S. H., & Pyrooz, D. C. (2014). *Confronting gangs: Crime and community* (3rd ed.). Los Angeles: Roxbury.

Curtis, R. (2003). The negligible role of gangs in drug distribution in New York City in the 1990s. In L. Kontos, D. Brotherton, & L. Barrios (Eds.), *Gangs and society: Alternative perspectives* (pp. 41–61). New York: Columbia University Press.

Dade County State Attorney. (1985, May 11). *Dade County gangs: 1984*. Final report of the Grand Jury, Circuit Court of the Eleventh Judicial Circuit of Florida in and for the County of Dade. Miami, FL: Dade County District Attorney.

Dade County State Attorney. (1988). *Dade County gangs: 1987*. Final report of the Grand Jury, Circuit Court of the Eleventh Judicial Circuit of Florida in and for the County of Dade. Miami, FL: Dade County District Attorney, May 11.

Davis, A. F., & Haller, M. H. (1973). *The people of Philadelphia: A history of ethnic groups and lower-class life, 1790–1940*. Philadelphia: Temple University Press.

Davis, M. (2006). *City of quartz: Excavating the future in Los Angeles* (2nd ed.). New York: Verso.

Dawley, D. (1992). *A nation of Lords: The autobiography of the Vice Lords* (2nd ed.). Prospect Heights, IL: Waveland.

Debarbieux, E., & Baya, C. (2008). An interactive construction of gangs and ethnicity: The role of school segregation in France. In F. van Gemert, D. Peterson, & I.-L. Lien (Eds.), *Street gangs, migration and ethnicity* (pp. 211–226). Portland, OR: Willan Publishing.

Decker, S. H. (1996). Deviant homicide: A new look at the role of motives and victim-offender relationships. *Journal of Research in Crime and Delinquency*, 33, 427–449.

Decker, S. H. (2007). Youth gangs and violent behavior. In D. J. Flannery, A. T. Vazsonyi, & I. D. Waldman (Eds.), *The Cambridge handbook of violent behavior and aggression* (pp. 388–402). Cambridge: Cambridge University Press.

Decker, S. H., Bynum, T., & Weisel, D. L. (1998). Gangs as organized crime groups: A tale of two cities. *Justice Quarterly*, 15, 395–423.

Decker, S. H., Katz, C. M., & Webb, V. J. (2008). Understanding the black box of gang organization: Implications for involvement in violent crime, drug sales, and violent victimization. *Crime and Delinquency*, 54, 153–172.

Decker, S. H., & Pyrooz, D. C. (2010). On the validity and reliability of gang homicide: A comparison of disparate sources. *Homicide Studies*, 14, 359–376.

Decker, S. H., & Van Winkle, B. (1996). *Life in the gang: Family, friends, and violence.* New York: Cambridge University Press.

De Genova, N. (2008). "American" abjection: "Chicanos," gangs and Mexican/migrant transnationality in Chicago. *Aztlán: A Journal of Chicano Studies*, 33, 141–174.

De León, A. (2001). *Ethnicity in the Sunbelt: Mexican-Americans in Houston.* Houston, TX: University of Houston Series in Mexican-American Studies.

Deutsch, L. (2000). Los Angeles police officer gets five years. *USA Today*, p. 6.

Diamond, A. J. (2001). Rethinking culture on the streets: Agency, masculinity, and style in the American city. *Journal of Urban History*, 27, 669–685.

Diamond, A. J. (2009). *Mean streets: Chicago youths and the everyday struggle for empowerment in the multiracial city, 1908–1969.* Berkeley: University of California Press.

Dinnerstein, L., & Reimers, D. M., (2009). *Ethnic Americans: A history of immigration.* New York: Columbia University Press.

Dmitrieva, J., Gibson, L., Steinberg, L., Piquero, A., & Fagan, J. (2014). Predictors and consequences of gang membership: Comparing gang members, gang leaders, and non-gang-affiliated adjudicated youth. *Journal of Research on Adolescence*, 24, 220–234.

Dooley, B., Seals, A., & Skarbek, D. (2014). The effect of prison gang membership on recidivism. *Journal of Criminal Justice*, 42, 267–275.

Drucker, E. (2011). *A Plague of prisons: The epidemiology of mass incarceration in America.* New York: New Press.

Drug Enforcement Administration. (1988). Crack cocaine availability and trafficking in the United States. *Bulletin*. Washington, DC: Author.

Drury, A. J., & DeLisi, M. (2011). An exploratory empirical assessment of gang membership, homicide offending, and prison misconduct. *Crime and Delinquency*, 57, 130–146.

Durán, R. J. (2008). Overview of project. *Southern New Mexico/Texas Gang Update*, 1, 1–2.

Durán, R. J. (2009). The core ideals of the Mexican American gang: Living the presentation of defiance. *Aztlán: A Journal of Chicano Studies*, 34, 99–134.

Durán, R. J. (2012). *Gang life in two cities: An insider's journey.* New York: Columbia University Press.

Durose, M. R., Cooper, A. D., & Snyder, H. D. (2014). *Recidivism of prisoners released in 30 states in 2005: Patterns from 2005 to 2010.* Special Report. Washington, DC: U.S. Department of Justice, Bureau of Justice Statistics.

Easton Gang Prevention Task Force. (2007). *222 corridor anti-gang initiatives.* Philadelphia: U.S. Attorney's Office, Eastern Pennsylvania District.

Eddy, P., Sabogal, H., & Walden, S. (1988). *The cocaine wars.* New York: W.W. Norton.

Egley, A., Jr. (2005). *Highlights of the 2002–2003 National Youth Gang Surveys.* OJJDP Fact Sheet (No. 2005–01). Washington, DC: U.S. Department of Justice, Office of Juvenile Justice and Delinquency Prevention.

Egley, A., Jr., & Howell, J. C. (2010). *Gang activity, subgroups, and crime.* Paper presented at the annual meeting of the American Society of Criminology, San Francisco, November.

Egley, A., Jr., & Howell, J. C. (2011). *Highlights of the 2009 National Youth Gang Survey.* Washington, DC: Office of Juvenile Justice and Delinquency Prevention.

Egley, A., Jr. & Howell, J. C. (2013). *Highlights of the 2011 National Youth Gang Survey.* *OJJDP Fact Sheet* (September). Washington, DC: Office of Juvenile Justice and Delinquency Prevention.

Egley, A., Jr., Howell, J. C., & Harris, M. (2014). *Highlights of the 2012 National Youth Gang Survey.* OJJDP Fact Sheet. Washington, DC: Office of Juvenile Justice and Delinquency Prevention.

Egley, A., Jr., Howell, J. C., & Major, A. K. (2006). *National Youth Gang Survey: 1999–2001.* Washington, DC: U.S. Department of Justice, Office of Juvenile Justice and Delinquency Prevention.

Esbensen, F., Brick, B. T., Melde, C., Tusinski, K., & Taylor, T. J. (2008). The role of race and ethnicity in gang membership. In F. V. Genert, D. Peterson, & I. Lien (Eds.), *Street gangs, migration and ethnicity* (pp. 117–139). Portland, OR: Willan.

Esbensen, F., Osgood, D. W., Peterson, D., Taylor, T. J., & Carson, D. C. (2013). Short and long term outcome results from a multi-site evaluation of the G.R.E.A.T. program. *Criminology & Public Policy*, 12, 375–411.

Esbensen, F., Peterson, D., Taylor, T. J., & Freng, A. (2010). *Youth violence: Sex and race differences in offending, victimization, and gang membership.* Philadelphia: Temple University Press.

Esbensen, F., Peterson, D., Taylor, & Osgood, D. W. (2012). Results from a multi-site evaluation of the G.R.E.A.T. Program. *Justice Quarterly*, 29, 125–151.

Esbensen, F., Winfree, L. T., He, N., & Taylor, T. J. (2001). Youth Gangs and Definitional Issues: When is a Gang a Gang, and Why Does it Matter? *Crime and Delinquency*, 47, 105–130.

Falk, W. W., Hunt, L. L., & Hunt, M. O. (2004). Return migrations of African-Americans to the South: Reclaiming a land of promise, going home, or both? *Rural Sociology*, 69, 490–509.

Federal Bureau of Investigation. (2009). *National gang threat assessment*. Washington, DC: Author.

Federal Bureau of Investigation. (2011). *National gang threat assessment: Emerging trends*. Washington, DC: Author.

Finestone, H. (1976). *Victims of change.* Westport, CT: Greenwood.

Fleisher, M. S. (1989). *Warehousing violence*. Newbury Park, CA: Sage.

Fleisher, M. S. (1995). *Beggars and thieves: Lives of urban street criminals.* Madison: University of Wisconsin Press.

Fleisher, M. S., & Decker, S. (2001). An overview of the challenge of prison gangs. *Corrections Management Quarterly*, 5, 1–9.

Florida Office of the Inspector General. (2013). *Annual Report: Fiscal Year 2011–2012*. Florida Department of Correction Tallahassee: Florida Department of Correction Security Threat Intelligence Unit.

Fong, R. S. (1990). The organizational structure of prison gangs: A Texas case study. *Federal Probation*, 54, 36–43.

Fong, R. S, & Buentello, S. (1991). The detection of prison gang development: An empirical assessment. *Federal Probation*, 60, 66–69.

Franco, C. (2010). *The MS-13 and 18th Street Gangs: Emerging Transnational Gang Threats?* (CRS Report RL34233, updated January 22, 2010). Washington, DC: Congressional Research Service, Library of Congress.

Fuentes, N. (2006). *The rise and fall of the Nuestra Familia*. Jefferson, WI: Know Gangs Publishing.

Gaes, G., Wallace, S., Gilman, E., Klein-Saffran, J., & Suppa, S. (2002). The influence of prison gang affiliation on violence and other prison misconduct. *The Prison Journal*, 82, 359–385.

Gannon, T. M. (1967). Dimensions of current gang delinquency. *Journal of Research in Crime and Delinquency*, 4, 119–131.

Garcia, J. R. (1996). *Mexicans in the Midwest: 1900–1932*. Tucson: University of Arizona Press.

Geis, G. (1965). *Juvenile gangs: Report to the President's Committee on Juvenile Delinquency and Youth Crime*. Washington, DC: U.S. Government Printing Office.

Gilfoyle, T. J. (2003). Scorsese's Gangs of New York: Why myth matters. *Journal of Urban History*, 29, 620–630.

Gilman, A. B., Hill, K. G., Hawkins, J. D., Howell, J. C., & Kosterman, R. (2014). The developmental dynamics of joining a gang in adolescence: Patterns and predictors of gang membership. *Journal of Research on Adolescence, 24*, 204–219.

Glaze, L. E., & Parks, E. (2012). *Correctional populations in the United States, 2011*. Washington, DC: U.S. Department of Justice, Bureau of Justice Statistics.

Goldstein, A. P., & Glick, B. (1994). *The prosocial gang: Implementing Aggression Replacement Training*. Thousand Oaks, CA: Sage.

Golub, A., & Johnson, B. D. (1997). Crack's decline: Some surprises among U.S. cities. *Research in Brief.* Washington, DC: National Institute of Justice.

Gordon, R. A., Rowe, H. L., Pardini, D., Loeber, R., White, H. R., & Farrington, D. (2014). Serious delinquency and gang participation: Combining and specializing in drug selling, theft and violence. *Journal of Research on Adolescence*, 24, 235–251.

Greene, J. A. (1999). Zero tolerance: A case study of police policies and practices in New York City. *Crime and Delinquency*, 45, 171–187.

Greene, J. A., & Pranis, K. (2007). *Gang wars: The failure of enforcement tactics and the need for effective public safety strategies.* Washington, DC: Justice Policy Institute.

Griffin, M. L., & Hepburn, J. R. (2006). The effect of gang affiliation on violent misconduct among inmates during the early years of confinement. *Criminal Justice and Behavior, 33,* 419–448.

Griffiths, E., & Chavez, J. M. (2004). Communities, street guns and homicide trajectories in Chicago, 1980–1995: Merging methods for examining homicide trends across space and time. *Criminology, 42,* 941–77.

Grogger, J., & Willis, M. (1998). *The introduction of crack cocaine and the rise in urban crime rates.* National Bureau of Economic Research Working Paper No. W6353. Cambridge, MA: National Bureau of Economic Research.

Gugliotta, G., & Leen, J. (1989). *Kings of cocaine.* New York: Simon & Schuster.

Haegerich, T. M., Mercy, J., & Weiss, B. (2013). What is the role of public health in gang membership prevention? In T. R. Simon, N. M. Ritter, & R. R. Mahendra (Eds.), *Changing course: Preventing gang membership* (pp. 31–49). Washington, DC: U.S. Department of Justice, U.S. Department of Health and Human Services.

Hagan, J. (1995). Rethinking crime and theory and policy: The new sociology of crime and disrepute. In H. D. Barlow (Ed.), *Crime and public policy* (pp. 317–339). Boulder, CO: Westview Press.

Hagan, J., & Foster, H. (2000). Making corporate and criminal America less violent: Public norms and structural reforms. *Contemporary Sociology, 29,* 44–53.

Hagedorn, J. M. (1988). *People and Folks: Gangs, crime and the underclass in a rustbelt city.* Chicago: Lakeview Press.

Hagedorn, J. M. (1998). Cocaine, kicks, and strain: Patterns of substance use in Milwaukee gangs. *Contemporary Drug Problems, 25,* 113–145.

Hagedorn, J. M. (2006). Race, not space: A revisionist history of gangs in Chicago. *Journal of African American History, 91,* 194–208.

Hagedorn, J. M. (2008). *A world of gangs: Armed young men and gangsta culture.* Minneapolis: University of Minnesota Press.

Hagedorn, J. M., & Rauch, B. (2007). Housing, gangs, and homicide: What we can learn from Chicago. *Urban Affairs Review, 42,* 435–456.

Hamilton, H.C. (1964). The Negro leaves the South. *Demography, 1,* 273–295.

Harrison, P. M., & Beck, A. J. (2006). Prisoners in 2005. *Bulletin.* Washington, DC: U.S. Department of Justice, Bureau of Justice Statistics.

Hartman, D. A., & Golub, A. (1999). The social construction of the crack epidemic in the print media. *Journal of Psychoactive Drugs, 31,* 423–433.

Haskins, J. (1974). *Street gangs: Yesterday and today.* Wayne, PA: Hastings Books.

Hawkins, D. (2011). Things fall apart: Revisiting race and ethnic differences in criminal violence amidst a crime drop. *Race and Justice, 1,* 3–48.

Hayeslip, D. W. Jr. (1989). Local-level drug enforcement: New strategies. *Research in Action* (No. 213). Washington, DC: U.S. Department of Justice, National Institute of Justice.

Hazen, J. M., & Rodgers, D. (Eds.). (2014). *Global gangs: Street violence across the world.* Minneapolis: University of Minnesota Press.

Hernandez, D. J., Denton, N. A., & Blanchard, V. L. (2011). Children in the United States of America: A statistical portrait by race-ethnicity, immigrant origins, and language. *The Annals of the American Academy of Political and Social Science, 633,* 102–127.

Hodgkinson J., Marshall, S., Berry, G., Reynolds, P., Newman, M., Burton, E., Dickson, K., & Anderson, J. (2009). *Reducing gang-related crime: A systematic review of "comprehensive" interventions. Summary report.* London: EPPI-Centre, Social Science Research Unit, Institute of Education, University of London.

Hong, J. S. (2010). Understanding Vietnamese youth gangs in America: An ecological systems analysis. *Aggression and Violent Behavior, 15,* 253–260.

Horowitz, R. (1983). Honor and the American dream: Culture and identity in a Chicano community. New Brunswick, NJ: Rutgers University Press.

Horowitz, R., & Schwartz, G. (1974). Honor, normative ambiguity, and gang violence. *American Sociological Review, 39,* 238–251.

Houston Intelligence Support Center. (2010). *Houston gang threat assessment.* Washington, DC: U.S. Office of National Drug Control Policy.

Houston Intelligence Support Center. (2011). *Houston HIDTA 2011 threat assessment.* Washington, DC: U.S. Office of National Drug Control Policy.

Howell, J. C. (1998). Youth gangs: An overview. *Juvenile Justice Bulletin.* Washington, DC: U.S. Department of Justice, Office of Juvenile Justice and Delinquency Prevention.

Howell, J. C. (1999). Youth gang homicides: A literature review. *Crime and Delinquency,* 45, 208–241.

Howell, J. C. (2003). *Preventing and reducing juvenile delinquency: A comprehensive framework.* Thousand Oaks, CA: Sage.

Howell, J. C. (2010). Gang Prevention: An Overview of Current Research and Programs. *Juvenile Justice Bulletin.* Washington, DC: U.S. Department of Justice, Office of Juvenile Justice and Delinquency Prevention.

Howell, J. C. (2012). *Gangs in America's communities.* Thousand Oaks, CA: Sage.

Howell, J. C. (2013a). GREAT results: Implications for PBIS in schools. *Criminology and Public Policy,* 12, 413–420.

Howell, J. C. (2013b). Why is gang membership prevention important? In T. R. Simon, N. M. Ritter, & R. R. Mahendra (Eds.), *Changing course: Preventing gang membership* (pp. 7–18). Washington, DC: U.S. Department of Justice, U.S. Department of Health and Human Services.

Howell, J. C., and Camacho, J. (2015). An early prevention and intervention continuum for gang involvement. Unpublished Report. Tallahassee, FL: National Gang Center.

Howell, J. C., & Decker, S. H. (1999). The youth gangs, drugs, and violence connection. *Juvenile Justice Bulletin.* Youth Gang Series. Washington, DC: U.S. Department of Justice, Office of Juvenile Justice and Delinquency Prevention.

Howell, J. C., Egley, A., Jr., & Gleason, D. K. (2002). Modern day youth gangs. *Juvenile Justice Bulletin. Youth Gang Series.* Washington, DC: U.S. Department of Justice, Office of Juvenile Justice and Delinquency Prevention.

Howell, J. C., Egley, A., Jr., Tita, G., & Griffiths, E. (2011). *U.S. gang problem trends and seriousness.* Tallahassee, FL: Institute for Intergovernmental Research, National Gang Center.

Howell, J. C., & Griffiths, E. (2016). *Gangs in America's communities* (2nd. ed.). Thousand Oaks, CA: Sage.

Howell, J. C., Lipsey, M. W., & Wilson, J. J. (2014). *A handbook for evidence-based juvenile justice systems.* Lanham, MD: Lexington Books.

Howell, J. C., & Moore, J. P. (2010). History of street gangs in the United States. *National Gang Center Bulletin No. 4.* Tallahassee, FL: Institute for Intergovernmental Research, National Gang Center.

Howell, J. C., & Young, M. A. (2013). What works to curb U.S. street gang violence? *The Criminologist,* 38, 39–43.

Howell, M. Q., & Lassiter, W. (2011). *Prevalence of gang-involved youth in NC.* Raleigh: North Carolina Department of Juvenile Justice and Delinquency Prevention.

Huebner, B. M. (2003). Administrative determinates of inmate violence. *Journal of Criminal Justice,* 31, 107–117.

Huebner, B. M., Varano, S. P., & Bynum, T. S. (2007). Gangs, guns, and drugs: Recidivism among serious, young offenders. *Criminology & Public Policy,* 6, 187–221.

Huff, C. R. (1989). Youth gangs and public policy. *Crime and Delinquency,* 35, 524–537.

Huff, C. R. (1993). Gangs in the United States. In A. Goldstein & C. R. Huff (Eds.), *The gang intervention handbook* (pp. 3–20). Champaign, IL: Research Press.

Huff, C. R. (2007). Gangs In R. Sisson, C. Zacher, & A. Cayton (Eds.), *The American Midwest* (pp. 1242–1243). Bloomington: Indiana University Press.

Hughes, L. A., & Short, J. F. (2005). Disputes involving gang members: Micro-social contexts. *Criminology,* 43, 43–76.

Hughes, L. A., & Short, J. F. (2006). Youth gangs and unions: Civil and criminal remedies. *Trends in Organized Crime,* 9, 43–59.

Hutchison, R. (1993). Blazon nouveau: Gang graffiti in the barrios of Los Angeles and Chicago. In S. Cummings & D. J. Monti (Eds.), *Gangs* (pp. 137–171). Albany: State University of New York Press.

Hutson, H. R., Anglin, D., & Eckstein, M. (1996). Drive-by shootings by violent street gangs in Los Angeles: A five-year review from 1989 to 1993. *Academic Emergency Medicine, 3,* 300–303.

Hutson, H. R., Anglin, D., Kyriacou, D. N., Hart, J., & Spears, K. (1995). The epidemic of gang-related homicides in Los Angeles County from 1979 through 1994. *Journal of the American Medical Association, 274,* 1031–1036.

Hutson, H. R., Anglin, D., Mallon, W., & Pratts, M. J. (1994). Caught in the crossfire of gang violence: Small children as innocent victims of drive-by shootings. *Journal of Emergency Medicine, 12,* 385–338.

Irwin, J. (1980). *Prisons in turmoil.* Boston: Little, Brown and Co.

Jacobs, J. B. (1974). Street gangs behind bars. *Social Problems, 21,* 395–409.

Jacobs, J. B. (1977). *Stateville: The penitentiary in mass society.* Chicago: University of Chicago Press.

Jacobs, J. B. (2001). Focusing on prison gangs. *Corrections Management Quarterly, 5,* vi–vii.

Jimenez, T. R. (2011). *Immigrants into the United States: How well are they integrating into society?* Washington, DC: Migration Policy Institute.

Joe, K. A. (1994). The new criminal conspiracy? Asian gangs and organized crime in San Francisco. *Journal of Research in Crime and Delinquency, 31,* 390–394.

Johnson, E. H. (1990). Yakuza (Criminal Gangs) in Japan: Characteristics and Management in prisons. *Journal of Contemporary Criminal Justice, 6,* 113–126.

Joint Crime Information Center. (2014). *Texas gang threat assessment.* Austin: Texas Department of Public Safety, Intelligence & Counterterrorism Division.

Jones, G. A. (2014). "Hecho en Mexico": Gangs identities, and the politics of public security. In J. M. Hazen & D. Rodgers (Eds.), *Global gangs: Street violence across the world* (pp. 255–280). Minneapolis: University of Minnesota Press.

Jones, N. (2004). It's not where you love, it's how you love: Young women negotiate conflict and violence in the inner city. *The Annals of the American Academy of Political and Social Science, 595,* 49–62.

Jones, N. (2008). Working the "Code": On girls, gender, and inner-city violence. *Australian and New Zealand Journal of Criminology, 41,* 63–83.

Jordan, M. (2009). *Florida STG Intelligence Unit aims to keep communities safe.* Tallahassee, FL: Florida Department of Correction, Security Threat Intelligence Unit.

Justice Policy Institute. (2000). *The punishing decade: Prison and jail estimates at the millennium.* Washington, DC: Justice Policy Institute

Jütersonke, O., Muggah, R., & Rodgers, D. (2009). Gangs, urban violence, and security in Central America. *Security Dialogue, 40* (4–5), 373–97.

Kassel, P. (1998). The gang crackdown in Massachusetts' prisons: arbitrary and harsh treatment can only make matters worse. *New England Journal on Criminal and Civil Confinement, 24,* 37–63.

Katz, C. M., Fox, A. M., Britt, C., & Stevenson, P. (2012). Understanding police gang data at the aggregate level: An examination of the reliability of the National Youth Gang Survey data. *Justice Research and Policy, 14,* 103–112.

Katz, C. M., & Webb, V. J. (2006). *Policing gangs in America.* New York: Cambridge University Press.

Katz, J. (1988). *Seductions of crime.* New York: Basic Books.

Keiser, R. L. (1969). *The Vice Lords: Warriors of the street.* New York: Holt, Rinehart & Winston.

Klein, M. W. (1995). *The American street gang.* New York: Oxford University Press.

Klein, M. W. (2004). *Gang cop: The words and ways of Officer Paco Domingo.* Walnut Creek, CA: AltaMira Press.

Klein, M. W., & Maxson, C. L. (1989). Street gang violence. In M. E. Wolfgang, & N. A. Weiner (Eds.), *Violent crime, violent criminals* (pp. 198–234). Newbury Park, CA: Sage.

Klein, M. W., Maxson, C. L., & Cunningham, L. C. (1991). Crack, street gangs, and violence. *Criminology*, 29, 623–650.

Klein, M. W., Weerman, F. M., & Thornberry, T. P. (2006). Street gang violence in Europe. *European Journal of Criminology*, 3, 413–437.

Kobrin, S., Puntil, J., & Peluso, E. (1967). Criteria of status among street groups. *Journal of Research in Crime and Delinquency*, 4, 98–118.

Kotlowitz, A. (1992). *There are no children here: The story of two boys growing up in the other America*. New York: Anchor Books.

Kubrin, C. E. (2005). Gangstas, thugs, and hustlas: Identity and the code of the street in rap music. *Social Problems*, 52, 360–378.

Kubrin, C. E., & Nielson, E. (2014). Rap on trial. *Race and Justice*, 14, 185–211.

Landesco, J. (1968). *Organized crime in Chicago*. Chicago: University of Chicago Press.

Langan, P. A., & Levin, D. J. (2002). *Recidivism of prisoners released in 1994*. Special Report. Washington, DC: U.S. Department of Justice, Bureau of Justice Statistics.

Leap, J., Franke. T., Christie, C., & Bonis, S. (2010). Nothing stops a bullet like a job: Homeboy Industries gang prevention and intervention in Los Angeles. In J. Hoffman & L. Knox (Eds.), *Beyond suppression: Global Perspectives on Youth Justice* (pp. 127–138). Santa Barbara, CA: Praeger.

Leland, J. (1993). Gangsta Rap and the culture of violence. *Newsweek*, 29, 60–64.

Levitt, S. D., & Venkatesh, S. A. (2000). An economic analysis of a drug-selling gang's finances. *Quarterly Journal of Economics*, 115, 755–789.

Lewis, O. (1961). *The children of Sanchez*. New York: Random House.

Lipsey, M. W., & Cullen, F. T. (2007). The effectiveness of correctional rehabilitation: A review of systematic reviews. *Annual Review of Law and Social Science*, 3, 297–320.

Lizotte, A. J., Krohn, M. D., Howell, J. C., Tobin, K., & Howard, G. J. (2000). Factors influencing gun carrying among young urban males over the adolescent-young adult life course. *Criminology*, 38, 811–834.

Lizotte, A. J., Tesoriero, J. M., Thornberry, T. P., & Krohn, M. D. (1994). Patterns of adolescent firearms ownership and use. *Justice Quarterly*, 11, 51–73.

Lobo, A. P., Flores, R. J. O., & Salvo, J. J. (2002). The impact of Hispanic growth on the racial/ethnic composition of New York City neighborhoods. *Urban Affairs Review*, 37, 703–727.

Lombardo, R. M. (1994). The social organization of organized crime in Chicago. *Journal of Contemporary Criminal Justice*, 10, 290–313.

Los Angeles Police Department. (2007). *2007 Gang Enforcement Initiative*. Los Angeles, CA: Los Angeles Police Department.

Lusane, C. (1993). Rap, race, and politics. *Race & Class*, 35, 41–56.

Lyman, M. D. (1989). *Gangland: Drug trafficking by organized criminals*. Springfield, IL: Charles C. Thomas.

Major, A. K., Egley, Jr. A., Howell, J. C., Mendenhall, B., & Armstrong, T. (2004). Youth gangs in Indian Country. *Juvenile Justice Bulletin*. Washington, DC: U.S. Department of Justice, Office of Juvenile Justice and Delinquency Prevention.

Manwaring, M. G. (2005). *Street gangs: The new urban insurgency*. Carlisle, PA: Strategic Studies Institute, The War College.

Manwaring, M. G. (2007). *A contemporary challenge to state sovereignty: Gangs and other illicit transnational criminal organizations in Central America, El Salvador, Mexico, Jamaica, and Brazil*. Carlisle, PA: Strategic Studies Institute, U.S. Army College.

Marks, C. (1985). Black labor migration: 1910–1920. *Critical Sociology*, 12, 5–24.

Mauer, M. (2004). Race, class, and the development of criminal justice policy. *Review of Policy Research*, 21, 79–92.

Maxson, C. L. (1998). Street gang members on the move: The role of migration in the proliferation of street gangs in the U.S. *Juvenile Justice Bulletin*. Youth Gang Series. Washington, DC: U.S. Department of Justice, Office of Juvenile Justice and Delinquency Prevention.

Maxson, C. L. (1999). Gang homicide: A review and extension of the literature. In D. Smith and M. Zahn (Eds.). *Homicide: A Sourcebook of Social Research* (pp. 197–220). Thousand Oaks, CA: Sage.

Maxson, C. L., Gordon, M. A., & Klein, M. W. (1985). Differences between gang and nongang homicides. *Criminology*, 23, 209–222.

Maxson, C. L., Woods, K., & Klein, M. W. (1996). Street gang migration: How big a threat? *National Institute of Justice Journal*, 230 (February), 26–31.

McGuire, C. (2007). *Central American youth gangs in the Washington D.C. area.* Working Paper. Washington, DC: Washington Office on Latin America.

McKay, H. D. (1949). The neighborhood and child conduct. *Annals of the American Academy of Political and Social Science*, 261, 32–41.

McKee, G.A. (2004). Urban industrialization and local public policy: Industrial renewal in Philadelphia, 1953–1976. *Journal of Public History*, 16, 66–98.

McKinney, K. C. (1988). Juvenile gangs: Crime and drug trafficking. *Juvenile Justice Bulletin.* Washington, DC: U.S. Department of Justice, Office of Juvenile Justice and Delinquency Prevention.

McWhirter, C. (2011). *Red summer: The summer of 1919 and the awakening of America.* New York: Macmillan.

McWilliams, C. (1943). Zoot-suit riots. *New Republic*, 108 (June), 818–820.

McWilliams, C. (1948/1990). *North from Mexico: The spanish-speaking people of the United States.* (Rev. ed.). New York, NY: Greenwood.

Miller, B. J. (2008). The struggle over redevelopment at Cabrini-Green, 1989–2004. *Journal of Urban History*, 34, 944–960.

Miller, J. (2002). The girls in the gang: What we've learned from two decades of research. In C. R. Huff (Ed.), *Gangs in America III* (pp. 175–197). Thousand Oaks, CA: Sage.

Miller, W. B. (1958). Lower class culture as a generating milieu of gang delinquency. *Journal of Social Issues*, 14, 5–19.

Miller, W. B. (1966/2011). *City gangs.* Phoenix: Arizona State University. Accessible at http://gangresearch.asu.edu/.

Miller, W. B. (1980). The Molls. In S. K. Datesman & F. R. Scarpitti (Eds.), *Women, crime and justice* (pp. 238–248). New York: Oxford University Press.

Miller, W. B. (1973). Race, sex, and gangs: The Molls. *Trans-Action*, 11, 32–35.

Miller, W. B. (1974a). American youth gangs: Fact and fantasy. In L. Rainwater (Ed.), *Deviance and liberty: A survey of modern perspectives on deviant behavior* (pp. 262–273). Chicago: Aldine.

Miller, W. B. (1974b). American youth gangs: Past and present. In A. Blumberg (Ed.), *Current perspectives on criminal behavior* (pp. 210–239). New York: Knopf.

Miller, W. B. (1975). *Violence by youth gangs and youth groups as a crime problem in major American Cities.* Washington, DC: U.S. Department of Justice, Office of Juvenile Justice and Delinquency Prevention.

Miller, W. B. (1980). The Molls. In S. K. Datesman & F. R. Scarpitti (Eds.). *Women, Crime, and Justice* (pp. 238–248). New York, NY: Oxford University Press.

Miller, W. B. (1982/1992). *Crime by youth gangs and groups in the United States.* Washington, DC: U.S. Department of Justice, Office of Juvenile Justice and Delinquency Prevention.

Miller, W. B. (2001). *The growth of youth gang problems in the United States: 1970–1998.* Washington, DC: Office of Juvenile Justice and Delinquency Prevention.

Miller, W. I. (1993). *Humiliation and other essays on honor, social discomfort, and violence.* Ithaca, NY: Cornell University Press.

Monti, D. J. (1993). Gangs in more- and less-settled communities. In S. Cummings & D. J. Monti (Eds.), *Gangs: The origins and impact of contemporary youth gangs in the United States* (pp. 219–253). Albany: State University of New York Press.

Moore, J. W. (1978). *Homeboys: Gangs, drugs and prison in the barrios of Los Angeles.* Philadelphia: Temple University Press.

Moore, J. W. (1985). Isolation and stigmatization in the development of an underclass: The case of Chicano gangs in East Los Angeles. *Social Problems*, 33, 1–13.

Moore, J. W. (1991). *Going down to the barrio: Homeboys and homegirls in change.* Philadelphia: Temple University Press.

Moore, J. W. (1993). Gangs, drugs, and violence. In S. Cummins & D.J. Monti (Eds.), *Gangs: The origins and impact of contemporary youth gangs in the United States* (pp. 27–46). Albany: State University of New York Press.

Moore, J. W. (1998). Understanding youth street gangs: Economic restructuring and the urban underclass. In M. W. Watts (Ed.), *Cross-cultural perspectives on youth and violence* (pp. 65–78). Stamford, CT: JAI.

Moore, J. W. (2000). Latino gangs: A question of change. *The Justice Professional*, 13, 7–18.

Moore, J. W. (2007). Female gangs: Gender and globalization. In J.M. Hagedorn (Ed.), *Gangs in the Global City* (pp. 187–203). Chicago: University of Illinois Press.

Moore, J. W., & Pinderhughes, R. (1993). Introduction. In J. W. Moore, & R. Pinderhughes (Eds.), *In the barrios: Latinos and the underclass debate* (pp. xi–xxxix). New York: Russell Sage Foundation.

Moore, J. W., & Vigil, D. (1993). Barrios in transition. In J. W. Moore & R. Pinderhughes (Eds.), *In the barrios: Latinos and the underclass debate* (pp. 27–49). New York: Russell Sage Foundation.

Moore, J. W., Vigil, D., & Garcia, R. (1983). Residence and territoriality in Chicano gangs. *Social Problems*, 31, 182–194.

Morales, G. C. (2011). *La Familia—The Family: Prison gangs in America* (2nd ed.). Des Moines, WA: Author.

Motel, S., & Patten, E. (2012). *Characteristics of the 60 largest metropolitan areas by Hispanic population*. Washington, DC: Pew Hispanic Center.

National Alliance of Gang Investigators' Associations. (2005). *National gang threat assessment: 2005*. Washington, DC: Bureau of Justice Assistance, U.S. Department of Justice.

National Alliance of Gang Investigators' Associations. (2009). *Quick guide to gangs*. Washington, DC: Bureau of Justice Assistance, U.S. Department of Justice.

National Drug Intelligence Center. (1994). *Bloods and Crips gang survey report*. Johnstown, PA: U.S. Department of Justice, NDIC.

National Drug Intelligence Center. (1996). *National street gang survey report*. Johnstown, PA: U.S. Department of Justice, National Drug Intelligence Center.

Ness, C. D. (2010). *Why girls fight: Female youth violence in the inner city*. New York: New York University Press.

Nielson, E. (2012). "Here come the cops": Policing the resistance in rap music. *International Journal of Cultural Studies*, 15, 349–363.

Olivero, J. M. (1991). Honor, violence, and upward mobility: A case study of Chicago gangs during the 1970s and 1980s. Edinburg: University of Texas–Pan American Press.

Olson, D. E., Dooley, B., & Kane, C. M. (2004). *The relationship between gang membership and inmate recidivism*. Research Bulletin, Vol. 2(12). Chicago: Illinois Criminal Justice Research Authority.

Orlando-Morningstar, D. (1997). Prison gangs. *Special Needs Offenders Bulletin*. Washington, DC: Federal Judicial Center.

Ousey, G. O., & Lee, M. R. (2004). Investigating the connections between race, illicit drug markets, and lethal violence, 1984–1997. *Journal of Research in Crime and Delinquency*, 41, 352–383.

Pachon, H. P., & Moore, J. W. (1981). Mexican-Americans. *The ANNALS of the American Academy of Political and Social Science*, 454, 111–124.

Passel, J. S., Cohn, D., & Lopez, M. H. (2011). *Census 2010: 50 million Latinos. Hispanics account for more than half of nation's growth in past decade* . Washington, DC: Pew Hispanic Center, Pew Charitable Trusts.

Papachristos, A. V. (2001). *A.D., after the Disciples: The neighborhood impact of federal gang prosecution*. Peotone, IL: New Chicago Schools Press.

Papachristos, A. V. (2009). Murder by structure: Dominance relations and the social structure of gang homicide. *American Journal of Sociology*, 115, 74–128.

Papachristos, A. V. (In press). *Street Corner, Inc. How the Evolution of a Street Gang Changed a City*. New York: Oxford University Press.

Papachristos, A. V., Hureau, D. M., & Braga, A. A. (2013). The corner and the crew: The influence of geography and social networks on gang violence. *American Sociological Review*, 18, 417–447.

Papachristos, A. V., & Kirk, D. S. (2006). Neighborhood effects on street gang behavior. In J. F. Short & L. A. Hughes (Eds.), *Studying youth gangs* (pp. 63–84). Lanham, MD: AltaMira Press.

Papachristos, A. V., & Kirk, D. S. (In press). Changing the street dynamic: Evaluating Chicago's Group Violence Reduction Strategy. *Criminology and Public Policy*, 14.

Papachristos, A. V., Wildeman, C., & Roberto, E. (2015). Tragic, but not random: The social contagion of nonfatal gunshot injuries. *Social Science & Medicine*, 125, 139–150.

Patterson, O. (2015). The real problem with America's inner cities. New York, the *New York Times*. Accessed May 10, 2015 from http://www.nytimes.com/2015/05/10/opinion/sunday/the-real-problem-with-americas-inner-cities.html?_r=0.

Park, R. E. (1936). Succession: An ecological concept. *American Sociological Review*, 1 (April), 171–179.

Parsons, T. (1951). *The social system*. New York: Free Press.

Parsons, T. (1967). *Sociological theory and modern society*. New York: Free Press.

Passel, J. S., Cohn, D., & Lopez, M. H. (2011). *Census 2010: 50 million Latinos. Hispanics account for more than half of nation's growth in past decade*. Washington, DC: Pew Hispanic Center, Pew Charitable Trusts.

Paz, O. (1961/1990). *The labyrinth of solitude*. London: Penguin.

Pearson, G. (1983). *Hooligan: A history of reportable fears*. London: Macmillan.

Perkins, U. E. (1987). *Explosion of Chicago's black street gangs: 1900 to the present*. Chicago: Third World Press.

Petersilia, J. (2003). *When prisoners come home: Parole and prisoner reentry*. New York: Oxford University Press.

Peterson, V. W. (1963). Chicago: Shades of Capone. *The ANNALS of the American Academy of Political and Social Science*, 347, 30–39.

Pew Charitable Trusts. (2008). *One in 100: Behind bars in America 2008*. Washington, DC: Author.

Phillips, I. (2007). Community re-entry challenges daunt ex-offenders quest for a fresh start. *Illinois Research Brief*, 2(1), 1–4.

Pihos, P.C. (2011). The racial politics of urban street gangs. *Journal of Urban History*, 37, 466–473.

Pincus, F. L., & Ehrlich, H. J. (1999). Immigration. In F.L. Pincus and H.J. Ehrlich (Eds.), *Race and ethnic conflict* (pp. 223–228). Boulder, CO: Westview Press.

Planty, M., & Truman, J. L. (2013). Firearm violence, 1993–2011 (NCJ 241730). *Special Report*. Washington, DC: U.S. Department of Justice, Bureau of Justice Statistics.

Polk, K. (1999). Males and honor contest violence. *Homicide Studies*, 3, 6–29.

Portes, A., & Rumbaut, R. G. (2005). Introduction: The second generation and the Children of Immigrants Longitudinal Study. *Ethnic and Racial Studies*, 28, 983–999.

Portes, A., & Zhou, M. (1993). The new second generation: Segmented assimilation and its variants. *The Annals of the American Academy of Political and Social Sciences*, 530, 74–96.

Pyrooz, D. C. (2012). Structural covariates of gang homicide in large U.S. cities. *Journal of Research in Crime and Delinquency*, 49, 489–518.

Pyrooz, D. C., Decker, S. H., & Fleisher, M. (2011). From the street to the prison, from the prison to the street: Understanding and responding to prison gangs. *Journal of Aggression, Conflict and Peace Research*, 3, 12–24.

Quinn, E. (2005). Nuthin' but a "g" thang: The culture and commerce of gangsta rap. New York: Columbia University Press.

Quinn, J. F., Tobolowsky, P. M., & Downs, W. T. (1994). Predictors of police perceptions of the severity of the local gang problem in large and small cities. *Journal of Gang Research*, 2, 13–22.

Ralph, P., Hunter, J., Marquart, W., Cuvelier, J., & Merianos, D. (1996). Exploring the differences between gang and non-gang prisoners. In C.R. Huff (Ed.), *Gangs in America* (2nd ed., pp. 241–256). Thousand Oaks, CA: Sage.

Redfield, R. (1941). *Folk culture of Yucatán*. Chicago: University of Chicago Press.

Reeves, J. L., & Campbell, R. (1994). *Cracked coverage: Television news, the anti-cocaine crusade, and the Reagan legacy*. Durham, NC: Duke University Press.

Rendon, A.B. (1971). *Chicano Manifesto*. New York: Macmillan.

Riis, J. A. (1902/1969). *The battle with the slum*. Montclair, NJ: Paterson Smith.

Rivera, F. P. (2012). The future of preventive public health: Implications of brain violence research. In R. Loeber and B.C. Welsh (Eds.). *The Future of Criminology* (pp. 159-165). Oxford, NY: Oxford University Press.

Ro, R. (1996). *Gangsta: Merchandizing the rhymes of violence*. New York: St. Martin's Press.

Rodgers, D., & Hazen, J. M. (2014). Introduction: Gangs in a global and comparative perspective. In J. M. Hazen & D. Rodgers (Eds.), *Global gangs: Street violence across the world* (pp. 1–25). Minneapolis: University of Minnesota Press.

Rosenbaum, D. P., & Grant, J. A. (1983). *Gangs and youth problems in Evanston*. Evanston, IL: Northwestern University, Center for Urban Affairs and Policy Research.

Rubel, A. J. (1965). The Mexican-American palomilla. *Anthropological Linguistics*, 4, 29–97.

Sanchez-Jankowski, M. (2003). Gangs and social change. *Theoretical Criminology*, 7, 191–216.

Sanders, W. B. (1994). *Gangbangs and drive-bys: Grounded culture and juvenile gang violence*. New York: Aldine de Gruyter.

Santana, E. L. (2007a). Corrections Connection Network News. "Gang culture: From the inside & out. Part I." Accessed May 14, 2013, http://www.corrections.com/news/article/17086.

Santana, E. L. (2007b). Corrections Connection Network News. "Gang culture: From the inside & out. Part II." Accessed May 14, 2013, http://www.corrections.com/news/article/17132.

Sante, L. (1991). *Low life: Lures and snares of old New York*. New York: Vintage Books.

Schlosser, E. (1998). The prison-industrial complex. *The Atlantic Monthly* (December), 51–77.

Schneider, E. C. (1999). *Vampires, dragons, and Egyptian kings: Youth gangs in postwar New York*. Princeton, NJ: Princeton University Press.

Seele, A., Arnson, C. J., & Olson, E. L. (2013). *Crime and violence in Mexico and Central America: An evolving but incomplete US policy response*. Washington, DC: Migration Policy Institute.

Seelke, C. R. (2012). *Gangs in Central America* (CRS Report RL34112). Washington, DC: Congressional Research Service, Library of Congress.

Seelke, C. R. (2014). *Gangs in Central America* (CRS Report for Congress RL34112). Washington, DC: Congressional Research Service, Library of Congress.

Sharbek, D. (2012). Prison gangs, norms, and organizations. *Journal of Economic Behavior & Organization*, 82, 702–716.

Shaw, C. R., & McKay, H. D. (1942/1969). *Juvenile delinquency and urban areas* (2nd ed.). Chicago: University of Chicago Press.

Sheley, J. F., & Wright, J. D. (1995). *In the line of fire: Youth, guns and violence in urban America*. Hawthorne, NY: Aldine De Gruyter.

Short, J. F. Jr. (1990). New wine in old bottles? Change and continuity in American gangs. In C.R. Huff (Ed.), *American gangs* (pp. 223–239). Thousand Oaks, CA: Sage.

Short, J. F. Jr. (1996). Foreword: Diversity and change in U.S. gangs. In C.R. Huff (Ed.), *Gangs in America* (p. vii–xviii). Thousand Oaks, CA: Sage.

Short, J. F., Jr. (2002). What is past is prelude: Gangs in America and elsewhere. In C.R. Huff (Ed.), *Gangs in America III* (pp. vii–xviii). Thousand Oaks, CA: Sage.

Short, J. F., Jr., & Strodtbeck, F. L. (1965). *Group process and gang delinquency*. Chicago: University of Chicago Press.

Short, J. F., Jr. (2006). Why study gangs? An intellectual journey. In J. F. Short & L. A. Hughes (Eds.), *Studying youth gangs* (pp. 1–14). Lanham, MD: AltaMira Press.

Short, J. F. Jr., & Strodtbeck, F. L. (1963). The responses of gang leaders to status threats: An observation on group process and delinquent behavior. *American Journal of Sociology*, 68, 571–579.

Simon, T. R., Ritter, N. M., & Mahendra, R. R. E. (2013). *Changing course: Preventing gang membership (NCJ 239234)*. Washington, DC: National Center for Injury Prevention and Control, Centers for Disease Control and Prevention, U.S. Department of Health and Human

Services, and National Institute of Justice, Office of Justice Programs, U.S. Department of Justice.

Skolnick, J. H. (1989). *Gang organization and migration*. Sacramento: Office of the Attorney General of the State of California.

Skolnick, J. H., Correl, T., Navarro, E., & Rabb, R. (1990). The social structure of street drug dealing. *American Journal of Police*, 9, 1–41.

Smith, C. M. (2014). The influence of gentrification on gang homicides in Chicago neighborhoods, 1994 to 2005. *Crime & Delinquency*, 60, 569–591.

Spergel, I. A. (1986). The violent youth gang in Chicago, IL: A local community approach. *Social Service Review*, 60, 94–131.

Spergel, I. A. (1990). Youth gangs: Continuity and change. In M. Tonry & N. Morris (Eds.), *Crime and justice: A review of research* (Vol. 12, pp. 171–275). Chicago: University of Chicago Press.

Spergel, I. A. (1995). *The youth gang problem*. New York: Oxford University Press.

Spergel, I. A. (2007). *Reducing youth gang violence: The Little Village Gang Project in Chicago*. Lanham, MD: AltaMira Press.

Spergel, I. A., Wa, K. M., & Sosa, R. V. (2006). The comprehensive, community-wide, gang program model: Success and failure. In J. F. Short & L. A. Hughes (Eds.), *Studying youth gangs* (pp. 203–224). Lanham, MD: AltaMira Press.

Starbuck, D., Howell, J. C., & Lindquist, D. J. (2001). Into the millennium: Hybrids and other modern gangs. *Juvenile Justice Bulletin. Youth Gang Series*. Washington, DC: U.S. Department of Justice, Office of Juvenile Justice and Delinquency Prevention.

Steinberg, J. (1996). George Bush, a crack cocaine kingpin? *Executive Intelligence Review*, 23 (September 13), 10–12.

Stewart, F. H. (1994). *Honor*. Chicago: University of Chicago Press.

Sullivan, J. P. (2006). Maras morphing: Revisiting third generation gangs. *Global Crime*, 7, 487–504.

Sullivan, J. P., & Bunker, R. J. (2002). Drug cartels, street gangs, and warlords. *Small Wars and Insurgencies*, 13(2), 40–53.

Sullivan, J. P., & Elkus, A. (2008). *Small Wars Journal*, "State of siege: Mexico's criminal insurgency." Accessed August 16, 2014, http://smallwarsjournal.com/jrnl/art/state-of-siege-mexicos-criminal-insurgency.

Sullivan, M. L. (1993). Puerto Ricans in Sunset Park, Brooklyn: Poverty amidst ethnic and economic diversity. In J. W. Moore, & R. Pinderhughes (Eds.), *In the barrios: Latinos and the underclass debate* (pp. 1–25). New York: Russell Sage Foundation.

Suttles, G. D. (1968). *The social order of the slum*. Chicago: University of Chicago Press.

Tapia, M., Sparks, C. S., & Miller, J. M. (2014). Texas Latino prison gangs: An exploration of generational shift rebellion. *Prison Journal*, 94, 159–179.

Taylor, C. S. (1990a). *Dangerous society*. East Lansing: Michigan State University Press.

Taylor, C. S. (1990b). Gang imperialism. In C. R. Huff (Ed.), *Gangs in America* (pp. 103–115). Newbury Park, CA: Sage.

Taylor, C. S. (1993). *Girls, gangs, women, drugs*. East Lansing: Michigan State University Press.

Telles, E. E., & Ortiz, V. (2008). *Generations of exclusion*. New York: Russell Sage Foundation.

Texas Fusion Center. (2013). *Texas gang threat assessment: 2012*. Austin: Texas Fusion Center, Intelligence & Counterterrorism Division, Texas Department of Public Safety.

Thompson, T. (2013). *The new mind of the South*. New York: Simon & Schuster.

Thrasher, F. M. (1927/2000). *The gang—a study of 1,313 gangs in Chicago*. Chicago: New Chicago School Press.

Tita, G. E. (1999). *An ecological study of violent urban street gangs and their crime*. Unpublished dissertation. Pittsburgh, PA: Carnegie Mellon University.

Tita, G. E., & Abrahamse, A. (2010). Homicide in California, 1981–2008: Measuring the impact of Los Angeles and gangs on overall homicide patterns. Sacramento, CA: Governor's Office of Gang and Youth Violence Policy.

Tita, G. E., & Cohen, J. (2004). Measuring spatial diffusion of shots fired activity across city neighborhoods. In M. F. Goodchild, & D. G. Janelle (Eds.), *Spatially integrated social science* (pp. 171–204). New York: Oxford University Press.

Tita, G. E., Cohen, J., & Endberg, J. (2005). An ecological study of the location of gang "set space." *Social Problems, 52,* 272–299.

Tita, G. E., & Radil, S. M. (2011). Spatializing the social networks of gangs to explore patterns of violence. *Journal of Quantitative Violence,* 27, 521–545.

Toch, H. (1978) Social climate and prison violence. *Federal Probation,* 42, 21–25.

Tonry, M. (1994). Racial politics, racial disparities, and the war on crime. *Crime & Delinquency,* 40, 475–494.

Travis, J. (2005). *But they all come back: Facing the problem of prisoner reentry.* Washington, DC: The Urban Institute Press.

Travis, J., & Petersilia, J. (2001). Reentry reconsidered: A new look at an old question. *Crime & Delinquency,* 47, 291–313.

Trulson, C. R., Caudill, J. W., Haerle, D. R., & DeLisi, M. (2012). Cliqued up: The post-incarceration recidivism of young gang-related homicide offenders. *Criminal Justice Review,* 37, 174–190.

Truman, J. L., & Planty, M. (2012). *Criminal Victimization, 2011.* Washington, DC: U.S. Department of Justice, Office of Justice Programs, Bureau of Justice Statistics (NCJ 239437).

Tuttle, W. M. (1996). *Race riot: Chicago in the Red Summer of 1919.* Chicago: University of Chicago Press.

United Nations. (2003). *The challenge of slums.* New York: Author.

United Nations Office on Drugs and Crime. (2007). *Crime and development in Central America: Caught in the crossfire.* New York: United Nations.

United States Government Accounting Office. (1989). *Nontraditional organized crime.* Washington, DC: U.S. Government Printing Office.

United States Government Accounting Office. (1996). *Violent crime: Federal law enforcement assistance in fighting Los Angeles gang violence.* Washington, DC: U.S. Government Printing Office.

United States Government Accountability Office. (2010). *Combating gangs: Federal agencies have implemented a Central American gang strategy, but could strengthen oversight and measurement of efforts.* Washington, DC: U.S. Government Accountability Office.

U.S. Agency for International Development. (2006). *Central America and Mexico gang assessment.* Washington, DC: Bureau for Latin American and Caribbean Affairs, U.S. Agency for International Development.

Valdez, A. (2007). *Mexican-American girls and gang violence: Beyond risk.* New York: Palgrave Macmillan.

Valdez, A., Kaplan, C. D., & Codina, E. (2000). Psychopathy among Mexican American gang members: A comparative study. *International Journal of Offender Therapy and Comparative Criminology,* 44, 46–58.

Valdez, A., Cepeda, A., & Kaplan, C. (2009). Homicidal events among Mexican-American street gangs: A situational analysis. *Homicide Studies,* 13, 288–306.

Valdez, A., & Sifaneck, S. J. (2004). "Getting high and getting by": Dimensions of drug selling behaviors among Mexican gang members in south Texas. *Journal of Research in Crime and Delinquency,* 41, 82–105.

Venkatesh, S. A. (1996). The gang and the community. In C. R. Huff (Ed.), *Gangs in America* (2nd ed., pp. 241–256). Thousand Oaks, CA: Sage.

Venkatesh, S. A, (2000). *American project: The rise and fall of a modern ghetto*(2nd ed.). Cambridge, MA: Harvard University Press.

Venkatesh, S. A. (2008). *Gang leader for a day: A rogue sociologist takes to the streets.* New York: Penguin Press.

Vigil, J. D. (1988). *Barrio gangs: Street life and identity in Southern California.* Austin, TX: University of Texas Press.

Vigil, J. D. (1990). Cholos and gangs: Culture change and street youth in Los Angeles. In C.R. Huff (Ed.), *Gangs in America* (pp. 116–128). Newbury Park, CA: Sage.

Vigil, J. D. (1993). The established gang. In S. Cummings & D. J. Monti (Eds.), *Gangs: The origins and impact of contemporary youth gangs in the United States* (pp. 95–112). Albany: State University of New York Press.

Vigil, J. D. (1998). *From Indians to Chicanos: The dynamics of Mexican-American Culture* (2nd ed.). Prospect Heights, IL: Waveland Press.

Vigil, J. D. (2002). *A rainbow of gangs: Street cultures in the mega-city*. Austin: University of Texas Press.

Vigil, J. D. (2007). *The projects: Gang and non-gang families in East Los Angeles*. Thousand Oaks, CA: Sage.

Vigil, J. D. (2008). Mexican migrants in gangs: A second-generation history. In F. van Gemert, D. Peterson, & I.-L. Lien (Eds.), *Street gangs, migration and ethnicity* (pp. 49–62). Portland, OR: Willan Publishing.

Vigil, J. D. (2010). *Gang Redux: A balanced anti-gang strategy*. Long Grove, IL: Waveland.

Vigil, J. D. (2011). *From Indians to Chicanos: The dynamics of Mexican-American culture* (3rd ed.). Prospect Heights, IL: Waveland.

Vigil, J. D. (2014). Cholo! The migratory origins of Chicano gangs in Los Angeles. In J. M. Hazen & D. Rodgers (Eds.), *Global gangs: Street violence across the world* (pp. 49–64). Minneapolis: University of Minnesota Press.

Vigil, J. D., & Howell, J. C. (2012a). *Gang subculture and locura: Variations in acts and actors*. Unpublished report. Tallahassee, FL: Institute for Intergovernmental Research, National Gang Center.

Vigil, J. D., & Howell, J. C. (2012b). *Immigration and gangs*. Unpublished Report. Tallahassee, FL: National Gang Center.

Vigil, J. D., & Long, J. M. (1990). Emic and etic perspectives on gang culture. In C. R. Huff (Ed.), *Gangs in America* (pp. 55–70). Newbury Park, CA: Sage.

Vigil, J. D., & Yun, S. C. (1990). Vietnamese youth gangs in Southern California. In C. R. Huff (Ed.), *Gangs in America* (pp. 146–162). Newbury Park, CA: Sage.

Visher, C., Yahner, J., & La Vigne, N.G. (2010). *Life after prison: Tracking the experiences of male prisoners returning to Chicago, Cleveland, and Houston*. Washington, DC: Urban Institute.

Voogd, J. (2008). *Race riots and resistance: The Red Summer of 1919*. New York: Peter Lang Publishing.

Wacquant, L. J. D. (2007). Three pernicious premises in the study of the American ghetto. In J. M. Hagedorn (Ed.), *Gangs in the global city* (pp. 34–53). Chicago: University of Illinois Press.

Wacquant, L. J. D. (2009). *Prisons of poverty*. Minneapolis: University of Minnesota Press.

Waldorf, D. (1993). When the Crips invaded San Francisco—gang migration. *Journal of Gang Research*, 1, 11–16.

Waldorf, D., & Lauderback, D. (1993). *Gang drug sales in San Francisco: Organized or freelance?* Alameda, CA: Institute for Scientific Analysis.

Ward, T. W. (2013). *Gangsters without borders: An ethnography of a Salvadoran street gang*. Oxford: Oxford University Press.

Washington Office on Latin America. (2010). *Executive summary: Transnational youth gangs in Central America, Mexico and the United States*. Washington, DC: Author.

Waters, M. (1998). Testimony of Maxine Waters before the House of Permanent Select Committee on Intelligence on the CIA OIG Report of Investigation: "Allegations of connection between CIA & Contras in cocaine trafficking to the US." Volume I: "The California Story" March 16.

Waters, T. (1999). *Crime and immigrant youth*. Thousand Oaks, CA: Sage.

Webb, G. (1999). *Dark alliance: The CIA, the contras, and the crack cocaine explosion.* New York: Seven Stories Press.

West, C. (1993). *Race matters*. Boston: Bacon.

Whyte, W. F. (1941). Corner boys: A study of clique behavior. *The American Journal of Sociology*, 46, 647–664.

Whyte, W. F. (1943a). Social organization in the slums. *The American Sociological Review*, 8, 34–39.

Whyte, W. F. (1943b). *Street corner society: The social structure of an Italian slum.* Chicago: University of Chicago Press.

Wilkinson, D. L., & Fagan, J. (2006). The role of firearms and violence "scripts": The dynamics of gun events among adolescent males. *Law and Contemporary Problems*, 59(Special Issue), 55–89.

Wilson, G. I., & Sullivan, J. P. (2007). *On gangs, crime, and terrorism, special to defense and the national interest.* February 28, 2007. Available at https://www.d-n.net/fcs/pdf/wilson_sullivan_gangs_terrorism.pdf.

Wilson, W. J. (1987). *The truly disadvantaged: The inner city, the underclass, and public policy.* Chicago: University of Chicago.

Winterdyk, J., & Ruddell, R. (2010). Managing prison gangs: Results from a survey of U.S. prison systems. *Journal of Criminal Justice*, 38, 730–736.

Wolf, S. (2014). Central American street gangs: Their role in communities and prisons. *European Review of Latin American and Caribbean Studies*, 96, 127–140.

Woods, R. A. (1898). *The city wilderness: A settlement study, south end, Boston.* Boston: Houghton Mifflin.

Woodward, C. V. (1951). *Origins of the new south, 1877–1913.* Baton Rouge: Louisiana State University Press.

Yablonsky, L. (1997). Gangsters: Fifty years of madness, drugs, and death on the streets of America. New York: New York University Press.

Yu, E.Y. (1987). Juvenile delinquency in the Korean community of Los Angeles. Los Angeles: Korean Times.

Zeigler, K., & Camarota, S. J. (2014). U.S. immigrant population record 41.3 million in 2013: Asian, Caribbean, and Middle Eastern immigrant populations grew most since 2010. Washington, DC: Center for Immigration Studies.

Zevitz, R. G., & Takata, S. R. (1992). Metropolitan gang influence and the emergence of group delinquency in a regional community. *Journal of Criminal Justice*, 20, 93–10.

Zilberg, E. (2011). *Space of detention: The making of a transnational gang crisis between Los Angeles and San Salvador.* Durham, NC: Duke University Press.

Index